December 2011

Merry Christmas

[signature]

D0961876

Additional Praise for *All for One*

"The concepts in Andrew Sobel's *All for One* are powerful and essential. The best professional service firms understand that achieving the position of trusted partner should be the goal of all of their efforts at building client relationships. Sobel's 10 strategies provide a very clear path to achieving that goal—for individual professionals and for their firms."

—Peter T. Regan
Executive Chairman, The ERM Group

"Andrew Sobel has once again broken important new ground for the professional services industry. *All for One* is a masterpiece that delivers dozens of pertinent examples of how the best in the business build trusted client partnerships, and all professionals can learn important lessons from it. My one regret in reading the book is the knowledge that my competitors also have access to it!"

—Donald Lowman
Managing Director and Board Member, Towers Perrin

"In today's marketplace, deep personal and institutional relationships have never been more important. In *All for One*, Andrew Sobel sets forth compelling relationship strategies for both the individual and the organization, and supports these strategies with insights into the how-to that is so often missing."

—Michael S. Hamilton
Partner, Chief Learning & Development
Officer—Americas, Ernst & Young LLP

"*All for One* offers high-impact, practical advice on building enduring client partnerships. Andrew Sobel once again shows us his amazing empathy and insight about client relationships."

—Jaideep Bajaj
Managing Director, ZS Associates

"*All for One* is a great, practical guide that provides an invaluable framework for building enduring, trusted client relationships. Andrew Sobel has delivered an essential read for all professionals, one that is deep with insights, advice, and leading-edge best practice."

—Diana Brightmore-Armour
Chief Executive, Corporate Banking, Lloyds Banking Group

"Trust is the grail for the professional advisor. And never has it been more important or elusive. In *All for One*, Andrew Sobel offers a master-class in building business relationships. Drawing on the experience of leading companies he lays out a clear path to achieve the ultimate advisory role as trusted partner. A must-read for anyone who purports to give business advice."

—Andrew Laurence
Chairman Worldwide Corporate Practice Committee, Hill & Knowlton

"Even the best relationship manager can learn from Andrew Sobel's *All for One*. It clearly demonstrates how the best institutional client relationships are developed, and shares practical advice that business books often promise but rarely deliver."

—Mark Read
Director of Strategy, WPP

"*All for One* lays out a highly practical framework for building a culture of relentless client focus and focusing a firm's human and financial capital to deliver real value to clients. Enduring client partnerships are essential to financial and reputational success, and Andrew Sobel delivers powerful insights about how to systematically cultivate and sustain them."

—James Bardrick
Co-Head, Global Industrials Banking, Citigroup

ALL FOR ONE

10 Strategies for Building Trusted Client Partnerships

ANDREW SOBEL

John Wiley & Sons, Inc.

Copyright © 2009 by Andrew Sobel. All rights reserved.

Published by John Wiley & Sons, Inc., Hoboken, New Jersey.
Published simultaneously in Canada.

No part of this publication may be reproduced, stored in a retrieval system, or transmitted in
any form or by any means, electronic, mechanical, photocopying, recording, scanning, or
otherwise, except as permitted under Section 107 or 108 of the 1976 United States Copyright
Act, without either the prior written permission of the Publisher, or authorization through
payment of the appropriate per-copy fee to the Copyright Clearance Center, Inc., 222
Rosewood Drive, Danvers, MA 01923, (978) 750-8400, fax (978) 646-8600, or on the web at
www.copyright.com. Requests to the Publisher for permission should be addressed to the
Permissions Department, John Wiley & Sons, Inc., 111 River Street, Hoboken, NJ 07030, (201)
748-6011, fax (201) 748-6008, or online at http://www.wiley.com/go/permissions.

Limit of Liability/Disclaimer of Warranty: While the publisher and author have used their best
efforts in preparing this book, they make no representations or warranties with respect to the
accuracy or completeness of the contents of this book and specifically disclaim any implied
warranties of merchantability or fitness for a particular purpose. No warranty may be created or
extended by sales representatives or written sales materials. The advice and strategies contained
herein may not be suitable for your situation. You should consult with a professional where
appropriate. Neither the publisher nor author shall be liable for any loss of profit or any other
commercial damages, including but not limited to special, incidental, consequential, or other
damages.

For general information on our other products and services or for technical support, please
contact our Customer Care Department within the United States at (800) 762-2974, outside the
United States at (317) 572-3993 or fax (317) 572-4002.

Wiley also publishes its books in a variety of electronic formats. Some content that appears in
print may not be available in electronic books. For more information about Wiley products,
visit our web site at www.wiley.com.

ISBN 978-0-470-38028-4

Printed in the United States of America.

10 9 8 7 6 5

To Mary Jane, Christopher, Elizabeth, and Emma.
Thanks for the love, laughter, and support.

Contents

PART III
The Five Institutional Strategies

PART IV
Frequently Asked Questions and
Conclusion

Introduction

Transforming Your Client Relationships

A variety of powerful forces are now creating unprecedented opportunities to partner with clients and add value in new ways. This book presents a road map for capturing these opportunities and building trusted client partnerships marked by depth, breadth, and longevity. It is organized around 10 fundamental strategies that combine to help you create a powerful, all-for-one, client-centered organization. These strategies have been identified and codified through an extensive, multiyear study of large-scale client relationships built by a wide range of highly successful services firms.

Why is this important? For your clients, these enduring, institutional relationships can increase value, reduce risk, and accelerate change. For you and your firm, they are the bedrock of your success. In good times they will fill your sails with wind, and in a difficult economy they provide essential ballast that will keep you on an even keel.

If you're in any type of service business, such as consulting, law, accounting, financial services, advertising, or technology services—you'll benefit from studying these essential strategies for building, growing, and sustaining long-term, trusted client partnerships.

Two analogies can help us to understand the challenge of building these flagship client relationships that usually account for a disproportionately large share of a firm's revenues and profits. Consider, for instance, the number of stars that we can discern in the night sky. From any one location on Earth, you can see about 2,000 stars with the unaided eye. In total, however, about 6,000 stars are visible from our planet. If we look at service firms, this raises a question: How can you ensure that, when the need arises, each individual professional can effectively see all 6,000 stars—that is, can possess a full understanding of your firm's complete capabilities and resources, or have an effective line of sight to a major client relationship and all the activities that surround it around the globe?

Consider as well the giant Redwood forests in northern California. These ancient trees can live to be 2,000 years old and reach over 350 feet in height. Although their roots are actually fairly shallow—growing only four or five feet into the ground—they spread out for up to 125 feet away from the base of the trunk. The roots interlock with those of all of the other nearby trees, thus creating a powerful defense against the storms and high winds that might topple them. This second analogy hints at the importance of collaboration and a sense of interconnection between professionals who must work together to create and sustain large, institutional client relationships—those "tall Redwoods" among your client base that need broad-based support in order to thrive and endure. In other words, the ability of individual professionals in a firm to see the whole picture, and their capacity to collaborate and live in a state of interdependence, are essential to the *All for One* approach.

Is it enough to have a cadre of skilled but individualistic rainmakers? Not any longer because developing trusted client partnerships is not a solo act. My first book, *Clients for Life*, articulated the journey from expert-for-hire to trusted client advisor. *All for One* sets out the next challenge, which is to evolve from a trusted advisor to a trusted partner. This is, in many ways, a more complex and challenging task; one that requires a comprehensive set of interlinked organizational capabilities rather than the simple derring-do of a single rainmaker. Today's large service firms—with their global infrastructure and substantial overheads—can only serve their clients effectively if they create a *whole* that is greater than the *sum of the parts.*

The title *All for One* captures the need to mobilize the right people, ideas, and resources from wherever they may reside in your organization—the *all*—into each client relationship—the *one.* The *one,* of course, could also be the individual relationship manager who must be supported by his or her entire firm. The phrase comes from *The Three Musketeers* by Alexander Dumas. "One for all, and all for one" is the motto of three inseparable young men—the musketeers of the title—who are members of the king's guard in France. Each of them puts the group's interests ahead of his own, and the group always comes to the aid of the individual. Isn't this how it should be in any great organization?

We face a number of trends that are dramatically affecting client relationships. Some of these are merely extensions of long-standing developments—for example, greater client sophistication and the use of procurement processes to buy services. Others are more recent and still unpredictable as to their eventual impact, such as the advent of technologies that are creating new opportunities to collaborate across boundaries and tap into the wisdom of crowds. I'll briefly mention the most important of these trends and pressures, which need to inform your relationship-building strategies:

- *Demands for more value for money:* Clients are under relentless pressure to do more for less, and they are passing this pressure on to their professional advisors. The increased use of procurement techniques to buy services is a manifestation of this pressure. If properly executed, a trusted client partnership can enable you to leverage your overheads and in fact deliver greater value for money.

- *Demands for more value for time:* Senior executives are now subject to so many demands that time has become a truly precious commodity. Only those professionals who understand how to add value for time will survive in the executive suite.

- *Service outsourcing and offshoring:* For example, GE and other large corporations routinely send legal work to India to be completed by U.S.-trained Indian lawyers at one-fifth the rates charged by their

U.S. counterparts. Some professional services are following the path of manufacturing jobs and are being either outsourced, which is an opportunity for domestic players (e.g., a Hewitt Associates or Towers Perrin will take over a variety of human resources [HR] services for a client), or sent to lower-cost centers in India or even China.

- *The need for foresight and risk reduction:* Executive turnover has accelerated, and corporations have become intolerant of financial, operational, or market surprises. Helping clients avoid these surprises through effective foresight and risk management has become an essential capability.

- *Simultaneous consolidation and fragmentation:* In the past five years, many clients have consolidated the number of service providers that they are willing to use in just about every market. Clients are moving from using hundreds of law firms to using a dozen; from dozens of banks to five or ten; from hundreds of marketing communications companies to one or two; and so on. If you don't have the scale and skill to land in the consolidated group that remains, you may be out of luck. At the same time, we continue to see the separation of "brains and brawn" as small boutiques split off from major firms and thrive by concentrating on specific niches.

- *The advent of Web 2.0 applications and advanced collaboration technologies:* These are just beginning to alter the way service firms work with their employees and their clients. Their ultimate impact is years away, but it will be profound. Firms that embrace these new tools will find it far easier to establish an all-for-one, collaborative culture and create more intimate connections with their clients.

Another way of thinking about the challenges that service providers face is to look at how the nature of client relationships is changing. Table I.1 summarizes these.

Service firms—especially those in traditional fields such as law and accounting—are generally slow to evolve. The most successful ones, however, are going to respond to the rapid evolution of

TABLE I.1 Three Epochs of Client Relationships

	PAST Tradition	PRESENT Performance	FUTURE Partnership
Drivers	▪ Tradition ▪ Schmoozing ▪ Politics	▪ Continuous performance ▪ Strategic selling ▪ Procurement	▪ Collaboration ▪ Partnership selling ▪ Transparency ▪ Unique relationship experience
Players	▪ One to one	▪ Many to many	▪ Interrelated networks
Nature of Value	▪ Core services ▪ Reduced political risk	▪ Core and add-on services ▪ Tangible value	▪ Continually increasing ▪ Tangible and intangible ▪ Multilayered, customized ▪ Embedded in the relationship experience

technology and changes in the competitive structure of markets by significantly altering the way they build and manage their client relationships. The rest of this book lays out a clear path that shows you how to do this by improving your existing practices and employing some new ones.

What are firms doing to respond to these growing client demands for more value? How are they innovating? What are they doing to put twenty-first century relationship-building capabilities into place? Chapters 2 through 13 include dozens of case studies that you'll find interesting. As a preview of what's to come, let me give you a quick sampling of some of the practices that you're going to read about in *All for One:*

- *Balancing short- and long-term goals:* Environment Resources Management (ERM), a major environmental consulting firm, has created leading-edge mechanisms to balance achievement of short-term financial results with long-term relationship-building goals. One of these programs is targeted at 50 of their senior partners, who are evaluated on two distinct balanced scorecards.

One scorecard, which drives cash bonuses, is for short-term financial goals; the second, which drives stock awards, focuses on growth and development goals that are directly tied to the firm's long-term growth and development agenda—including relationships and service excellence. Everyone's scorecard—both before and after the evaluation process is completed—is posted on an intranet and can be reviewed by any one of the 50.

- *Enhancing dialogue with your clients:* Bain & Company, a global consulting firm, uses its Net Promoter Score (NPS) methodology to strengthen relationships with its own clients. Dispensing with traditional market research, where third-party agencies ask clients dozens of tedious questions, Bain asks every executive it works with in each client organization a simple question: "On a scale of 0 to 10, how enthusiastically would you recommend Bain to a friend or colleague?" Research shows that only clients scoring 9 and 10 will become active promoters and spread positive word-of-mouth about the firm; the rest are "passives" or "detractors." Follow-up phone calls with active promoters and detractors create an ongoing dialogue that has proven invaluable to Bain in its relationship-building efforts.

- *Accessing innovation:* Citigroup's Global Corporate Bank has created an innovation network comprised of 50 up-and-coming Citibankers from all around the globe. On a regular basis, this group surfaces innovative ideas and practices from all different parts of the bank, which are then codified and shared with relationship managers who are leading Citigroup's key client relationships. A complementary program called "Passing Down the Wisdom," led by senior bankers, helps to further improve bankers' relationship-building skills by formalizing the apprenticeship process.

- *Leveraging collaboration technologies:* IBM uses online technology to hold "innovation jams" that link employees, clients, and other collaborating parties in virtual brainstorming sessions. The first innovation jam was held in 2006. Subsequently, $100 million was allocated to fund the new ideas that emerged from this 72-hour session, many of which have been successfully implemented.

- *Supporting relationship managers:* HR consulting firm Towers Perrin maintains an extensive support network for its client relationship managers (CRMs). This includes a knowledge management system that gives any CRM immediate access to a wide array of service offering content, best practices, and intellectual capital; a highly structured series of monthly conference calls with all 400 of their CRMs; and a special fast-track program to develop emerging CRMs.

- *Bringing new ideas to clients:* Cognizant, one of the fastest growing technology services companies in the world, implements "big ideas" programs for key clients and has earned an enviable reputation for innovation in a commoditizing market. Using collaboration technologies, they draw new ideas for improving the client's business from their project teams on a monthly basis, filter and develop them, and then present them to senior management each quarter.

- *Customizing the relationship experience:* WPP, a leading $12 billion marketing services company, is creating an entirely new advertising agency—from scratch—to serve Dell Computer. Called Enfatico, it will replace nearly 800 individual marketing services agencies that Dell previously worked with. Enfatico is being tailor-designed to serve the Dell account, and it will eventually be staffed with 1,000 professionals drawn from multiple disciplines and locations around the world.

- *Creating new service delivery models:* Entirely new approaches for adding value to clients and lowering the cost of doing business are emerging in a variety of markets. For example, London-based Eden McCallum has created a new consulting firm model based on 400 independent consultants, most of whom have worked for leading general management consulting firms. They charge about one-half the rates of established firms and give clients greater ownership over the staffing and delivery process. Alternative legal services companies have developed along similar lines. These offer—on a contract basis—experienced attorneys (who have often worked at top-tier law firms) to clients who want lower rates, flexibility, and more control over the work.

You will read about these and other examples in *All for One*, which is based on five years of extensive research I have conducted into the foundations of trusted client partnerships. Through the Client Leadership Forum, a peer-to-peer best practices sharing group that I direct with my colleague James Kelly, I have had the opportunity to conduct in-depth studies of a dozen leading service firms in a variety of markets. I have drawn additional examples and findings from another 20 organizations with which I have either worked or interviewed for this book. I have not tried to select the absolute "best" firms in the world at all aspects of building an all-for-one, client-centered organization because they don't really exist; each firm has different strengths. Instead, I have identified a series of *best practices* that I've drawn from a large sampling of truly excellent service firms. Some of these companies, such as Citigroup and IBM, are large and well known; others, like ZS Associates, Parthenon Group, and ERM, are smaller but exceptionally innovative.

In many of the examples and case studies, I provide the name of the company and the individuals involved, but not always; sometimes I have been asked not to disclose these details. In many cases, I have simply used the title *relationship manager* to identify a variety of partners, managing directors, account managers, and client service officers I have worked with over the past several years.

This book is divided into four parts:

- *Part One* presents case studies of two extraordinarily successful trusted client partnerships, defines the six levels of professional relationships, and summarizes the 10 strategies required to arrive at Level 6.
- *Part Two* contains the first five of 10 strategies for building trusted client partnerships. These five are mostly, but not exclusively, the responsibility of the individual professional.
- *Part Three* contains the last five strategies that have to be driven mostly at the firm level; you can think of them as institutional strategies that require specific commitment and support from senior management.

- *Part Four* changes the pace and presents the 17 most commonly asked questions that have been posed to me about building long-term client relationships, along with their answers. This section complements the 10 strategies with tactical advice on how to deal with a variety of vexing relationship issues. Chapter 14 concludes the book.

This book serves as a guide and road map to creating an all-for-one culture and developing more trusted client partnerships. Whether you are an individual professional responsible for managing client relationships or a member of your firm's leadership, you'll find, in almost every chapter, ideas that you can apply immediately.

PART

I

A Road Map for Building Trusted Client Partnerships

1

Reaching Level 6: Trusted Client Partner

This book describes the 10 essential strategies that are required to build long-term, institutional client relationships—what I call *trusted client partnerships*. These partnerships are broad and deep, and they are characterized by many-to-many relationships at multiple levels. They usually endure for years. They account for a small percentage of most firms' client relationships, but they contribute a disproportionately large share of their growth, profits, and intellectual capital. They can be hugely beneficial to clients, and often result in greater value, lower risk, and faster execution. You need them in good times, but even more so in tough times. The 10 strategies that I introduce in the coming chapters are largely the result of an extensive study I have conducted of large, institutional client relationships; they also reflect my personal experiences in building senior executive relationships during my 28-year career in management consulting.

What exactly *is* a trusted client partnership? Let's define this term by first examining two striking but typical examples.

Citigroup and Royal Dutch Shell

Less than 10 years ago, the idea of having Royal Dutch Shell as a major client was little more than a gleam in the eyes of the top executives of Citigroup's Global Corporate Bank. Today, Shell is one of Citigroup's largest worldwide clients. Citigroup has built a network of relationships with dozens of Shell executives around the world and is a major partner in helping Shell to achieve its strategic objectives. The way in which this happened is a practical illustration of the power of the *All for One* strategies and philosophy set out in this book.

In the beginning, two Citigroup investment bankers had some contacts in Shell's mergers and acquisitions department. Rather than going it alone, they brought in the then-chairman of Citigroup Europe, Sir Win Bischoff, as a senior advisor to the team. Sir Win did not simply push aggressively to be included in an upcoming transaction, as bankers sometimes do, but rather offered to conduct a complete analysis—at no charge—of Shell's upstream (refining and distribution) business. Working with a division head who would later become the Shell CEO, the Citigroup team spent three months looking at the future of the business. The ideas that emerged from this work, combined with the trust that developed, eventually earned Citigroup the right to participate in three major Shell deals.

Some top executives were replaced the following year; and it turned out that two of the newcomers had worked for other Citigroup clients. The Citigroup team worked hard to successfully transfer those relationships. The new CEO, however, had no relationship with Citigroup. Sir Win called on his extended network and asked a former finance minister to introduce him to the new CEO and to give Citigroup advice on how to build the relationship. Shortly afterward, Citigroup was one of nine banks invited to bid on a major restructuring assignment. The Citigroup team members invested heavily in preparing their proposal. They even took the unusual approach of interviewing Shell's auditors and lawyers in an attempt to understand every aspect of the restructuring challenge. Through the quality of their proposal and their intimate knowledge of Shell's business, they won the mandate. Shell not only picked them for the assignment, but they also insisted on paying them for the planning work because they wanted it to be a fair deal and hoped to secure Citigroup's full commitment to the program.

The relationship expanded over time, and Citigroup began doing brokerage, trading, and cash management for Shell. It would be one-sided to say that the relationship has always been a bed of roses—in fact, there have been ups and downs, as there invariably are between a major investment bank and a large corporate client. There have been times, for example, when each side had to say no to a request by the other party. Equally, there have been moments when deposits of trust were made—such as when Citigroup helped Shell out by liquidating a particular bond position.

Citigroup employed a number of *All for One* strategies in fostering the Shell relationship. Some were explicit —for example, carefully leveraging firm-wide networks, coordinating between product units, putting a senior advisor on the team, and investing heavily to build intimate client knowledge. Others, however, were more hidden in the fabric of the institution, and included things like a sophisticated, multilevel relationship management structure and a performance evaluation system that balances achieving short-term financial goals with commitment to cultural values such as collaboration and client focus.

> Successful long-term relationships are based on a combination of the individual and the company. In order for there to be continuity, you really must have a relationship at the firm level. This is why having the right culture is essential. It's where teamwork comes in, it's about how people are measured and evaluated, and even about how information flows—these things are extremely important. The individual actually delivers the relationship, but the firm backs it up. If the culture doesn't support the individual's efforts, then it will fail.
>
> **—Sir Win Bischoff, Chairman, Citigroup**

Booz Allen Hamilton and the U.S. Navy

A second example of an extraordinary trusted client partnership is Booz Allen Hamilton's relationship with the U.S. Navy. Talk about a "client for life"—the U.S. Navy has used this consulting firm for nearly *70 years*, a period of time equal to about three professional lifetimes. In 1940—as the Axis powers tightened their grip on Europe and Asia—the U.S. Navy found itself grossly underequipped, with no permanent headquarters and less than half the ships it needed to conduct the war. The two founders of Booz Allen Hamilton—Ed Booz and Jim Allen—personally took on the assignment to help the Navy expand and modernize. They assisted the Navy to create a more effective management structure and cut red tape, and then worked side by side with Navy personnel to implement a series of recommendations designed to speed up decision making and accelerate manufacturing processes. Good work is always the foundation of a trusted client partnership; and indeed, Secretary of the Navy Frank Knox—who had hired Booz Allen Hamilton—was later quoted by *Fortune* magazine as saying that in using the firm, he had never spent the government's money more effectively. Since that initial engagement, Booz Allen Hamilton has worked with the U.S. Navy on a continuous series of projects, helping it confront an array of strategic, operational, and technology issues through the Cold War and beyond. The firm helped the Navy launch the Polaris missile program in the 1950s, and develop shipboard communications and computer technologies in the 1970s. Today, a dedicated group of partners lead Booz Allen Hamilton's work with the Navy across multiple locations around the world.

Like Citigroup's Corporate Bank, Booz Allen Hamilton employs a variety of organizational practices, processes, and systems that enable it to develop, grow, and sustain trusted partnerships with its clients. These include an ability to work with and support—rather than disdain—the procurement managers who evaluate new proposals; an authentic talent for aligning with their client's agenda ("your mission is our mission" is a commonly used phrase at the firm); a set of well-developed best practices for institutionalizing and building many-to-many relationships with the client's organization; a skilled cadre of project managers (principals) and client service officers (vice presidents) who are empowered to lead major engagements; and rigorous quality control processes.

Booz Allen Hamilton's relationship with the Navy is the rule for them, not the exception. Over the past decade, the firm's now $3 billion public sector consulting business has grown at the remarkable pace of 20 percent per year. Its success cannot simply be ascribed to a rapidly growing market for government contracts. In fact, it faces intense—even brutal—competition. For some bids (and over 80 percent of Booz Allen Hamilton's government work is won through formal, competitive procurement processes) there can be 10 or even 20 large competitors such as Boeing, IBM, Accenture, and other behemoths, who have nonetheless been unable to achieve Booz Allen's growth rates.

What's their secret—besides a highly structured approach to building and managing large-scale relationships? One of Booz Allen Hamilton's senior vice presidents described to me his view of their competitive advantage:

> *It's very simple: Collaboration is built into our DNA, and so we always compete as one team. When a large opportunity presents itself, we discuss it as a partner group. We decide together whether or not to commit the resources needed to win the bid. If every head in the room nods, then we go for it. We do whatever it takes, and everyone helps each other out. If I need a particular person who is engaged elsewhere—if they are really critical to help us win and then deliver—my partners will almost always make the sacrifice. The fact is, we are much smaller than almost all of our competitors. But they compete as isolated business units, and we compete as one firm. So even though we are not as large, we do a better job of marshalling the right resources and concentrating them onto the opportunity. We effectively bring to bear the clout of a much larger organization.*

Relationships like these are the envy of any large services firm. They don't happen by accident, however; and they are not the work of a single talented individual. They must be systematically cultivated and grown. As I described in the Introduction, the capacity of a firm to develop these trusted client partnerships rests on an entire *system* of organizational capabilities. You can become a trusted advisor by developing your own skills and working on your own client relationships, but you need to employ a multiplicity of strategies and a team approach in order to become a trusted partner—it's not a solo act. The journey is well worth it, however. The rewards, for both service provider and client, are huge.

Underpinnings of Trusted Client Partnerships

To cultivate a relationship of this stature, two key dimensions must be developed: the individual professional's role, and the firm's overall relationship. Here's what has to happen:

- First, the individual professional who is leading the relationship must evolve his *role* from that of an expert for hire to a trusted client advisor. This is the essential first step.
- Second, the firm's *relationship* must develop from a single point of contact and a single service to multiple contacts and a broad range of services.

These two dimensions are shown in Figure 1.1.

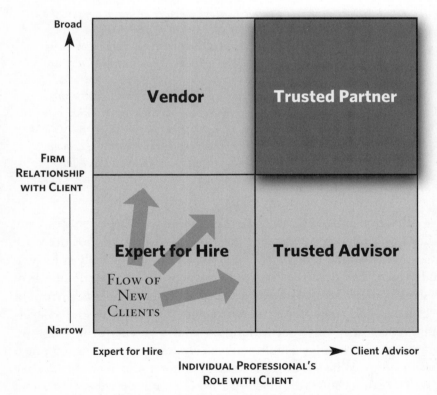

FIGURE 1.1   The Client Development Matrix

If you reflect on it, you'll see that this Client Development Matrix—where each quadrant represents a particular positioning with the client—makes intuitive sense. However, to create a complete progression of professional relationships, we need to consider individuals who are not yet clients—people who have not even entered the matrix. Nonclients include what I call *contacts* and *acquaintances*. If we add these into the mix, we end up with six levels of professional relationships. My clients have found it extremely useful to think about these as a progression from one to six.

Level 1: *Contact*

This is the starting point. We meet someone, have a brief conversation, and exchange business cards. We may stay in touch over the years, but there is little interaction. The individual is primarily just a name in our contact database.

Level 2: *Acquaintance*

Acquaintances are contacts we have gotten to know a bit better or friends we have carried with us through the different stages of our lives. We know something about each other, and may have actually spent a fair amount of time together, but the individual has never become a client. He or she may be important to us for other reasons, however, perhaps as source of friendship, information, and insight about markets and competitors, or as resources that we can introduce to our clients.

Level 3: *Expert*

At the beginning of your relationships with them, some contacts and acquaintances become clients for whom you are invariably hired in a narrow, expert role. The client has a problem she wants solved, and you have the specific knowledge and experience to deal with it. Almost all relationships begin in this way and, in this quadrant, the trust and mutual understanding that enable a relationship to deepen simply have not developed yet. It's not a "bad" position to be in, but over time, you're going to want to move to the right and upward in the matrix.

Level 4: *Vendor or Steady Supplier*

If you do a good job on the first engagement or transaction, you will probably be asked to do some follow-up work; and you may eventually end up managing a very large, multifaceted set of programs. Don't kid yourself, however, you're still in "request-for-proposal territory," just as you were when you were a solitary expert for hire. At this point, you may be spending a lot of your time with procurement managers or lower-level buyers, without the benefit of having an anchor into senior management. You are by no means part of this client's inner circle; you're more like a contractor who is managing many tradesmen or experts.

Level 5: *Trusted Advisor*

You earn this coveted role—which was the subject of my first book, *Clients for Life*—by exemplifying a series of essential qualities that set you apart from the expert for hire or vendor. These include things like personal trustworthiness, independence, judgment, big-picture think-ing, empathy, and others. The challenge at this point is to move up the other axis and broaden the relationship at a firm level—to grow it from an individual relationship to an institutional one. You don't always progress linearly from Level 3 through Levels 4 and 5—sometimes you move directly from Expert to Trusted Advisor, skipping the Vendor stage altogether.

Level 6: *Trusted Partner*

This is the ultimate goal: to be a trusted advisor to your client *and* to harness the full power of your organization to address a variety of client issues. Finding yourself in this upper-right quadrant means that you have built a true partnership. You are helping to shape your client's agenda, you've developed many-to-many relationships, and you are meeting an array of client needs with different services or products. It's not an easy task to play this role with a client, but if you succeed, you and your firm will probably have a client for life—and a highly profitable one at that. You'll also experience great personal satisfaction in the role of a trusted counselor who is having a significant impact on client success.

These six levels, and the way in which a client would describe them, are summarized in Table 1.1.

How Do You Know You've Reached Level 6?

In a Level 6 trusted partner relationship, you typically:

- Have developed multiple relationships between your firm and the client's organization, both horizontally and vertically;
- Have several, Level 5 trusted advisor relationships with the client;
- Have strong relationships with one or more key economic buyers;
- Have broadened the relationship so that you provide the client with a variety of services or products and there is a breadth of revenues; and
- Are doing work that is aligned with the most critical issues on the client's agenda.

There are no hard-and-fast, scientific criteria to identify a Level 6 trusted client partnership, but these are some of the key factors you need to look for.

We have three foundations that contribute to sustaining our long-term, institutional client relationships: the team; client results; and our approach to creating value. Our competitive spirit is turned toward our client's competition—not toward each other. Many of our consultants were at the top of their class, but we emphasize our team approach and collaboration every chance we can. When we recruit we look for teamwork skills, and collaboration is reinforced in the performance feedback process and in almost every communication from our managing partner. As a result, we have a culture where individuals don't try to "outshine" a peer; and the slogan "One Bain partner never lets down another Bain partner" is engrained in our behavior.

—Wendy Miller, Director, Bain & Company

TABLE 1.1   The Six Levels of Professional Relationships

Level	How a Client Would Describe It
1. Contact	"We've met. I think he works for . . ."
2. Acquaintance	"I've known her for a while. We have some things in common and know some of the same people."
3. Expert For Hire	"He's very knowledgeable in that area and did excellent work for us on a project."
4. Steady Supplier	"We've had a relationship for a while now. She and her firm consistently deliver, and I've recommended her to a few colleagues. For this type of work, we'll continue to use them."
5. Trusted Advisor	"I've known him for a long time. He's superb at what he does, and has great business sense. I really trust his judgment, and I will definitely use him as a sounding board for tough issues."
6. Trusted Partner	"I view them as a long-term partner in growing our business. They've built many strong relationships with our people, and they consistently add value. I feel we get the best that their firm can offer."

Importance of Reaching Level 6

How would you or your firm's client relationships map against the client development matrix and these different levels of relationships? How many of your clients would fall in each of the quadrants? When I have worked with my clients to position their client base in this matrix, they typically find that between 10 and 20 percent of their relationships fall into the Level 6 trusted partner quadrant. These relationships are in the minority; but as I've mentioned, they make an outsize contribution to the growth and prosperity of any firm, and they are often the source of your most innovative intellectual capital.

What if you had just a few more of these Level 6 relationships? What kind of an impact would this have on your organization? I have frequently seen a single Level 6 client transform a career or an office. For example, when I moved to Rome to become Gemini Consulting's Country Head and Managing Director for Italy, I was able to succeed in growing the practice and adding staff mainly because of two Level 6 relationships that I developed early in my tenure there. And during their early days, Bain & Company based its international expansion strategy on the development of Level 6 relationships. Bain would only open a new office outside the United States when it had developed a "consolidated" client in that geographic location, that is, a major flagship client that would provide ballast and a steady revenue stream to support the hiring of staff and investment in local office infrastructure.

Why It Matters to Clients

I've made it clear how important Level 6 relationships are for the service provider. But what about the client? In the hundreds of interviews that I have conducted, client executives cite a variety of benefits to these long-term, institutional relationships, some of which include:

- *Impact:* Often, it takes a significant concentration of resources from an outside service provider to help clients actually achieve their strategic goals.
- *Continuity:* The trust and continuity that are part of the fabric of a trusted client partnership increase speed and enable more efficient project completion.
- *Value:* By developing intimate client and industry knowledge, the service provider can add value in multiple dimensions and create more tailored solutions.
- *Ease of use:* It can be extremely unwieldy and inefficient for large clients to use dozens—even hundreds—of banks, law firms, or advertising agencies all around the world. By concentrating their

business with a smaller number of strategic partners, clients can dramatically decrease the friction of relationship management.

- *Cost:* All of the factors cited here can combine to reduce overall costs for the client.

Not surprisingly, the investment required to develop Level 6 client relationships is commensurate with their importance and payback. Building and sustaining them requires the application of the integrated set of strategies that are summarized in the next chapter.

2

Employing 10 Integrated Strategies

O ver the past five years, I have studied, in depth, about 50 Level 6 relationships across a variety of service markets—including consulting, accounting, law, financial services, advertising, public relations, and technology services. I have also reviewed several hundred additional client relationship case studies that have provided supporting data to the 50 detailed reviews. Two things became apparent as I analyzed these relationships. First, a multiplicity of strategies contributed to their development. Second, these strategies were successful because they were able to take root in a culture of collaboration and client focus. Let's look first at the strategies that were used, which form the core of this book.

There are 10 distinct strategies that contribute to the development of Level 6 trusted partner relationships. They are not all used at once and, depending on the individual client, they may vary somewhat in importance. Five of them tend naturally to be the individual professional's responsibility, while the other five must be driven more by the institution:

Strategies That Are Mostly the Responsibility of the Individual Professional

1. *Become an agenda setter.* Evolve from agenda reacting to agenda setting by identifying, aligning with, and helping to shape your client's most critical issues and priorities.

2. *Develop relationship capital.* Identify and cultivate a group of *critical few* relationships, drawn from five key constituencies, and understand how to link these to your clients' and colleagues' own networks.

3. *Engage new clients.* Cross the bridge from contact to client as you develop rapport, identify the other person's agenda, and build trust in your ability to solve their problems.

4. *Institutionalize and grow.* Turn individual relationships into institutional ones as you mobilize the right people, ideas, and resources into your client relationship, and build a team behind you.

5. *Add multiple layers of value.* Deliver tangible and intangible value as well as institutional and personal value, and leverage your firm's organization and resources to tap into six distinct value levers for your client.

Strategies That Are Mostly the Responsibility of the Firm

6. *Target the right clients.* Develop a shared view about which clients, issues, and individual executives you want to engage with in the first place.

7. *Build a client leadership pipeline.* Systematically develop the next generation of client leaders and actively support your current relationship managers.

8. *Promote collaboration.* Enable firmwide collaboration that allows the right people and ideas to cross organizational and geographic boundaries easily and rewards them for doing so.

9. *Engage in systematic client listening.* Implement multiple channels of client listening activities to connect with clients at the top, understand their issues, and ensure quality.

10. *Create a unique client experience.* Develop a truly differentiated client experience in which your client interactions themselves represent significant sources of value, and work with clients to co-create the relationship experience that is most beneficial to them.

You may ask, "What do some of these individual strategies have to do with developing a large-scale, trusted partnership?" They are, in fact, *essential* ingredients for our recipe. At the molecular level, large-scale relationships are composed of many individual ones. The ability of each professional to build his or her own relationship capital, for example (Chapter 4), and to successfully engage contacts and acquaintances and turn them into clients (Chapter 5) is critical to laying the foundations for a client partnership.

These strategies are additive and mutually reinforcing. You can pursue them individually, and they will certain provide benefit to you. But it's when you are able to put them all into place together that you create an entire organizational system that allows you to develop and nurture trusted client partnerships on a consistent basis.

These 10 strategies can be loosely overlaid on the Client Development Matrix that we looked at in Chapter 1 (see Figure 2.1).

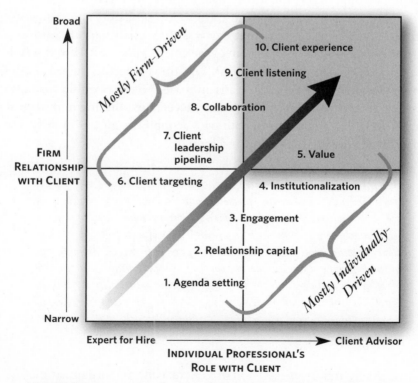

FIGURE 2.1 Ten Strategies to Build Trusted Client Partnerships

Chapters 3 through 12 explain each of these 10 strategies in depth, providing practical examples, best practices, and suggestions for implementing them in your own organization.

Do You Have a Client-Centered, Collaborative Culture?

I was recently in London for a meeting of the Client Leadership Forum, a group of leading service firms that meet regularly to share best practices on how to develop a client-focused organization and build long-term client relationships. I co-founded this Forum with my colleague James Kelly as a means to create peer-to-peer sharing and to drive innovative research on this topic. The meeting was held at the corporate headquarters of one of the Forum participants, Lloyds Banking Group, one of the top 25 banks in the world. Around the table were the leaders from these firms, a mixture of CEOs and managing partners. One of our guests that day was then-chairman of Citigroup Europe—and soon to be chairman of the entire bank—Sir Win Bischoff (see the earlier sidebar on Sir Win). Did this powerful, quintessential banker start off by talking about his approach to relationship management, or the skills he has honed over the years in advising and negotiating with CEOs in dozens of countries around the globe? Hardly. He began by addressing the group and saying:

> *When I arrived at the reception downstairs, I was struck by how professional, friendly, and inviting the receptionists were. They were expecting me, knew where I was going, addressed me by name, and made me feel immediately at home here in Lloyds TSB's offices. In truth, the capacity to build great client relationships starts with the culture, and that means being client focused in every part of the organization. You can give relationship managers all the training you want, but unless the culture is aligned with the goal of collaborating to deliver great client service and investing in long-term relationships, it just won't work. It all starts with the culture.*

The very first manifestation of a client-centered organization may well be the reception desk as you walk in. But the process, as we'll see in Chapter 10, definitely starts at the top. Ed Nusbaum, the chief executive of accounting firm Grant Thornton, puts it this way:

> *Building a collaborative firm starts with the tone set by leadership and the messages you send out to your people. At every level, in every practice, I try to promote a mindset and culture where our professionals help each other out. You need a matrix to manage the organization, but we've really tried not to create silos so that the client remains our main focus. Our metrics, which include client service quality and working as one firm, reflect this.*

Most service firms *claim* to be collaborative and client-focused. But are they really? Is your own organization's culture truly relationship and client-centric? Are your values shared from the executive suite right through to your receptionist? Without the right culture, as Sir Win tells us, all of the strategies and initiatives and training programs in the world will fall on deaf ears and on barren soil. There is no definitive litmus test for what constitutes a client-centered culture; but there is a series of questions I suggest you ask yourself about your own firm in order to assess its readiness to adopt the *All for One* strategies described in this book:

Some Questions to Ask

- What fraction of their time do your top executives actually *spend* with clients? (5 percent? 20 percent? 50 percent?)
- Are clients regularly discussed in executive forums and at the management committee level?

After I joined Lloyds TSB three years ago, the first thing we did to create a more collaborative, client-focused organization was to merge our relationship and product organizations. We created a corporate markets business centered on our clients, from product development through to relationship management. We also aligned our measurement and reward system with our goal of building broad-based relationships, and created a scorecard that includes financial measures for cross-selling as well as relationship development. I personally try to role model our values—this year, for example, I have personally met with 360 of the bank's clients. When you have client focus coming from the top, it really lifts the game of your relationship managers throughout the organization.

—Diana Brightmore-Armour, CEO of Corporate Banking, Lloyds Banking Group

- How much power are relationship managers given in order to act on their clients' behalf ?
- Is there a gap between senior management's pronouncements about "client focus" and its actual policies and actions?
- Does the firm do anything to independently verify the success of its relationships (e.g., market research, independent reviews)?
- Does the firm have metrics to assess relationship health (e.g., retention, breadth, relationships with decision makers, number of referrals)?
- Are professionals allowed discretionary time and budget to build networks and relationships that may have little short-term payoff?
- Does an interest in and focus on clients pervade the organization and extend beyond those professionals who are managing client relationships (e.g., to receptionists, administrative and support staff, functional specialists in IT and legal)?
- How easy is it for clients to do business with the firm?
- Is your organization structure client centric? Are single clients and client markets major focal points for the organization?
- What is the sense of balance between working for the firm's interests (achieving short-term financial return) versus serving the client's agenda?
- Do your professionals willingly and naturally collaborate around client relationships?
- At the end of the year, how much arguing or conflict is there around getting credit for revenue generation and client relationship success?

Conclusion

Traditionally, we celebrate and hold in awe those individuals who are accomplished rainmakers or trusted counselors to top executives. Reaching Level 6, however—building trusted client partnerships—requires more. *All for One* is a philosophy that, when operational, allows you to mobilize the right people, ideas, and resources

TABLE 2.1　Do You Have a Level 6 Client Relationship?

	No	Some-what	Yes
1. We have developed *many-to-many* relationships, at multiple levels, between our firm and this client.			
2. We have established several or more *trusted advisor* relationships.			
3. We have strong relationships with senior executives who are *economic buyers*.			
4. This client buys a *broad range* of services from us.			
5. Our work is aligned with and supports one or more of this client's most *critical priorities*.			
6. This client considers us a *partner* in accomplishing its strategic and operational goals.			
7. This is a *multiyear* relationship.			
8. This client's executives would enthusiastically *recommend* us to their colleagues and friends.			

into each and every client relationship. It enables you to deliver the whole firm, all the time, to every client. In good times, these Level 6 relationships will lead your growth; in tough times, they will ensure that if your clients have to cut back, you will be the last one standing among your competition.

A good way to start this journey is to select a current client that has the potential to develop into a Level 6 relationship; or, alternatively, one that you believe is already at this stage but needs more attention and investment. As you go through the chapters, you can then apply the strategies to this specific client. Table 2.1 sets out a series of questions that will help you determine how close you are to Level 6.

PART II

The Five Individual Strategies

3

Strategy One: Becoming an Agenda Setter

*Understanding and Shaping Your Client's
Most Critical Priorities*

After six months of unsuccessful attempts, the senior business development team at a large technology services company finally procured a meeting with a high-potential customer: the chief executive of a major telecommunications provider. Four executives from the technology services firm went to the meeting with the CEO. They had prepared carefully—or so they thought—and had developed a well-honed presentation on how they could provide a mission-critical, state-of-the-art system to the CEO's company. They traveled from three different countries to attend the meeting.

Fifteen minutes into the discussion, however, the CEO appeared unengaged and distracted. His knee rocked from side to side, and he peered at his Blackberry. He finally glanced at his watch, and then abruptly interrupted the presentation. "Look, it's been very nice meeting you, but I've got an urgent appointment and I have to leave." He thanked his guests and left them, speechless and forlorn, in the meeting room. His assistant led them out.

One of the executives later confessed to me that they had discovered, a few days after the meeting, a video of the CEO on a financial news web site. It had been filmed only a week before their meeting, and in it, the CEO had laid out a new set of strategic priorities for his organization. These focused on things like value-added services, customer retention, and improved responsiveness in their call centers. The technology company's new system was definitely not part of, nor aligned in any clear way, with the CEO's new agenda. Given the crushing demands on his daily schedule, the CEO quickly decided that the meeting did not align with his priorities and was not a good use of his scarce time—so he unceremoniously bolted.

Were my friends from the technology firm simply unprepared for the meeting with the CEO? Were they too eager to sell? Possibly. In any event, the point is clear: Understanding a client's agenda is the first and in some ways *most critical* step that you must take in order to connect with them and eventually develop a Level 6 trusted partner relationship. That's why *Agenda Setting* is the first of the 10 strategies for building a client-centered firm and reaching Level 6. Almost everything else flows from a deep understanding of and connection to your client's core agenda.

What Is an Agenda?

Every client executive has, or should have, an agenda of important priorities that he or she is focused on. The word "agenda" derives from the Latin verb *agere*, "to do," and means a list of things to do.

An agenda usually describes a set of major priorities or goals. It may be formally written out, but sometimes it's simply kept inside your client's head. It usually includes more than one or two items, but probably not more than six or seven. It can consist of broad, strategic aspirations ("globalize our consumer business"), focus on operational priorities ("reduce costs by 10 percent"), or comprise both types of objectives.

If a client doesn't have an agenda, he or she needs to develop one. A well-thought-out agenda is an essential tool that helps executives use their time effectively and focus on their most important priorities in a world where there are innumerable and unrelenting demands for their attention.

There are always several levels of agendas in any client organization. There will invariably be an overarching strategy for the organization, owned by the CEO and his top team; but then each individual client will have a more specific set of issues and goals. You need to have a strong understanding of both levels.

It's your job to engage with your client's agenda. But why is this subject so important? There are many reasons:

- *Relevance:* In order to be truly relevant to a client, your work must directly relate to and support that client's agenda of critical priorities. If you cannot demonstrate this, you will be sidelined: senior management won't care about your work, and your fees will always be under scrutiny. You'll be a nice-to-have but nonessential vendor.

- *Impact:* If you want to impact a client's success, your work needs to somehow affect or tie to the company's most important levers for growth and value creation. I started in the consulting profession during the 1980 to 1982 recession, and I can still remember how some consulting firms were selling "culture change" projects—a poor use of scarce cash for companies that were losing money—because it was the latest intellectual fad.

- *Ensuring that the agenda is the right one:* The wrong agenda can be disastrous. At this writing, General Motors' market capitalization

> ## A Famous Agenda at IBM
>
> In 1993, Lou Gerstner became the CEO of IBM, a company whose performance was dismal at the time. IBM was considered unmanageable, and Gerstner was under intense pressure to break it up into pieces. He spent the first couple of months of his tenure visiting IBM customers all over the world. Their message to him was clear and consistent: "We need help using your products, and breaking yourself up isn't going to make our life any easier." Gerstner firmly rejected calls to dismantle the company, and developed an agenda that is now lore. Starting from the customer perspective, he created a clear plan for IBM based on customer focus, growing services, helping customers run their computer systems, better integrating the different divisions of IBM, and instigating a tougher, more engaged leadership style. To further his agenda, Gerstner founded IBM Global Services, which today is a $50 billion consulting and systems integration business.

is a fraction of Toyota's, and bankruptcy is a distinct possibility—a consequence of spending decades following the wrong agenda (a wasted robotics program in the 1980s; lack of investment in hybrid technologies; an excessive focus on large SUVs and trucks as oil prices climbed; and so on). Clearly, General Motors' agenda has not been the right one.

- *Breadth:* You may be initially asked to work on a relatively circumscribed, narrow issue for a client. Your ability to broaden the relationship over time depends on understanding and being able to engage with the client's broader agenda. If all of your conversations with the client are about the specific project at hand, it's unlikely you will be able to discern additional needs, introduce other colleagues, and therefore grow the relationship.

Principal Concerns of Senior Executives

To help your clients shape and set their agendas, you need to understand the broader set of concerns shared by almost all executives. It's useful to think about two categories: institutional concerns and personal concerns. While their relative emphasis will vary from person to person and situation to situation, they tend to cut across industries and markets. Let's start with the personal concerns because these are often ignored in favor of the more easily accessible business issues.

Personal Concerns

All clients have a personal agenda that, in some respects, may be even more important than their business agenda. Major concerns include:

1. *Career:* All executives are deeply concerned about their careers. They're wondering: "How am I doing in my current role? What does my boss think about my performance? What should my next move be? Do I have broader support in the organization? Should I think about leaving for a new company?"

2. *Wealth:* While executives think a great deal about personal wealth creation, they discuss it very little. Given today's levels of executive

compensation, the stakes for some are very high indeed. Their personal wealth is directly impacted by their company's stock price and by their ability to hit certain performance targets. The success or failure of your work could in fact have a measurable impact on a client's net worth.

3. *Relationships and network:* When it comes to investing their personal time, one criterion that executives often consider is: "Can this individual or organization extend my network and provide valuable contacts for me?" Everyone can offer opera tickets and seminars, but truly valuable personal contacts are proprietary and not subject to gift rules or other corporate restrictions.

4. *Personal life:* In the end, every client has a personal life that usually revolves around family, friends, and personal pursuits. If you'd like to connect more deeply with your clients, you *must* understand and appreciate this aspect of their lives.

Institutional Concerns

At the most basic level, senior clients usually have five major institutional concerns:

1. *Growth:* Profits drive stock price, and the perennial concern of the corporation's top officers is: "Where is our future growth going to come from?" They direct a laser-like focus on investors' expectations for growth, on how much *organic* revenue growth they can realistically achieve, and on how they can fill the gap—if there is one—with acquisitions, partnerships, licensing, and other means. Advisors who can squarely and convincingly connect their service offering to increased growth will get management's attention.

2. *Costs:* Cost cutting, in many organizations, has gone from a periodic exercise to an ongoing program of cost review and management. Nearly all managers are under continual pressure to do more for less, and almost no area of a corporation is exempt from these demands. There are two implications of this: First, any service professional must be cognizant of the cost pressures that clients experience and put a singular focus on value. Second, any

proposal that will help a client control costs and use assets more efficiently is going to get noticed.

3. *Capital markets:* The investors and credit institutions that provide equity and debt financing to a company are crucial constituencies, and executives—especially CEOs and CFOs—spend a lot of their time focused on what their investors think, their access to additional funds, and their stock price.

4. *Risk:* There is no question that today's business environment is fraught with risks for executives at every level. Many factors have contributed to this, including regulatory changes (e.g., Sarbanes-Oxley, which gives the CEO additional liability for the accuracy of financial statements), the volatility of financial markets, the transparency and immediacy created by the Internet, and so on. No one wants to have to face his or her boss or the company's board and say, "Something very bad has happened that we did not anticipate."

5. *The senior team:* All executives think long and hard about their team of senior managers. Are they the right individuals for the job? Are they aligned to the strategy? Do they work as a team and collaborate? Can their performance be improved? What can be done about conflicts? This is an area where you can often add additional value by offering insights about how to improve the performance of your client's senior team.

Other issues of concern, depending on the particular executive and the company's strategy, include employee engagement and alignment, competition, innovation, and external constituencies (e.g., the government, NGOs, unions).

Pressures on Senior Executives

In addition to the various business and personal issues that may impact a client's agenda, it's important to keep in mind that today's clients are subject to a variety of relentless pressures—some of which are unprecedented. The first of these is extremely *high expectations.* As CEO salaries have grown, so has the compensation for the next tier of executives and functional heads. Performance expectations have grown dramatically, as has the amount of intense *time pressure* under which executives are expected to accomplish their ambitious goals. Not surprisingly, they are demanding corresponding speed from their advisors. Fifteen years ago, it would have been normal to spend six or even nine months "studying" a problem. Now, clients may allot a month—or even a week—for the upfront study phase, with implementation expected to swiftly follow.

More than ever, top executives are in a *media spotlight*. Today, senior corporate executives are fair game to be pulled into the middle of a media circus that now includes not just press reporting but millions of Internet sites, blogs, and video-hosting services like YouTube. The slightest misstatement, angry e-mail sent in haste, bad joke, gaffe, or misstep can quickly ruin a career.

Given the pressure cooker environment in which executives find themselves, it's not surprising that *executive turnover* has grown significantly. Recent studies of accelerating CEO turnover illustrate this inspades. There is not only intense pressure to meet financial and operational goals, but also to do so without making any mistakes. As noted earlier, executives cannot afford to go to their boards and shareholders with a major surprise, because it may just mean the end of their tenure.

Clients also face *more choices* than ever. Many factors—including the Internet, technology, and improved communications and transportation—have "flattened" the world and created previously unavailable opportunities for companies of any size. Even a small-town or local business can become global today. Executives thus have a plethora of choices available to them, many of which are the wrong choices. Deciphering complex issues such as globalization and the impact of technology means that executives have to put more time,

> As a CEO, I do have a long-term agenda of goals and programs. However, my priorities also shift as I have to deal with crises, organizational issues, customers, and so on. So the issue you want to see me about this week may not resonate, and therefore I won't make time for it in my calendar. However, you have to be persistent—that issue could resurface in a month or two and then I may be very interested in talking to you.
>
> **—Chief Executive Officer**

energy, and thought into separating the wheat from the chaff in order to make the right decisions. This is why trusted advisors will not become anachronisms any time soon.

A final point about the pressures on client executives is that their priorities are both *fixed* and *fluid*. While it is true that most good business leaders operate under a set of strategic priorities that they are constantly driving forward, it's also fair to say that top executives' immediate priorities can change from week to week—as the quote on page 41 illustrates. In other words, you have to be very flexible and adaptive as you interact with your clients around their agenda.

Agendas and the Executive Life Cycle

Tenure and career stage can also have a strong influence on the nature of a client's agenda. When executives are new in a position, they are more open to outside suggestions; and they will often begin by setting a higher-level, strategic agenda for change. In the middle of their tenure, they are more likely to be focused on achieving specific operational objectives and results. Toward the end of their tenure, they become concerned about their legacy in the role. What have they really achieved? How will others view their contributions?

The stage of the executive's career is also relevant. The first half of an executive's career lends itself toward a focus on personal accomplishment and on demonstrating that he has the requisite talent and drive to accomplish difficult objectives. As he is promoted into senior management, he often realizes that it's no longer about his own skills, but rather his ability to get things done through others—to motivate, inspire, and lead rather than personally break down brick walls. This will lead to major shifts in the focus on the agenda he is pursuing.

Evolving through Three Stages

To reach the point where you have earned the right to help a client shape and set his or her agenda, you typically move through the following stages:

Stage 1—Agenda reacting: In stage 1, you react to a client's request for work. You get a call asking for help with an issue. Your client has identified the need, not you—you're reactive, not proactive.

Stage 2—Agenda sensing: In this phase, you invest time to deeply understand your client's needs, issues, and goals. This may happen as a natural consequence of working with her, or it may require a special effort to get to know her as an individual, learn about her business, and understand the markets and industries in which her organization competes.

Stage 3—Agenda setting: At this point, you have earned the requisite trust to be able to help your client shape and set her agenda. You have a "seat at the table" when your client is thinking about her most important issues.

Stage 1 is self-evident, and doesn't require huge amounts of skill. However, there is a knack—as one of my clients says—to "being there when the dam breaks." In other words, you need to be visible and accessible when the client has a need. To do this, you'll want to draw on the "staying in touch" strategies that you'll read about in the next chapter.

Stages 2 and 3, agenda sensing and setting, are a complex blend of art and science; so let's look at specific strategies to help you improve at these latter two stages.

Getting Better at Agenda Sensing

It's not always easy to understand an executive's priorities; and the more senior the client, the harder it can be to really tease apart his complete agenda. Potential barriers include a client's own lack of clarity about his agenda, or, commonly, a lack of trust and confidence in the advisor. If a prospective client doesn't sense that you are a credible—and trustworthy—source of help, then he is just not going to open up.

There are two principal approaches to uncovering your client's agenda in order to undertake Agenda Sensing. The first is through direct conversations; the second draws on secondary research.

Executive Conversations

Client agendas are uncovered through open-ended questions that probe for key priorities, problems, and opportunities. Here are some suggested questions that may be helpful as you explore and try to uncover a client's agenda:

1. In talking to our other clients in your industry, we find that there are three major issues that they are grappling with right now ... how would these resonate with you and your management?

2. How is your organization reacting to ... [a recent, important development in this client's industry or function]?

3. How are you handling ... [new competition, low-cost imports, a new regulatory framework, etc.]?

4. Can you share with me your thoughts about the most pressing issues that you're focused on right now?

5. Can you say more about what you mean by ... [organizational transformation, globalization, cultural change, innovation, etc.]. Do you have some specific goals? What programs are you trying to implement to achieve them?

6. At the end of the year, how will you be evaluated? What accomplishments or goals will you be judged by?

7. What are your key priorities this year? What do you need to accomplish?

8. As you look at your plan for this year, what do you feel is working well? Where are you making less progress?

9. What are your biggest opportunities over the next several years?

10. What issues do you wish you could spend more of your time on? Less time on?

11. How would you describe your organization's priorities for the next year?

12. When you eventually leave this position and take on a different role, what would you have most liked to accomplish?

There are some additional questions that can help you better understand a client's *personal* agenda. Obviously, you need to gauge the appropriate moment to use them; however, I'd encourage you to do so because almost all great professional relationships also have a personal component to them. For example:

13. You've had such a successful career ... what further aspirations do you have? Is there anything else you would like to achieve?

14. What's the most enjoyable part of your job? Least enjoyable?

15. When you look back on the different positions you've held, what's been your most memorable or personally rewarding one?

16. Where, in the organization, would you like to go from here?

There are several important things to remember when having exploratory conversations about executives' agendas. First, be careful about being too direct when you're not well acquainted with a client. Some will respond forthrightly to direct questions about their agenda, but others will be reluctant to open up with someone they don't know well. Try to avoid sitting down in someone's office and immediately asking, "What are your top three priorities?" Worse yet is the now over-used, "What keeps you up at night?" (Someone once responded to one of my clients, "The traffic noise." And recently, the CEO of Amtrak told a reporter, "People ask CEOs what keeps them up at night—in my case, it's my four-year-old."). These questions are very blunt and direct, and if used too early in the conversation, may really put someone off. Inquire about your client's agenda in a way that shows that you know what you are talking about. That's why I prefer what I call "issue-based queries," such as questions 1 and 2 in

I track our top 100 clients on a daily basis, and I look for news and developments that may affect them. You also have to *ask* about your client's issues. I will often say, "Could I spend a half hour with you to better understand your challenges?" Obviously, you do your homework and have to be prepared. But I have never met a client who said "No, I don't want to spend time talking to you about my business." It's just never happened—ever. When I go to meet with a CEO or CIO at one of our clients, I always try to understand what their agenda is and how our work is supporting that agenda. Whether it's a cost reduction or time-to-market issue, I map our work to that objective and try to articulate how we are helping the client to achieve it.

—Francisco D'Souza, Chief Executive Officer, Cognizant

the previous list. These kinds of thoughtful questions—which, by their formulation, demonstrate your knowledge and experience—are a good way to rapidly establish your credibility and instill belief in your ability to help. Without that trust and confidence in your capabilities, clients won't open up.

Second, one of the barriers to grasping clients' agendas is that they don't always articulate them very clearly. Clients' descriptions of their agenda will often change and evolve over a number of different conversations, partly because the process of talking out loud often helps deepen their own understanding of the agenda, and partly because they open up more as they get to know and trust you. It's an organic progression. Just be careful about latching onto the very first iteration of an agenda that they give you.

Secondary Research

There is absolutely no substitute for talking in person to clients about their agendas. A great deal can be done, however, to illuminate agendas through well-executed secondary research. There are many sources for this type of research—company financial statements and annual reports, banking or brokerage reports and reviews, articles and books, speeches by company executives, videos of senior executives, and other sources such as former employees, customers, journalists, industry pundits, and bloggers. There are also many free retrieval services available today that can deliver daily news to you that is specific to your client or a particular topic.

Secondary research has its role, but it also has significant limitations. It can provide important information about a client's background and context, but it's hard to contribute truly significant insight during a client conversation when this kind of information is all you have to go on. If you are overconfident about your understanding of a company's agenda based on secondary sources, there is a serious risk of coming across like a know-it-all about a client's issues. At worst, your ideas could seem simplistic, or even wrongheaded.

Imagine if someone you've never met showed up at *your* office and told you, "I've read a lot about you and your firm, and I understand you are facing four critical issues." Your first reaction would probably be, "But you haven't even spoken to me yet. What the heck do you know?"

On the other hand, if you are unprepared and start asking a client questions that can easily be answered from a web site, annual report, or the *Wall Street Journal*, you'll come across as unprofessional and unprepared. One client of mine confessed that he went to a first meeting with a prospective client several years ago, and found himself woefully underprepared. The client's first question was, "So what do you think about our stock price?" He was caught completely flat-footed, having neglected to check such basic background information about the company. In short: Secondary research is absolutely necessary to build an initial foundation of understanding; but it is rarely sufficient to uncover a client's most pressing agenda.

Industry Knowledge

Deep industry knowledge can be essential to effective agenda setting, and many services firms have moved toward strengthening their specialization around industries in order to have the requisite understanding of the issues. In some fields, such as law, there has historically been more of a focus on developing a core expertise that can be generalized across many types of companies, but this is changing. A good example of this is the law firm Milbank Tweed, whose project finance department is one of the largest in the world. Managing Partner Eric Silverman, who chairs this highly successful group, tells us:

> How do you help to shape a client's agenda? First, you *earn the right* to serve it. You do this through the quality and integrity of your work. There is only one way in, and it's not on the golf course! It takes time and hard work to earn the right to engage the senior agenda with senior people.
>
> **—Shumeet Banerji, Chief Executive Officer, Booz & Company**

After the downturn in 2002, we refocused our practice around discrete industry sectors. We didn't want to just position ourselves as finance lawyers, but rather lawyers who are experts in sectors such as space and satellites; natural resources; and power and energy. These industry sectors have also provided a focal point for collaborating with our other legal departments such as litigation, restructuring, M&A, and others. This approach has given us a distinct competitive advantage, and more flexibility to move from issue to issue within an industry group.

Approaches for Engaging in Agenda Setting

An agenda can be discerned, and then ultimately shaped, through a variety of processes:

- *Exploratory conversations:* You explore the client's agenda using the questioning techniques set out earlier. Chapter 5, on engagement, also describes a number of best practices for understanding a prospective client's key issues.
- *Bottoms-up:* After you've won the assignment, you slowly build up an intimate knowledge of the issues, becoming thoroughly familiar with the client's organization.
- *Top-down:* You engage in agenda setting based on a top-down understanding of the business that might take in board members, the CEO, and divisional or functional heads.
- *Market-back:* You define an agenda that is driven from an understanding of customers and their needs (which is what Gerstner did at IBM when he took over as CEO).
- *Investor-back:* You help shape the agenda through a solid understanding of investor sentiment and expectations.
- *Workshop-based:* You create a formal workshop designed to discuss, debate, and shape the client's agenda. This could involve one or more offsite planning sessions with the client's entire team.

Tools of Influence

Sensing a client's agenda and helping them achieve it is by itself an important role for an external advisor. Improving a client's agenda, however—or helping them to create a compelling agenda in the absence of one—can be an extraordinarily valuable service. Since many senior executives have firm ideas about what they want to accomplish already, you are going to have to influence and persuade in order to be effective.

There are at least eight strategies that can be utilized to influence a client's agenda and persuade them to modify their position:

1. *Goal alignment:* The most compelling way to influence is to demonstrate that your idea or proposal will help the other person accomplish one of his goals—especially one that is critical to his career success. This means that you have to have a clear understanding of your client's aspirations.

2. *Quality and acuity of judgment:* People can reach different conclusions with the same data. But sometimes there is a clear-cut, "right" way; and then a second-best way that represents a distinctly inferior approach. Forming a correct judgment, and then successfully demonstrating the soundness of that judgment, is essential to effective influence. A quality judgment incorporates four major components: The use of solid facts; sound analysis; relevant experience; and a good understanding of the client's values, beliefs, and decision-making process.

3. *Peer pressure:* In some situations, an outside professional may have inherently limited powers of influence. Even if there is a good deal of trust in the advisor, the client may feel that an outsider does not—and never will—know the business as well as an insider; and that after all is said and done, the advisor does not have to live with the decision. However, a client will often listen carefully to respected peers, and influencing *those peers* can be an effective strategy.

4. *Expert opinion:* We are a culture of experts and authorities, and a client may well be influenced by other particularly well-regarded voices. This could be an important customer, an executive at another company, an experienced board member, a well-known industry expert or commentator, or perhaps some other individual who is regarded as sage and insightful.

5. *Values alignment:* Sometimes a particular action is the right one to take because it aligns squarely with your or your client's closely

held values and beliefs. For example, in 1995, the Malden Mills factory in Lawrence, Massachusetts, burned to the ground two weeks before Christmas. The owner, Aaron Feuerstein, could have pocketed the insurance money and happily retired. Instead, he not only rebuilt the mill, but continued to pay the salaries of all 3,000 workers for six months. The factory thrives today, and Feuerstein has subsequently been the recipient of many humanitarian awards.

Franklin D. Roosevelt and Lend-Lease

In 1939, President Franklin D. Roosevelt needed to convince a skeptical and isolationist congress that the United States needed to come to the aid of Britain, which was besieged by the Nazis. The turning point was a famous news conference in which he said, "If a neighbor's house was on fire, wouldn't you lend him your garden house to help put out the fire?" This analogy paved the way for the president's lend-lease program, which enabled the United States to provide military equipment to Britain under the guise of lending it to them.

6. *Stories, analogies, and metaphors:* Storytelling is an elemental form of human communication. Stories are vivid and memorable, and can have an impact well beyond their words. A story could be as simple as an anecdote about how another client dealt with a similar situation, or it could draw on a fable, parable, or even a joke that helps underscore the point you are trying to get across.

7. *Emotions:* It's often said that facts tell, but emotions sell. One should be careful about emotional appeals; but when framed properly, a reference to the emotional aspects of an agenda can be appropriate and effective. For example, consider Shakespeare's portrayal of King Henry V's speech to his troops before the battle of Agincourt. The English were outnumbered at least two to one by the French forces, wracked by illness, and exhausted from weeks of marching through the sodden French countryside. Does Henry V encourage his troops by talking about how effective their longbows will be, or how the rain and mud will disadvantage the French knights, who will be bogged

down in the muddy ground? No, he appeals to their emotions by saying,

> "This day is call'd the feast of Crispian.
> He that outlives this day, and comes safe home,
> Will stand a tip-toe when this day is nam'd"

In other words, "If you live through this battle, you'll be remembered on this day and be able to stand proudly in every year to come. Your names will become as famous as those of the great figures in English history!" He appeals to their sense of pride, to their chance to make history, and their desire for immortality. A similar appeal to a client executive might refer to recognition of his or her leadership, to leaving a legacy, to being an iconoclast, and so on.

8. *A contextual or paradigm shift:* Sometimes, the environment, market dynamics, and competitive landscape have changed so dramatically that business-as-usual is no longer an option. Demonstrating this to clients can have a powerful influence on their agenda. Former Intel CEO Andy Grove, in his classic book *Only the Paranoid Survive,* refers to these specific times as "inflection points." At the time that Grove wrote the book, memory chip manufacturing was a major business for Intel, but it was slowly being commoditized. Intel executives, however, would not accept that the business had no future—they didn't see it at all. Grove changed their minds, not by showering them with detailed analysis, but by helping them to realize that "the world had changed" and that Intel was facing an entirely new set of market dynamics within which the memory chip business could no longer prosper. Bill Gates, the co-founder and former chairman of Microsoft, tried to do the same thing with his now-famous 1995 memo on the "Internet Tidal Wave," which he sent to Microsoft's top executives. The memo outlined Microsoft's failure to grasp the importance of the Internet. In it, Gates exhorted his troops to give "the Internet the highest level of importance" going forward. While it did instigate major changes in the company's strategy, it may not have done enough given the rise of Google and its emergence as Microsoft's most potent competitor.

Helping Your Client Implement an Agenda

Understanding a client's agenda and helping to improve it is a huge first step. But what happens—or doesn't happen—afterward is even more important. For some clients, an outside advisor's ability to help them actually *implement* their agenda is the ultimate measure of whether that advisor can really add value.

There are a number of considerations to successfully implementing an agenda, whether the client in question is a c-level executive or the director of a department. These are expressed next as a series of questions that you ought to ask about your client's agenda. You may feel that your area of expertise does not qualify you to discuss these issues with your client, but remember two things: First, this type of conversation can be very helpful to an executive who has an ambitious set of goals; and second, if you only talk about the technical details of your work, you'll never broaden the relationship and be perceived as a deep generalist who can bring both technical skills and big-picture thinking to the table.

> *Does the client's agenda clearly link to the organization's overall set of strategic goals?* If it doesn't, your client may at best be at odds with the mainstream strategy of his or her company; and at worst become irrelevant in his or her own organization.
>
> *Does the agenda take into account the views of major constituencies?* These constituencies will vary depending on the level and position of your client. For a CEO, they will certainly include investors, the board, employees, and customers. For a head of human resources, they might include the CEO, the company's senior line executives, front-line employees, and unions.
>
> *Is the client's senior team aligned around the agenda?* Do the executives agree with the priorities, and do they feel a sense of joint responsibility for their accomplishment? Are there conflicting agendas among team members?
>
> *Are the right people in place to accomplish the agenda?* In his book *Good to Great*, author Jim Collins calls this "getting the right people on the bus." Are there key executives who are aligned against the different priorities and the programs that are in place to support them?

Have ambitious objectives been established to drive the agenda forward? Sometimes agendas can contain very broad statements about a client's priorities. These priorities need to be turned into specific objectives that directly address a company trend or issue.

Have specific measures been developed so that you know whether you are succeeding? Measures are more specific than objectives. They describe behaviors and outcomes, and they will tell you if things are really on track.

Are there programs and initiatives in place to support the achievement of the agenda? Each agenda item needs to be supported by a specific program of activities. You might ask your client something as simple as, "How is this going to actually get done?" or, "Which programs do you feel are directly supporting the achievement of this particular goal?"

Is there a management process in place to facilitate the implementation of the agenda? You need to encourage clients to think about how they are going to manage the process of implementing their agenda. Is this a radical or ambitious agenda that requires an ad hoc "change coalition" to drive it forward? Can it be managed through normal management processes such as an executive committee or senior team?

Are you taking the opportunity to periodically discuss your client's progress? Sitting down regularly to discuss progress against the agenda represents a high-impact client conversation. This will allow you to see which areas are coming easily to them, and which might require more input or additional help from you.

Agenda Setting: What Successful Trusted Advisors Say

I would like to share with you some of the comments that my clients have made about successful—and unsuccessful—agenda setting:

- "I always spend considerable time thinking through the client's strategic business situation as well as his or her personal career situation."

- "I read analyst reports and often take a capital market perspective during our conversations: 'Why are people buying their stock/others' stock?' "
- "I always ask for and study my clients' planning documents to understand their priorities."
- "I have learned to be less tentative about setting 'the big meeting' where we get the client to talk about his agenda and provide our perspectives on it."

There are also pitfalls:

- "If you drive an agenda too hard or too soon, you risk being perceived as not objective or as making a marketing push. It turns people off."
- "We understood only what the client wanted, not what he or she really *needed* for their institutional and personal success."
- "I made an assumption that I had fully understood the agenda, but actually I did not really appreciate the client's complete set of priorities."
- "We were not bold enough about getting to the client's agenda, and we hesitated to follow up out of fear of 'over selling' "

Conclusion

If you are responsible for developing and managing client relationships, it is imperative to hone your skills at sensing and shaping client agendas. The art of growing a relationship is very much founded on the capacity to deliver high-quality work in a specific area of expertise, while simultaneously conversing intelligently with your client about their broader agenda and connecting your work to it. A profound understanding of your client's most critical issues and goals, in short, is essential to building the Level 6 trusted partnerships described in Chapter 1.

1. Agenda Reacting	2. Agenda Sensing	3. Agenda Setting
✓ Stay in touch regularly so you are top of mind with your contacts. ✓ Be selective about the requests you agree to react to. Do they align with your client's critical priorities?	✓ Invest to understand your client's personal and business agendas. ✓ Use both face-to-face conversations and secondary research. ✓ Build relationships at multiple levels and walk the halls with existing clients. ✓ Don't always accept a client's agenda at face value— explore it over time to clarify it.	✓ Earn the right to influence an agenda. ✓ Build knowledge of your client's organization, markets, industry, competitors, customers, and environment. ✓ Be proactive about scheduling agenda-setting conversations. ✓ Employ multiple tools of influence to help shape and persuade. ✓ Ask challenging questions about your client's implementation of the agenda.

FIGURE 3.1   Becoming an Agenda Setter

Figure 3.1 summarizes some of the major considerations that we have covered that are necessary to evolve from agenda reacting to agenda setting.

Your ability to help shape and set your clients' agendas depends very much on your understanding of their business and the environment their companies compete in. Figure 3.2 "How Well Do You Really Know Your Client's Business?" asks about the 10 basic areas in which you should have some understanding. It doesn't matter whether you are a consultant, lawyer, accountant, or banker, if you want to advise at the highest levels, you cannot hide in your expert silo. You need to offer both your core expertise *and* a big-picture understanding of your client's world.

✓ **Strategy and goals**
What is the stated strategy, and what long-term goals have been set?

✓ **Financial performance**
What is the client's performance in terms of revenue and profit growth, stock price trends, market share, and competitive rankings?

✓ **The organization**
Who are the key executives? What are their responsibilities?

✓ **Key operational initiatives**
What initiatives are planned for the next year? (e.g., new products, cost-cutting, etc.)

✓ **Major competitors**
Who are the major competitors, and what is the industry structure?

✓ **Industry and market trends**
What are the four to five most important trends for this client's business?

✓ **The customer base**
Who are the key customers? How concentrated is their purchasing power? Why do they buy from your client?

✓ **The suppliers**
Who are major suppliers? How much leverage do they have?

✓ **Partnerships and alliances**
Which are the major partnerships? How well do they function?

✓ **Culture**
What is the organizational culture like today? What core values does the client espouse? What does it aspire to in the future?

✓ Plus relevant information about the particular function or organizational unit you work with most directly.

FIGURE 3.2 How Well Do You Really Understand Your Client's Business?

Figure 3.3 challenges you to extend your knowledge and understanding to your clients' environment, which will powerfully influence the agenda of almost any executive within the organization.

Whenever you have a client meeting in the future, ask yourself: "Does the work we are discussing connect to and align with my client's priorities? Does this conversation resonate with his or her institutional or personal concerns?"

If you aren't connecting to your client's agenda, the signs will be clear. He will seem less than fully engaged. He'll be a bit distracted, perhaps thinking about something else that is more pressing. His voice will lack energy and enthusiasm. He'll look straight at you, but not really see you. If you sense this lack of interest, change course quickly. You could ask, "What's the most important thing we should be talking

✓ **The economy and key economic trends**
What are the views of leading economists and commentators?

✓ **The capital markets**
What's happening in the stock and bond markets?

✓ **Technology**
What major technology trends may affect your client's business?

✓ **Management practice**
What basic ideas and frameworks should you understand about perennial topics like leadership, strategy, and teamwork?

✓ **Demographic trends**
How will these affect the workplace and consumer buying habits?

✓ **Government and politics**
How does government policy influence your client's business?

✓ **The regulatory environment**
What changes are ocurring?

✓ **Legal trends**
What risks does your client face? (litigation, labor issues, etc.)

✓ **The media**
How do the media view your client?

✓ **Nongovernmental Organizations (NGOs)**
Can any NGOs affect your client's business, either positively or negatively?

FIGURE 3.3   How Well Do You Really Understand Your Client's Environment?

about today?" or, "I'd like to make sure we're covering what's really important to you—are there some other issues that you want to discuss before we finish this morning?"

When you strike the right chord, you'll know it. Your client will be talkative, animated, and energetic. You'll probably go over your allotted time. She may ask you about some additional things you can do to support her, or a few next steps she'd like to see come out of the meeting. She'll already be looking forward to your next session. You'll be energized, too.

4

Strategy Two: Developing Relationship Capital

Building the Vital Relationships That Drive Your Career and Your Firm

How do you develop a vibrant professional network that will support a successful career? Where should you focus your relationship-building efforts if your goal is to ultimately develop a handful of trusted client partnerships? These are essential questions for any service professional. They are also directly relevant to our task of creating an all-for-one organization. Ultimately, it is the combined impact of all of your professionals' individual networks that help to support and grow your Level 6 clients. As we see in Chapter 7, *network leverage* can become a key source of value to these institutional clients.

The advent of social networking technologies and other ways of staying in touch with large numbers of people have definitely made this subject more interesting but also more confusing than ever. I'll use myself as a case study. Right now, I have a mere 41 connections on LinkedIn, a web-based professional networking tool. Yet through those 41 I can, according to LinkedIn, get warm introductions to 1,275,300 people among the tens of millions who subscribe to the service. Is this relevant? Should I spend more time focusing on these million-plus professionals who *may* want to meet me? Pundits often cite "Metcalfe's law," developed by Robert Metcalfe, as they exhort people to create large numbers of personal connections. His law states that the value of a network is equal to the square of its connected nodes—in other words, if you double the number of people you know, the value of your network quadruples. Metcalfe, however, articulated this principle in the early 1980s, and he was talking about fax machines and other nodes within a telecommunications network—not interpersonal relationships.

Do more connections mean more value for you? If we're talking about online businesses like MySpace or Amazon, the answer is undoubtedly yes; but for the average business professional, more is not necessary better. In an age where people are nearly as famous for their networking prowess as their innate talent, where you can instantly have hundreds or thousands of "friends" on Facebook, and where we are led to believe that we are only a few network connections away from even the most glamorous celebrities, it is easy to be led astray from our primary goal: to form deep, trusted relationships with a relatively small group of clients and colleagues. Metcalfe's law and the media hype surrounding web-based social networks are, in many ways, a distraction from the real task of developing long-term, consultative relationships with a selected group of senior executives. In Chapter 10, we see how networking and collaboration technologies do have the potential to transform the way we work with each other and with clients; but in the end, most of us still want a few good clients, rather than thousands of "connections."

An article in the *New York Times Magazine*, written by a young man who lives in a major city, poignantly underscored how superficial some of our twenty-first century relationships can be. He had accumulated 700 "friends" on Facebook and decided to invite them all to an evening get-together at a local bar. Only 1 out of 700 showed up—and that person only briefly stopped by—even though dozens had indicated they would come. He sipped his drink until midnight, and returned home, more lonely than ever (Niedzviecki, "Facebook in a Crowd," October 24, 2008).

How Many Is Enough?

If you are a consultant, banker, lawyer, or other business professional who manages sophisticated client relationships, consider the following three stories. Each one is significantly representative of the feedback I've received from the tens of thousands of service professionals I have worked with on this subject. They form an interesting counterpoint to the "more is better" theory:

> *Over the last 15 years, I have cultivated a relationship with one particular lawyer in New York. We continually refer deals to each other. We talk once or twice a week. I would say that 20 percent of the business I have developed in my entire career has in some way touched this person. He has gotten to know many of the managing directors here, and I have now dealt with nearly 15 partners at his firm. The relationship has, to some extent, become institutionalized.*
>
> —Head of M&A, Investment Bank

> *There is one executive that I have worked with for over 20 years, and during this time he has held five different top management and board positions with major companies. Each time he moved to a new role, he called me, and engaged my firm for a major project. This relationship has not only resulted in a very large revenue stream over time—well over $100 million in fees—but this person has served as a reference and referred a number of other important clients to me.*
>
> —Senior Partner, Consulting Firm

> *As I think back, there have been four particularly critical relationships that have been instrumental in helping me to succeed and build my career. Three of these were internal relationships with senior partners. One of these three left the firm to take a leadership position in a client organization. The fourth was a client who later sat on a number of boards.*
>
> —Chairman, Law Firm

The Critical Few versus the Many

In each of these examples, a select few relationships have been hugely influential. I call these *Relationship Hubs*—the *critical few* individuals who are or can be truly important to you, and for whom you can also make a real difference. In the course of my research and ongoing client work, I have interviewed several hundred highly successful professionals on this subject, and also collected data from another 3,000 relationship managers who have completed a Relationship Capital exercise that I sometimes conduct during workshops. What I have found is that for someone in mid-career, there are typically between 15 and 20 relationships that account for probably 80 percent of their success and growth. Try this exercise yourself: Approach someone in your firm who has been working for 25 or 30 years—nearly a lifetime of work—and ask them how many relationships truly counted for them; how many *really* made a difference. The answers will vary, but you'll usually hear somewhere between 15 and 30. I have never, ever heard someone say 75 or 100.

A consultant or accountant actually only needs a handful of good clients to have a great career, and Figure 4.1 explains *why* this is so.

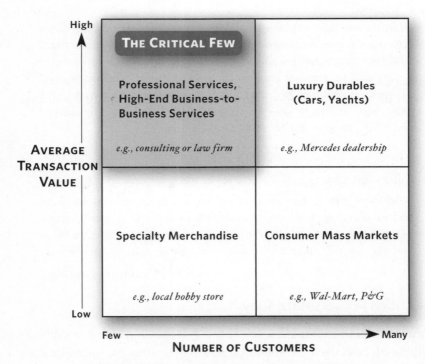

FIGURE 4.1 The Critical Few versus the Many

Figure 4.1 looks at two dimensions of your business: the average transaction or sale value, and the number of customers you deal with. Most of the people reading this book are in the upper-left quadrant, where you find service professionals and account managers for high-end, business-to-business products and services. Your average sale value is *high*, and you have *few* customers whom you get to know really well.

What does this say about my one million potential contacts on LinkedIn? While these might be useful for selling a book (which would move me to a position in the lower-right quadrant), they would not aid in marketing and delivering my consulting services.

There is another aspect to your network, which I call the *many*. This is your broader network, and it might contain 500 or 5,000 names of individuals you've met or known over the years. This network is also essential to maintain, not least because it is the pool from which the *critical few* emerge. It's important to continually add to this larger group of contacts—one reason being that one of the things you can offer people is connection value, or valuable introductions to others in your orbit. The *many* is a different from the *critical few*, however, and you need to separate the two in your mind because they require very different strategies to develop.

In the rest of this chapter, I'm going to give you some overall strategies for building your broader network, but my focus will be mostly on the *critical few*—on how to develop your 15 to 20 Relationship Hubs. I will address questions such as:

- Who should be on your list of Relationship Hubs?
- How do you become a valuable, interesting person to those in your network?
- How can you stay in touch with and add value to your key relationships on a regular basis?
- What should your personal network-building model be?

Many networking experts put a focus on constantly getting out and meeting people, or even making dozens of phone calls a day to individuals on your contact list. One author on the subject talks about making 80 calls each day to stay in touch, wish people happy birthday, and so on. These activities—at least in anything but small doses—are neither useful nor practical for most professionals whose careers may thrive on a foundation of 5 or 10 great client relationships spread over many years. Get out there and form new relationships—yes, but just remember that the pot of gold you seek lies at or near your feet, not in some far-off, exotic country.

The Critical Few: Developing Your Relationship Hubs

The process of developing your Relationship Hubs—those 15 to 20 *critical few* relationships that can make a significant difference to you and your firm, and for whom *you* can make a difference—comprises five basic steps:

1. Clarify and develop your personal brand.
2. Identify your relationship hubs.
3. Consider weak links and potentials.
4. Assess loyalty and connectivity.
5. Stay in touch.

    Let's look at each step in detail.

Step 1: Clarify and Develop Your Personal Brand

Why would someone be interested in a relationship with *you* to begin with? It starts with your personal brand. Clearly, the concept of a personal brand in a service business is less exact and precise than it might be in the consumer goods marketplace. Nonetheless, almost everyone who is successful at attracting and keeping clients has an implicit or explicit personal brand.

    Spurred by consultant Tom Peter's writings, the idea of personal branding has gained currency over the past 10 years, and there are many good books on the topic. Most of my clients are service professionals, however, who have a somewhat more focused, practical view of branding than what is presented in these tomes. So I'm going to spend a few pages on the essentials.

In the simplest terms, personal brands for most professionals have two dimensions: (1) their professional expertise and (2) the personal qualities that clients know and admire them for. I have asked client executives about the concept of a personal brand, and they find it easy to talk about their trusted advisors in terms that comprise both professional and personal qualities (e.g., "She is a top-flight litigator who really knows the pharmaceutical industry. She's an excellent listener, but at the same time is always direct and candid.").

If you want to think about your personal brand in somewhat more scientific terms, there is a classic brand definition framework that states that a brand has four aspects to it. These are:

1. *Differentiation:* How distinctive, in the minds of clients, is your brand? Does it imply a unique or special set of benefits?
2. *Relevance:* How useful do clients perceive your brand to be? How well does it meet clients' needs?
3. *Esteem:* To what extent does your brand command the respect and regard of clients?
4. *Knowledge (or familiarity):* How well does the market understand your brand? How widely has your brand been experienced?

There are some well-known professionals who are strong on all of these dimensions—Alan Dershowitz and Robert Shapiro in law, for example, or Bruce Wasserstein in the mergers and acquisitions world. But most of us fall short in one or more of them.

Often brands can have very different strengths—Apple Computer (now just Apple) was always *differentiated* as a brand, but for many years it lacked *relevance* to many consumers and businesses. On the other hand, ATT had strong *knowledge*—it was a widely known brand—but low *esteem* because people just didn't think that highly of its service and innovation.

Service professionals are often high on relevance and esteem, but low on differentiation and knowledge/awareness. Take a management consultant: His clients may perceive his services to be very helpful, and they will have great respect for him. But in reality his service offering is not very differentiated—there are hundreds if not thousands of other consultants who can do similar work—and he may not be known outside of a small group of loyal clients.

Here are some questions you should ask yourself about your personal brand:

- Can you articulate your personal brand in a few sentences or less?
- How differentiated is what you do for clients compared to your competition?
- How well known are you? Are you a valuable brand that is still undiscovered by the marketplace?
- What would be proof of your brand's success?
- What brand-building activities are you planning in the next six months (speaking, writing, networking, conducting research, etc.)?

Your brand is important; it's the reason that people want to associate with you professionally. Clients, colleagues, and other individuals in your professional life will always be attracted to you in part because you have experience, knowledge, and skills that are helpful to them, and in part because you have attractive or interesting personal qualities—in short, because it's stimulating and enjoyable to be around you.

Step 2: Identify Your Relationship Hubs

So who should be on your list of the *critical few*? When I do this exercise with groups of client-facing professionals, I find that very few instructions or criteria are needed to get people going on their lists. I usually tell them: "Make a list of your most important—or potentially important—professional relationships." To help shape and expand the list, think about your relationships in five groups:

1. *Clients (former, current, and prospective):* These are the people with whom you do business. When professionals think about their key relationships, they usually focus on these past, current, or potential clients. You will probably have many of your names under this category. This is a very important starting point, but there's more.

2. *Colleagues:*It's always been necessary to have a supportive group of colleagues, but as organizations become more global and the delivery of services more complex, this category of Relationship Capital takes on renewed importance. New research indicates that workplace "stars" don't always transition well to new companies, because they leave behind the supportive, internal networks they have developed with coworkers. In any large organization, your success with clients will ultimately be predicated on your ability to build these internal relationships—especially if you are a relationship manager whose job it is to bring your client the best that your firm has to offer. Depending on your area of practice, your internal relationships could be as or more important than your external ones (a tax attorney, for example, might get most of her leads from other partners in the firm who are doing corporate work).

3. *Counselors:* Counselors advise and mentor us during our careers and provide support, encouragement, and guidance. Many studies have affirmed the importance of these mentors, but the effectiveness of formal corporate mentoring programs is less clear. You should not wait to be

---

An Invaluable Catalyst

In European and Asia, Catalysts are not just valuable, but *essential* to doing business, as I learned when I was Country Manager for Gemini Consulting in Italy. After some effort, I once procured an appointment with the CEO of a leading Italian company. The day before the meeting, my Italian partner found out about the meeting. "You can't just go in there," he exclaimed, "He doesn't know you! You need an introduction." He then called an even more famous CEO, who later entered the world stage as Italy's prime minister. My partner had worked with him extensively, and he knew me as well. That afternoon, my partner's contact—a true catalyst—called the head of the company I was going to meet with, and sang our praises. When I showed up in the CEO's office I was greeted like an old friend instead of yet another annoying consultant. What would have been a perfunctory meet-and-greet turned into a substantive conversation; and the CEO became a major, ongoing client for nearly five years.

—Andrew Sobel

"assigned" a mentor—you have to actively develop relationships with your counselors, both inside and outside the firm. Many figures can play this role: a former boss, a senior executive from within your firm, or even a retired executive.

4. *Catalysts:* A rare breed, these individuals can introduce us to others and make deals happen. Catalysts are often bankers, venture capitalists, board directors, and agents, but they can come in many guises. It is no accident that extremely well-connected Catalysts like Robert Rubin—the former Treasury Secretary—are so highly sought after for corporate boards and other advisory roles.

5. *Collaborators:* Most companies are aided and abetted by an extensive network of collaborators—business partners who really go well beyond the mere role of supplier. A law firm might be an important collaborator for an investment bank or an accounting firm—or a business school professor for a consulting firm—just as family practitioners are collaborators for the medical specialists they recommend to their patients.

On average, I have found that if people come up with 20 names, they will usually break down into the five categories as follows:

Clients (former, current, prospective)	10
Colleagues	5
Counselors	2
Catalysts	1
Collaborators	2

What you will find is that it's easy to come up with a list of 10 or 15 current or prospective clients—setting aside whether they are the right names or not. It is much harder, however, to identify important Catalysts or Collaborators. You may have other categories that you think about, but I have found these five are very useful in stimulating peoples' consideration of how they ought to be focusing their relationship-building efforts.

Some of your Relationship Hubs will no doubt fit into several categories, just as you may fulfill different roles for your own clients. A client could also be a catalyst for you, and a colleague could also be a counselor or mentor. In making your list, just put each name in the *most* appropriate category.

I am often asked two questions about the *critical few:* "Do you only know who they are in retrospect?" And, "Does this group change over time?" The vast majority of the seasoned professionals I have interviewed have said that they *knew* these individuals were important at the time—their significance was pretty clear from the beginning. And yes, the group will change over time; but the further you are into your career, the more slowly it will happen. Each year, one or two people may drift out of your inner circle, and one or two new individuals may come in. But this group should not turn over very much, unless you are in a very transactional product or service area where you have completely different clients each year. In this case, a portion of your list may turn over (e.g., clients) but some people should remain the same (e.g., colleagues, catalysts, collaborators).

Step 3: Consider Weak Links and Potentials

While there are great rewards to be reaped by focusing on a core set of relationships with clients, prospects, colleagues, and other key figures, you don't want to become insular or overly reliant on a small group of what sociologists call "strong ties." It's also important to have relationships with people who come from completely different social and professional circles. This idea was set out in a 1973 groundbreaking paper entitled "The Strength of Weak Ties," by sociologist Mark Granovetter. Granovetter did a study of people looking for new jobs and discovered that more often than not, they found a new position not through someone in their close circle of friends and acquaintances; but through individuals they did not know very well at all—the so-called "weak links" in the title of his original paper. These weak links enable you to access other networks, which you are not in daily contact with.

In a later article, Granovetter describes the problem of relying solely on your close buddies:

> *It follows, then, that individuals with few weak ties will be deprived of information from distant parts of the social system and will be confined to the provincial news and views of their close friends. This deprivation will not only insulate them from the latest ideas and fashions but may put them in a disadvantaged position in the labor market.* (Sociological Theory, *volume 1, 1983*)

Other, later research has validated Granovetter's findings. One study of corporate bankers, for example, showed that when the bankers went outside their normal circle of colleagues to seek advice and input on a deal, their closing rates were higher. This is why, for example, I always recommend that a client account planning meeting include an experienced colleague who is *not* involved with the client; and who therefore is likely to have a fresh perspective on how to improve the relationship.

The lessons here are straightforward: Be eclectic, and include individuals—both in your *critical few* and in your broader network—who are quite dissimilar from you, and who run in very different circles.

In addition to including and using some weak links in your network, it's good to have a few "aspirational" relationships in view. A *potential* Relationship Hub could be someone who is:

- A young, high-potential manager who in 5 or 10 years will be in senior management
- A senior executive at a company you would like to build a relationship with
- A highly connected Catalyst

While you probably have many relationship-building opportunities at your front door, it's always good to ask the question, "Whom *should* I be working with?" The clients you have today may not be the ones you want to have in the future.

Step 4: Assess Loyalty and Connectivity

Once you have articulated your list of *critical few* Relationship Hubs, you need to assess each person's loyalty and connectivity. I have found that this additional step provides important insights into strategies for improving your relationship with each individual.

Connectivity simply refers to the extent to which the person is "plugged in" to a broader set of networks and communities. Some executives, for example, by dint of personality and temperament, love to connect with others through an endless variety of memberships and activities—board directorships, round tables, conference participation, an active personal social network, and so on. In his book *The Tipping Point*, for example, Malcolm Gladwell makes the case that Paul Revere's "ride" to alert Bostonians to the invading British was successful precisely because Revere was highly connected. Other leaders, in contrast—often introverts—focus almost exclusively on their own organizations, eschewing this type of extroverted networking. These individuals, to use our terms, have low connectivity.

Loyalty can be to you personally and/or to your firm—it's hard to distinguish between the two, and they always overlap somewhat. Loyalty is a surrogate for the overall closeness and strength of the current relationship. Keep in mind that loyalty in this sense does not mean exclusivity. A client of yours may be quite loyal to you, but that loyalty is typically contained to a specific sphere of business; and it is granted in exchange for ongoing value that you add. "Blind loyalty" hardly exists in business today. Evidence of loyalty can include sustained, repeat business with you or your firm; spontaneous word-of-mouth recommendations; specific referrals; formal references; and being invited into a trusted advisor role with the client.

If you look at your list of critical few relationships, you can probably easily rate each person based on loyalty and connectivity, from low to high. If you put these two dimensions together in a matrix, you get Figure 4.2.

Potentials

Potentials are, in a sense, the pool from which your Relationship Hubs are ultimately drawn. They could be people you just don't know enough

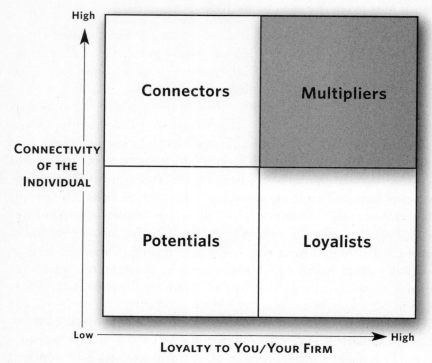

FIGURE 4.2 Segmenting Your Relationship Hubs

about to catalog properly in the matrix, or they could be younger professionals whose ultimate potential—and proclivity to connect or become loyal to you—is still undeveloped. They also comprise the "aspirational" hubs described under Step 3.

Connectors

These individuals can make a huge difference with a phone call, or even a fleeting reference to you or your company. Connectors represent a well-documented social phenomenon. They are usually "boundary spanners" between different groups or networks, and serve as conduits for information. The question here is, "What can you do that is of value for this individual?" Loyalty, in the complex world of business-to-business relationships, is based on a subtle blend of demonstrated value added, personal trust, and reciprocity. By cultivating these three factors, you may be able—if only around a specific transaction or niche—to move a connector to the right.

Loyalists

Loyalists are often current or past clients that you have worked closely with and done a great job for. They fall into the lower-right quadrant because—like many—their connectivity is only average to low. The questions you must ask yourself about Loyalists include, "How can I continually add value and sustain their loyalty?" and also, "How can I help make this person more connected?" One way of adding value to an individual in your own circle is to plug him or her into a broader network of relationships. For example, the vice president of business development for a Fortune 500 company told me, "One of the most valuable things that some of our outside consultants and bankers have done is to introduce me to my counterparts at other companies. They have connected me into their network."

Multipliers

In the upper-right quadrant are those rare but exceedingly influential relationships with highly connected individuals who are loyal to you. Many professionals have only a few relationships in this category. These are especially important relationships, and they need to be carefully nurtured and protected. There are several questions to ask about your Multipliers:

- How can you partner with Multipliers in innovative ways? For example, co-authoring an article together; jointly developing intellectual capital; bringing the Multiplier into a deal or business opportunity; creating many-to-many relationships so that there is an institutional bond as well as a personal relationship; and so on.
- What can you do to encourage or facilitate Multipliers to spread the word about your services and abilities? Are they willing to act as a reference and provide referrals?

When I ask groups of professionals to map their Relationship Hubs on this matrix, they are spread asymmetrically across the four quadrants. Most people, for example, have relatively few Connectors and Multipliers (perhaps two or three in each), whereas they typically have quite a few names in the Loyalist quadrant.

You can take this framework to an office or practice level by having each person map their relationships and then compare and contrast them. My clients have found it quite useful to look, for example, at a complete list of Multipliers for an industry group or office and see what connections exist between them. To the extent you have a natural affinity group within your pool of Multipliers, it begets an opportunity to create an event to which you invite all of those individuals. A colleague may also have a Relationship Hub that can help you develop one of your own relationships, or vice-versa.

Step 5: Stay in Touch

Finally, remember that the point is not what your Relationship Hubs can do for you—but what you can do for them. You need to think about each individual on your list, and consider these questions:

- Is there a particular issue this person is working on or a goal she is pursuing?
- Do you understand her agenda of critical priorities, both on a business and personal level?
- What can you do to help her accomplish her agenda and succeed?
- How well do you *really* know these individuals, on both a personal and a professional level?
- Do you have a sustaining program for each of them? How will you stay in touch and develop the relationship over time?

Staying in touch with current clients is relatively easy; staying in touch with past clients or other contacts, when there is no obvious reason to be interacting, is far tougher, and it is one of the most common problems of busy professionals. If there is a magic formula for staying in touch, it is pretty straightforward: Treat this like diet and exercise—do a few things every week, without fail. Ingrain it into your daily life. Understand the essential interests of the other person, and follow up in ways that are helpful to them. A successful program of diet and exercise is not a one-off event, but rather it is based on daily discipline.

In Chapter 7, we examine the question of value in much greater detail. Here, I'd like to give you some ideas for how you can add value on a more personal level as you strive to stay current with and useful to each of your Relationship Hubs. Fundamentally, you should think about four categories of sustaining activities:

1. *Ideas and content:* Follow up with ideas, suggestions, perspectives, articles, white papers, firm publications, research studies, books, and so on. Lunch or dinner can be time consuming and intrusive for some people, whereas a cup of coffee during the early morning or mid-afternoon is a more digestible interlude. A phone call and a simple, "We've just completed some work that I'd like to share with you" may be enough. If you feel that you need a more compelling reason, then you may have to do some homework. When a client gets a call and the advisor says, "I've been thinking about that issue you mentioned during our last conversation, and I've got a couple of ideas I'd like to share with you," the client will rarely turn you down.

> When you talk to a client every day or every week, you have plenty to say. The conversation can go on and on. When you talk to them every six months, you've got nothing to say.
>
> **—Kenneth D. Moelis, CEO, Moelis & Co.**

2. *Connection:* You can add great value by connecting your Relationship Hubs to other people in your network. Remember that there are no laws against making a valuable introduction for someone—unless the other person is a known terrorist or on the FBI's Most Wanted list. Your and your firm's networks are proprietary—no one else can copy them and offer them to your clients.

3. *Personal help:* Occasionally you will have the opportunity to give a helping hand to a client or colleague. Are they new in town, and need help navigating private schools and health clubs? Do they have a son or daughter who is applying to college and would benefit from talking to you about your alma mater? Are they in between jobs, and need help refining their resume and gaining introductions to executive search firms? Could you help identify a medical specialist for someone? There are endless ways you can be helpful to your most important contacts. Just do it sincerely and without any expectation that you'll get something in return beyond a "Thank you."

4. *Fun:* The age of schmoozing seems to be over. Today, clients have less and less time for extracurricular activities, and in many countries statutory barriers have been put into place to prevent corporate executives from accepting gifts or entertainment from service providers. That said, some people still do like to have fun and would enjoy an invitation to a special sports event, concert, gallery opening, dinner, and so on. Ironically, these types of social activities are often more acceptable—especially to clients—once they know you fairly well. Anyone who is trying to acquire a client can offer tickets to a playoff game, but when the offer comes from someone they know and like, it's different.

I recommend that you draw up a relationship-building plan that encompasses the 15 to 20 names on your list of the *critical few.* Use the four categories just outlined to stimulate your thinking about how you can stay in touch with each person. For current clients, you'll no doubt be in touch quite frequently. For others, map out staying-in-touch activities that you can commit to on at least a monthly or quarterly basis.

Finally, as you review your list of Relationship Hubs, ask yourself, "How well do I really know each of these individuals?" Figure 4.3 is a checklist of things you might want to know about any individuals with whom you are trying to build a meaningful relationship, be they clients or colleagues. You won't know all of these things about everyone, but it's a good place to start.

As a **Person**

The Basics

✓ Spouse or partner, children

✓ Parents' vocations and interests, siblings

✓ Educational background

✓ Where they grew up

✓ Avocations: hobbies, interests

✓ Favorites: favorite restaurant, author, movie, etc.

Deeper Knowledge

✓ Formative life experiences

✓ Personal issues they may be dealing with

✓ Personal ambitions and aspirations

✓ Nonprofit or charitable involvement

✓ Personal style: introvert vs. extrovert, detail oriented vs. focused on the big picture, etc.

✓ Risk tolerance

As a **Professional**

The Basics

✓ Preferred means of communication (email, phone, memos, etc.)

✓ Work style (early/late? weekends?)

✓ Personal assistant: background, interests

✓ Career history: accomplishments, positions held

✓ Most concerning issues right now

✓ Professional and alumni associations

✓ Conference participation

Deeper Knowledge

✓ Strengths and weaknesses as an executive

✓ Role models, mentors

✓ Career goals and aspirations

✓ Quality of relationship with their boss

✓ Relationships with key direct reports (do you know them?)

✓ Corporate directorships

✓ Other executives they associate with

✓ Their most important networks and relationships

FIGURE 4.3   How Well Do You Really Know Your Client?

The Critical Few: Conclusion

It is a thought provoking and also intimidating exercise to sit down and to try to identify your most important relationships. It takes a bit more work to go even further and examine how well you really know each individual on your list and develop a plan to deepen your relationship with them. But the rewards for doing so are substantial. If you'd like to do this systematically, you can download a set of forms I have prepared from the tools section of my web site (www.andrewsobel.com).

The Many: Developing Your Broader Network

As I mentioned earlier, our main focus in this chapter is on the *critical few*—on identifying a small group of relationships where you'd like to focus your relationship-building efforts. There are a number of good books on the broader subject of networking, although you will find they tend to concentrate mainly on two different areas. On the one hand, they discuss academic theories about how networks function in large organizations; on the other hand, they explain the practical but usually fairly obvious aspects of how you get out and meet people. Here I give you just a few suggestions about managing the *many*, as I call this extended network.

First, several times a year, sit down and scroll through every contact in your database. I tend to do this at night, sitting in my kitchen. It takes a couple of hours; I just click through my list of contacts and occasionally take notes. I usually end up flagging 5 or 10 names that deserve attention. Sometimes they are old clients that I haven't talked to in years, and so I decide to send them an e-mail or call them to re-establish contact. Sometimes I find a name that really should go into my list of Relationship Hubs. Small actions like this will occur to you as you review all your names.

Second, try to stay in touch with this broader group through efficient broadcast channels that, if possible, have a personal touch to them. If you send a monthly company publication to your network, it should come with *your* name on it, not just the name of your company. Better yet, have a short list of people who also receive a personal note from you that accompanies the publication and that highlights one of the articles that may be of interest to them. Bain & Company's *Results Brief* is an e-zine, which is e-mailed to its large network of relationships via an e-mail that is addressed to each recipient by his or her first name. It also comes from the e-mail mailbox of the Bain consultant who has the main relationship with the individual, giving the communication a personal feel to it.

Use any excuse to reach out: If you have an article published, send a reprint to everyone in your broader network. I stay in touch with my own network through my monthly newsletter, *Client Loyalty*, which is often reprinted and circulated by other newsletters to a much larger audience. It contains a new, 1,000-word article each month on some aspect of building long-term client relationships, with a link to an audio podcast that I personally narrate. I also try to send annually—to a slightly smaller group than my entire contact database—a useful tool of some sort. The most recent of these was an $11'' \times 14''$ color laminate with a list of 75 best practices for developing clients for life. Holiday cards are fine, but if you don't take the time to personalize them with a short note or personal greeting, they are not very effective, or even appreciated.

Finally, continually seek to expand your broader network—the *many*—through what I call *traffic-building* activities. Figure 4.4 sets out a number of these, although I'm sure you could add many more. Each year, you should pick a few of these activities that fit your interests, temperament, and particular market, and commit to them.

Turning the Tables

One of the tax partners at Osler, a leading Canadian law firm, has a powerful way of staying in touch with his contacts. He maintains a core list of around 150 clients and key contacts. Every morning, he carefully reviews the latest developments and news that could possibly be of interest to the individuals on this list. He then creates customized, value-added e-mails that he sends out to them. These missives don't just summarize the news, but rather what the implications are for the recipients. Over the years, being on this partner's e-mail list has become highly coveted. People routinely call him up and complain that they are no longer on the list, or would like to be on it. "Well," he tells them, "if you aren't doing any business with us it's impossible for me to know what your particular needs are." He regularly gains new clients—and wins back old ones—who want to be subscribers.

—Andrew Sobel

INTELLECTUAL CAPITAL
DEVELOPMENT
✓ Primary research

✓ Surveys

✓ Service offering innovation
& codification

PUBLISHING
✓ Commercial articles
(newspapers & magazines)

✓ Books or book chapters

✓ White papers

✓ Firm publications

✓ Web-based content

✓ E-newsletters or
monthly bulletins

✓ Blogs

SPEAKING
✓ Industry/practice
conferences

✓ Client-specific events

✓ Firm-sponsored
conferences

✓ Media events

NETWORKING
✓ Industry and professional
associations

✓ Non-profit leadership

✓ University/graduate school

✓ Personal events
(e.g., dinners)

✓ Social/cultural events

✓ Content-based events
(private seminars)

✓ Media and journalists

Collaborating firms

✓ "Brokers" (banks, private
equity, VCs)

✓ Alumni

✓ Academics

✓ Retired executives

✓ Advisors/advisory boards

OTHERS
✓ Media interviews
(print, TV, radio, etc.)

✓ Targeted mailings

✓ Third-party endorsements

✓ Capability alliances

✓ Academic alliances

✓ Teaching

FIGURE 4.4   Potential Traffic-Building Activities

Note: This chart was inspired by author Alan Weiss's Marketing Gravity Planner, and the concept of traffic building derives from my conversations with Bill Jackson at Booz & Company.

Models for Building a Network and a Client Base

Over the years that I've spent working with many different types of service professionals in a multitude of markets, I have noticed that there are different focal points for building a network, and, ultimately, a client base. Some people publish a lot, and create a stream of leads based on regular idea generation. Others—particularly outside of major centers such as London and New York—are very involved with the local community and civic causes. Yet other professionals build their entire careers on large clients, developing their network within and around a single multinational. There are, in fact, six principal models for building a client base. They overlap, and most professionals will implicitly focus on at least two and possibly three of these. However, it's not feasible or practical to pursue all of them. The six focuses are:

1. *Industry:* These professionals become extremely knowledgeable about one major industry, such as telecommunications, chemicals, or financial services; and build a network of relationships in and around the companies in it. Their know-how and relationships may extend across the entire value chain to suppliers on one end and customers on the other.

2. *Functional, product, or practice:* This could include a concentration on a function such as information technology or operations, but also on a process like innovation or change management. In pursuing this strategy, your internal network is often as or more important than your external network.

3. *Intellectual capital:* All service professionals need to develop and accumulate intellectual capital—ideas, insights, frameworks, and concepts—that clients find valuable. Only a minority of service professionals, however, will make this a *primary* means of building

> My practice's client development efforts draw heavily on what we call the "market-back intellectual capital model." For the last 15 years we've been publishing books, articles, and viewpoints. The key is consistency in getting these out, year after year. You can't simply write one article and quit, because you just never know which one is going to be a hit. Sometimes, something you wrote eight years ago resonates with an executive today—and results in a new client. Our entire team leverages this output, and often, individual consultants will take an existing article and tailor it for their particular client base.
>
> **—Gary Neilson, Senior Vice President, Booz & Company**

an inquiry stream from clients. When you have an intellectual capital focus, you create interesting ideas, get them out into the marketplace through books, articles, and speeches, and then see who is interested.

These next three models often complement the first three:

4. *Very large clients:* Some professionals are able to focus relentlessly on one or perhaps two very large clients. They become a trusted confidant of key executives at this client, and deliver a broad range of their firm's capabilities to them. You have to be highly credible with top executives, but also able to build bridges at middle management levels. When you pursue this model, a single client organization—and the people and companies that orbit around it—becomes the focus of your network-building efforts.

5. *Social networking:* Some people—usually extroverts—excel at networking through social get-togethers. They are always "in the flow," hosting dinners, joining associations and clubs, going to cultural events, attending various happenings, and getting involved in nonprofit causes. They are also good at using these connections to unite with decision makers in prospective client organizations.

6. *Geography:* In a time when functional specialists may fly all over the world to work with clients in far-flung locations, there are still geographically oriented business communities. If you live in Houston, Atlanta, Rome, or Stockholm, there are many opportunities to develop roots in the local community and focus on potential clients in your city. Knowledge of who in your firm is good at what—and then building bridges to them and drawing them into your local relationships—is a key success factor for making this model work.

Often, these six models combine into three major clusters, although other combinations are found as well:

1. Industry + Very large client
2. Functional/Practice/Product + Intellectual capital
3. Geography + Social networking

The questions are: Which model or combination of models represents your chosen focus; and how can you even more explicitly develop and exploit the approach you've taken?

In the end, a firm's ability to build and sustain Level 6 relationships is very much based on the strength of the individual networks developed by its professionals. A large, complex institutional relationship, for example, may well draw on individuals who have each pursued a different network model and therefore have something unique to offer the client.

Conclusion

If you want to develop Level 6 relationships, you are going to have to focus. You will need to create an appropriate balance between the *critical few* and the *many* when it comes to developing your network, with an emphasis on the former. Remember: Someone you already know is probably the future core of a large-scale trusted client partnership. As the following story illustrates so well, you don't want to wait until that individual is a top executive somewhere before you start paying attention to them.

A client of mine had worked her way up the corporate ladder in the legal department of a $25 billion Fortune 100 company to eventually become the general counsel. Later, she left the corporate world and became a partner in a major law firm. One day I asked her about her experiences as general counsel, when she was a client to many external advisors. Her response truly struck me. She said,

> The day that I was promoted to general counsel, and it was announced in the newspapers, the calls flooded in from lawyers and other professionals who wanted to meet with me. Some very big law firms that hadn't been interested in me before now suddenly wanted to meet. Do you know what I asked them? "Where were you five years ago?"

Follow the person—not the position. Build relationships with interesting, ambitious, bright individuals, and over time they will go places and accomplish things. Develop your relationship capital over time, nurture it carefully, and the rewards will be plentiful.

5

Strategy Three: Engaging New Clients

Evolving Your Relationships from Contacts to Clients

One of my clients, a partner at a leading management consulting firm, used to visit the North American CEO of a large multinational corporation on a regular basis. One day, as he was leaving his client's office, the CEO's executive assistant stopped him.

"You know," she said, "You really ought to come more often. He enjoys talking with you."

"Well," the partner replied, "I do visit quite regularly. And when I come, I always bring some very good analyses to show him." He pointed to a PowerPoint deck that he still held in his left hand.

"But your competitors come more often," The assistant added. "And he does really enjoy your conversations."

"Well, I see what you're saying," the partner insisted, "but I think we add a lot of value in these sessions, and we do bring a lot of good ideas to him," nodding toward his briefcase.

"You don't understand," the sympathetic but exasperated assistant responded. "He has confessed to me privately that he views those PowerPoint slides as the price he has to pay to have a *good conversation* with you!"

Indeed, many of us have misplaced notions about what clients really value. In this case, my talented friend did not realize that he possessed an undervalued asset (undervalued by him, that is)—which was his ability to act as an objective sounding board and provide his client with ideas, perspectives, and insights through vibrant, unscripted conversation.

In a sense, *good conversations* are the key to evolving your client relationships through the six levels that I described in Chapter 1. Reaching Level 6—trusted partner—obviously requires a more sustained, firmwide effort; but converting a contact into a client and then earning a seat at the table as a trusted advisor are very much about having engaging conversations that inherently add value. So you might think about moving your and your firm's relationships through these different levels in terms of the question, "How can my team and I have more interesting and valuable conversations with our contacts and clients?" You always want to leave the other person wanting more and looking forward to your next encounter.

Engagement is the process of winning a client for the first time, and then deepening that relationship as you work together. I'm not going to focus on selling techniques, which are well covered elsewhere, but rather on fundamental rapport-building skills and strategies that will help you be successful in the early stages of any relationship. I've carefully chosen six areas to cover—some of which are particularly problematic for the professionals with whom I work—and all of which will help you jump-start your early interactions with clients. These are:

1. Holding successful first meetings
2. Creating dynamic conversations
3. Engaging with senior executives
4. Getting to know clients as people
5. Accelerating trust
6. Living by core relationship-building principles

First meetings? Conversational techniques? Does this sound too basic? Steve Pfeiffer, chair of the executive committee at the law firm of Fulbright & Jaworski, says this about first meetings:

> *Virtually every large, institutional client relationship that we have today began with a single, one-on-one conversation between one of our partners and a prospective client. The trust and confidence built during those early meetings are essential. You simply must be skilled at handling these initial conversations.*

In my experience, even the most accomplished professionals can improve their skills at the engagement process by 30 to 40 percent.

First Meetings

I recall participating in a conference call with five client executives, that was intended to prep me for an upcoming phone conversation with their chairman. By the end of the discussion, the group had made a list of 10 things they hoped I would accomplish during what would be my very first introduction to the head of their firm. I pulled back, realizing that their overzealousness was setting me up for failure. "Look," I told the group, "I've never even spoken to your chairman before. I think we need to set more modest objectives. Step one is just for us to get to know each other!" Upon reflection, the group agreed with me, and we scaled back our aspirations for the call. Be careful about over-reaching in a first encounter; you don't want to overextend yourself *or* overwhelm a new client. At the same time, however, it's important to remain disciplined about what you are trying to accomplish.

The overall focus of a first meeting—whether with a new prospective client or a new executive who works at an existing client—should be to begin the trust-building process. We know that clients do business with people they trust, and lack of trust is the first big barrier that has to be overcome in the early stages of a relationship. Building trust is a very broad aspiration; however, and you have to approach first meetings with a far more specific plan. You should have *four* main goals for any first meeting:

> The truth is that you cannot actually develop trust in a very first meeting. What you *can* do is to get a sense for whether or not the other person is someone in whom you *could* develop trust over time. Do they ask thoughtful questions and listen well? Are they asking for business *today*—or showing they are willing to invest in getting to know our business and build a relationship in the future? If they bring one or more colleagues, how do they get along together? This gives me a hint about what a long-term relationship with them *might* be like.
>
> **—Chief Financial Officer**

1. Build rapport.
2. Understand the other person's issues.
3. Demonstrate credibility.
4. Establish a next step.

Trust is something that will begin to develop *if you accomplish* these four objectives. In other words, it's an outcome that derives from certain behaviors. Most client executives have told me that they don't believe you *can* build trust in a first encounter (see sidebar); but you can get an impression about the *potential* to build trust.

Let's look at strategies to accomplish each of these four goals.

Goal one: Build Rapport

Rapport refers to a feeling of connection, trust, and understanding based on similar interests or character. When you have rapport with someone, there is a harmonious, mutual understanding that develops. The word *rapport* comes from a French phrase (and originally from Latin) meaning "to bring back." This is an interesting origin, and it hints at the idea of recalling shared interests, experiences, and memories ("Oh, I grew up in New York also!"). Rapport begins to form when you identify things that you have in common with others, and engage in discussion about each other's interests and experiences.

The person whom you are meeting for the first time might—depending on their temperament—want to spend five minutes on the up-front small talk that starts the rapport-building process;

or they might want to spend 30 seconds on it, and get right down to business. Alternatively, they might only feel comfortable engaging on this more personal level at the very end of the meeting as you are walking out. It's your job to sense this and react accordingly. It can be downright annoying for someone to be asked a lot of personal questions about their family and hobbies when they're anxious to get to the business at hand.

> I have no special talents. I am only passionately curious.
>
> —**Albert Einstein**

Curiosity is an important aspect of the engagement process, both in terms of being curious about others and—as we'll see later on—evoking the other person's curiosity to continue the dialogue. Some of my own clients confess to being inept at what they call "small talk." But small talk comes naturally when you are curious about the other person and willing to share something about yourself. Later on in the chapter, I provide some questions that can help you be curious in a nonthreatening manner.

The New Neuroscience of Empathy

Empathy, which is one of the core attributes of client advisors, is clearly at the heart of the rapport-building process. It has long been believed that empathy is about 50 percent inherited and 50 percent learned; in other words, while some people are naturally more empathetic, everyone can get better at it. Recently, some groundbreaking research into the human brain's *mirror neurons* has begun to lift the veil on the actual mechanism of empathy. Mirror neurons are specialized brain cells that become activated when you engage in any particular action or movement, such as reaching for a cold soft drink, getting up out of your chair, or scratching your ear. Researchers have discovered that these mirror neurons fire in exactly the same patterns whether *you* are performing the action or *someone else* is performing it. So in essence, these specialized brain cells allow you to actually *experience* what the other person is experiencing.

Furthermore, it appears that mirror neurons enable you to understand *intent*. For example, in one experiment, when a subject reached for a coffee mug on a table as if to clear it off but with no intent to drink from the mug, the mirror neurons of the person observing the scene barely activated. When the subject reached for the mug with the intention of drinking from it, the mirror neurons began firing actively, even though the movement was almost exactly the same.

Professor Mark Thompson at UCLA has remarked that mirror neurons "re-create the experience of others within ourselves." They basically allow us to walk in the other person's shoes. Interestingly, they also let us feel others' pain. For example, mirror neurons in the region of the brain that registers disgust also fire when you observe expressions of disgust on other peoples' faces.

The neuroscience of empathy has some powerful implications for building rapport, and also for relationships in general. First of all, we are all innately programmed to empathize with others, and when we fail to do so, it's because we are letting other things get in the way. These could include an excessive focus on our own expertise, or just plain anxiety. A person may seem to lack empathy, but as we've learned, *everyone* has the basic genetic wiring that enables him or her to walk in other peoples' shoes. Second, your own mood and emotions can have a powerful, visceral effect on clients. If you frown, look repulsed by an idea or suggestion, or are just plain depressed, you may, via the other person's mirror neurons, impart your emotions to him without realizing it. It's good to be authentic and open with clients; but if you're having a bad day or harboring negative thoughts about something, you may want to be careful about how you express yourself in your gestures, expressions, and tone of voice. In short, it looks like Dale Carnegie was right. Seventy-five years ago, he wrote about the positive impact of a smile on others, although at the time he was unaware of the underlying science that has been discovered.

Mimicry Revisited

The concept of mimicry, or mirroring another person's body language in order to establish rapport, has been around for quite a while. I receive a lot of questions about this concept in terms of its potential use in relationship building in business. I've always been somewhat skeptical of mimicry because I'm concerned that if it is used as a conscious strategy, it can be manipulative and come across to the client as contrived and insincere. However, new research has underscored just how powerful the role of mimicry is in establishing social bonding between two people.

In one recent experiment conducted by Rick van Baaren in the Netherlands, students were asked to present their opinions about a series of advertisements. As some of them spoke, researchers mimicked their posture and body language, while trying not to be too obvious about what they were doing. At a certain point, one of the researchers would drop a handful of pens. The students who had been mimicked were two to three times more likely to lean over and pick up the pens as those who had not been mimicked—in other words, they were more inclined to be helpful to the researchers. The study found that the greatest results were achieved when the researchers put a short delay into their mimicking behavior.

In another study conducted at Duke University, researchers had 37 students drink a beverage that was touted as a new sports drink. The researcher who subsequently interviewed them about the drink mimicked their posture and movements, using a one- or two-second delay. If a student crossed her legs, the interviewer would wait a second or two and also cross his legs. If the student scratched her nose, the interviewer would also scratch his nose, trying to approximately but not precisely copy the gesture. At the end of the interviews, students who had been mimicked with a delay were far more likely to say that they would buy the new sports drink, compared to students who were not mimicked.

Our knowledge of the science behind human interaction has been rapidly evolving. Despite the power of these findings, I would be cautious about making this your main rapport-building strategy. I like to think about this aspect of rapport in terms of tuning into and reflecting the other person's style and approach. Do they stand up from their desk and walk around the room, and actively gesticulate? Then I tend to walk around the room also. Are they more formal and reticent, and sit compactly at a conference table without moving very much? Then I adapt my own style to be more subdued.

Achieving an initial level of rapport is your first goal in any first encounter. You do this by briefly engaging in casual small talk and identifying interests, experiences, or people you may share in common;

being curious about the other person and their work; and tuning into their body language, tone, and style.

Goal two: Understand the Other Person's Issues

In Chapter 3 I highlighted the importance of understanding a client's agenda of priority issues and goals, and I set out a number of techniques for doing so, including specific questions that you can use during senior executive conversations. Let's take another look at this because it is such an important skill.

In a first meeting, there are (at least) five distinct approaches to getting a prospective client—or anyone—to talk about their issues. I've listed each of these below, and I've described the most commonly used one last, for reasons I will explain:

1. *What we find:* In this approach, you share with the client some specific experience or best practices that relate to their issue, and then you let them react. You might say, "What we find is that there are usually three potential obstacles to implementing a program like this," or, "What we find is that behavioral change is an important but often-ignored ingredient in this situation."

2. *Smart questions:* In this context, a smart question is one in which you demonstrate your own knowledge of the issues while getting your client to open up and tell you more about theirs. It works well when you ask the client to place their organization on a scale of extremes—for example, I might say, "Some of my clients, which have historically had tenure-based compensation systems, are now moving toward more individually driven rewards. On the other hand, other clients are trying to get away from an emphasis on individual performance and are moving toward team-based incentives. I'm curious, where is your organization on this continuum?"

3. *What are the implications?* Implication questions are almost always fruitful as a means to explore a client's issues. You can simply ask, "How is this affecting...(morale, sales, productivity, risk exposure, communications, speed of decision making, etc.)?"

4. *Let me give you an example:* This approach to gleaning your prospective client's issues involves simply sharing several case examples of other clients you've worked with, and getting the other person to react to those stories. This works best in response to questions like, "So tell me something about your firm," in which case you respond by saying, "The best way to talk about what we do is to give you one or two examples of recent work we've completed." After you recount a short, sharp case study (100 to 150 words, no more), the client will usually say something like, "That's interesting. Actually, we're facing a similar issue." Or, "That's really not our issue. What we are up against is quite different."

> I can always tell how experienced a consultant or banker is by the quality of the questions they ask me. Experience is best conveyed indirectly—it's more credible then.
>
> **—Chief Executive Officer**

5. *What are your priorities?* I still hear people asking questions like "What keeps you up at night?" or "What are your three most pressing issues right now?" As I've mentioned, these are shopworn, overused, and with some clients, possibly intrusive. Many clients have told me that they need to feel more comfortable with an outsider before opening up, and that the other person needs to "earn the right" by first establishing that they actually know what they are talking about. If you choose the direct route and want to dive right in, try a more understated approach. For example, "To understand if and how we can be helpful, it would useful to get a sense from you about some of the high-priority issues you are working on right now." Or, "I know you have a lot on your plate right now. In your view, what would you say are the *most* critical issues on your agenda?" You can also turn this over to the client and say, "I understand that we've got 30 minutes this morning—are there some particular issues you'd like to focus in on during our discussion?"

If you have done a skillful job of uncovering your potential client's issues, you will also have gone a long way toward establishing your own credibility and competence. Let's look at this next step in more detail.

TABLE 5.1 Building Your Credibility: The Client's View

Common Statements Intended to Build Credibility	Unspoken Reactions That Clients Have Shared
"We are the largest, with over 60 offices worldwide."	*Of course—I knew that already, and I'm concerned that I won't be an important client to you.*
"We've worked for most of the major companies in your industry."	*I'm not sure I'm going to get any fresh thinking from you. Besides, how can you do a good job for both my competitors and for me?*
"If you go to page 1 of the presentation, this gives you an overview of our firm."	*Of course I know about your firm. When are we going to get to my issues?*
"We are number 1 or 2 in these markets."	*I know, that's why I'm talking to you. But I'm also not impressed with league tables—I think people manipulate them.*
"Let me introduce you to my four colleagues."	*That's a lot of people to bring to a get-to-know-you session. Who would I work with, anyway?*
"After graduating from Duke with honors, I earned my MBA at Harvard."	*Big deal. I went to my state university. I hope your firm isn't full of Ivy-League snobs.*

Goal three: Demonstrate Credibility

Let's start by talking about what *does not* build credibility with a client during a first meeting. All of the statements in Table 5.1 are well meaning, and while they may work with some people on some occasions, they generally do not impress client executives.

Professionals gravitate toward using statements like these for several reasons. First, they believe that these descriptions of success—size, market share, league tables, degrees, and so on—must be impressive to clients. Second, it's much easier to sell "features" than to sell a solution that delivers benefits. The former only requires a list, whereas the latter requires a far more subtle process of exploration with the client.

Clients, however, want to know if they can really trust you to fix their problems. At home and at work, they are bombarded with all sorts of claims by people wanting to sell them something, and they are naturally skeptical.

So if these statements do not build credibility, what does? If I could boil it down to a handful of things that help build your credibility in first meetings, they would be: Be prepared. Know your stuff. Demonstrate *indirectly* that you know your stuff. Tell them something they don't already know, or at least help them discover a new insight as a result of your conversation. And finally, demonstrate honesty and straightforwardness in your answers to clients' questions. As soon as a client senses any equivocation or obfuscation on your part, or has any doubt about your competence, your credibility is lost.

> I am not interested in seeing league tables, market share rankings, or other such charts designed to show that someone's firm is number one in something or is very big and global. I wouldn't be talking to you in the first place if I didn't already know you were a large organization with lots of offices. What I'm interested in is your understanding of and insight into *my* issues. Do you understand my company and me?
>
> **—Chief Executive Officer**

I'd like to focus for a moment on two of these points: demonstrating competence *indirectly* and helping the client discover something that they didn't know before you walked in the door.

The main way you demonstrate your competence indirectly is by *showing* rather than *telling*. When you tell, you make assertions about your capabilities and you describe the assets you can bring to bear (e.g., "We are the best at . . ."). When you show, you use examples, case histories, descriptions of specific best practices, and so on. It's that simple. Showing is tangible, realistic, and palpable to the client; telling is intellectual and wordy.

An additional "showing" strategy is to use and leverage independent or third-party endorsements. Think about it: If *you* say you're great, it will come across as bragging and puffery. If a credible *third party* says you're great, it's a lot more believable. If a prospective client calls a past client who then raves about you, that's a very powerful independent endorsement. If a magazine publishes your article, that's also an implicit endorsement. When you use third-party endorsements, you are saying, in effect, "Don't listen to me—listen to these other people who have no axe to grind and no special interest at stake!"

Here are a number of things you can do in a conversation to indirectly demonstrate your credibility and, hopefully, to communicate something to the client that they don't already know:

- Describe short, pithy examples of successful client assignments that you have completed.
- Use or evoke third-party endorsements.
- Share ideas, experiences, and best practices you have observed.
- Ask thoughtful questions that implicitly demonstrate your knowledge of the issues.
- Politely challenge the other person's assumptions and assertions.
- Introduce interesting market, competitive, or trend data.
- Suggest counter-intuitive or unusual approaches.
- Synthesize rather than summarize (a summary is boring; a synthesis adds value by clarifying and framing the gist of the discussion).
- Make it a conversation, not a presentation, and use documents as leave-behinds, not the main course.

> Let another praise you and not your own mouth; a stranger, and not your own lips.
>
> **—Proverbs 27:2**

Finally, always walk into a first meeting with what I call the *mindset of independent wealth*. If you think about it, someone who is independently wealthy would be healthily detached from the outcome of a first meeting, taking the attitude that "If it works out, great; if not, that's okay, too." They would be objective about whether the other person really needed their services. They would give their opinions honestly and even bluntly, without dancing around the real issues. They would not be too distracted thinking about their own agenda, and would therefore listen carefully to the other person. They would not focus on the clock, or become concerned that they were wasting time or not getting to a sale quickly enough.

Wouldn't these be an effective set of attitudes in *any* relationship? If you are not yet independently wealthy, you should at least carry the *mindset* around with you. You can do this by exemplifying three specific behaviors:

1. Treat your clients like peers. Don't be either sycophantic or condescending.
2. Demonstrate great enthusiasm for your work. Through your energy and passion, show your clients that you love what you do.
3. Never act as if you have the meter running. Be completely present in the moment.

If you do these things, you will present an attractive appearance—aura, even—that others will notice from across the room.

Goal four: Establish a Next Step

If you ask any veteran salesperson, he or she will tell you that the objective of a first meeting is to get a second meeting. Author and sales expert Neil Rackham has a nice word for this—he calls it an "advance." It may not necessarily be a second meeting, but it is something that advances the relationship and the sale.

Be careful, however, about setting your expectations too high. If you and the client do not identify a clear next step or advance, there may be a very good reason for it. Sometimes, a first meeting is purely a get-to-know-you session, and nothing specific or actionable emerges from it. You may simply decide that you are going to stay in touch and perhaps meet again in three or six months.

The key to a next step is curiosity. Earlier, I talked about how your *own* curiosity helps fuel your empathy and interest in the other person. Now, we are talking about evoking the *client's* curiosity to want to meet again with you or someone else from your firm. You can evoke your client's curiosity in a variety of ways, such as:

- Clearly making the connection between a tough issue they are trying to solve and a specific capability or experience you can bring to bear on that issue (client is thinking: *Maybe they have the skills to help us*).

- Suggesting that you can bring back some data or research that is either just plain intriguing, or that will shed light on one of the issues the client is dealing with (client is thinking: *They've got some interesting data I'd like to see*).

- Offering an introduction to a colleague—or even someone outside your firm, such as a client—who has first-class expertise and experience (client is thinking: *I'd like to meet this person. She's a real expert*).

- Showing that you have a perspective or angle on the client's problem that no one else has come up with, for example, "This sounds like a bold program that you are rightly proud of. There are a couple of significant risks, however, that you may not have considered. Let me explain." (Client is thinking: *This is the kind of fresh perspective I need. I'd like to explore this further.*)

A next step may naturally emerge from your conversation, but sometimes you may have to suggest what the advance should be: "Why don't I put some thoughts together on that issue, and then we could have another conversation next week"; or, you could turn it back to the client and say, "From your perspective, what do you think an appropriate next step would be?"

Conversational Techniques

Some people seem like natural-born conversationalists. They never lack for something interesting to say, they draw others out of themselves and into the conversation, and they change the subject at just the right time. However, I don't think that anyone is *born* with these skills. You may by nature be more or less extroverted, but in truth, anyone can learn basic conversational techniques. There are three ingredients required to sustain a good, interactive dialogue. First—as we have mentioned repeatedly in this chapter—curiosity about and interest in other people, which you manifest by asking questions; second, a willingness to engage in disclosure—to share your thoughts, feelings, and experiences; and third, the common sense to know when you've exhausted the topic or line of inquiry and should move on.

Here are some listening or conversational techniques that I have found useful:

- *Synthesizing:* Pulling the conversation together and clarifying the issues, as opposed to just summarizing.
- *Active listening:* Interjecting "okay, uh huh; I see; what happened then?" and so on.
- *Nonverbal listening:* Leaning over, using strong eye contact, focusing completely on the other person.
- *Echoing:* Repeating the last word of the other person's sentence, to encourage elaboration.
- *Self-disclosure:* Saying things like "I know what you mean—I missed my husband's birthday one year, too."
- *Open-ended questions:* "How do you think this is affecting your customer service?" as opposed to "What is your market share?"
- *Provocative questions:* "Why?" "So what?" "Does that really matter?"
- *Questions about the meaning of words:* Encouraging the other person to elaborate: "What exactly do you mean by dysfunctional?"
- *Questions about the past, the present, and the future:* "How and when did this start?" "What are you doing now about it?" "In a year's time, what kind of progress do you hope to achieve?"
- *Personal questions:* "Where did you grow up?"; "Going forward, is there another role you'd like to play in the organization?"
- *Questions about feelings:* "How did people feel about that decision?"

- *Admitting that you don't know:* "I don't know your company well enough to answer that. I can tell you what I'll be looking for, however."
- *Letting the client answer provocative or difficult questions:* Wait five seconds before answering, and another client executive in the group may jump in and answer before you do.

Listening Pitfalls

There are a number of bad habits that I have observed—starting with some of my own—that can get in the way of effective listening and, therefore, good conversations. Ask yourself how often you indulge in any of the following:

- *Thinking ahead:* Our minds often race ahead to the next question or issue while the person we're with is still talking.
- *Believing that you're the most insightful person in the room:* We tend to forget that it's not always about being right or having the perfect idea, but rather about helping clients make changes that will improve their business.
- *Being in love with your own ideas:* After spending weeks or months analyzing the problem, it's easy to become enamored of the conclusions you're trying to present—as opposed to creating a give-and-take with the client as you socialize and test your ideas.
- *Listening without giving back:* Good listening is about mutual disclosure, not just sitting there and taking notes. The conversation has to be interspersed with sharing of your own thoughts, feelings, ideas, and experiences.
- *Not affirming or validating:* Affirmation is a powerful reinforcement for the person speaking. Paraphrase and synthesize as you go along. Affirm that you have understood your client.
- *Lack of mindfulness:* We are often distracted, rushed, and judgmental; and not "present" in the current moment. All of your

body language has to reinforce that this is the most important conversation happening in your world today.

- *Indulging your biases:* We all have biases, and even prejudices, which inhibit our ability to listen. Some studies have shown, for example, that doctors give inferior care to certain minority groups. Why? Most likely because their unconscious biases prevent them from listening well—from taking these patients as seriously as they should.

- *Not allowing silence:* Silence gives the client a chance to think and reflect, and it can make you seem thoughtful and considered in your judgments. Don't rush to fill every second of airtime— embrace the occasional pause or break in the conversation.

Engaging with Senior Executives

Think about the senior executives that you know. What are they like, inside and outside the office? What pressures are they under? In their careers, they are most likely highly driven and successful. You will probably find that many of them read widely and pursue—with passion and vigor—an eclectic variety of outside interests. At work, they have access to vast amounts of information because they tend to be collection points for a broad array of market and competitive data that cross their desk. They will value your expertise, especially if you are truly good at what you do. But if you are one-dimensional and have few professional or personal interests outside your core specialty, it's unlikely that your relationship with them will grow very close. As one of my clients said to me, "In order to be interesting, you've got to have interests."

A recent *New York Times* article about the libraries of CEOs starts with the headline, "In personal libraries, more literature and poetry than business best sellers." The library of Nike founder Phil Knight is filled with volumes on Asian history, art, and poetry. Dee Hock, the founder of Visa, built a large library and then spent years trying to find the one book that provided the most wisdom for him—which turned

> If you are not spending 50 percent of the time you have with a senior executive talking about things *other than* the immediate project you are working on, you're probably not really developing a relationship with that person.
>
> —**Relationship Manager**

out to be *The Rubaiyat*, by Omar Khayyam, a great Persian poem about the dangers of greatness. Apple CEO Steve Jobs apparently has an intense interest in the English poet, artist, and mystic William Blake. Shelly Lazarus, the chairwoman of Ogilvy & Mather, says that "As head of a global company, everything attracts me as a reader; books about different cultures, countries, problems. I read for pleasure and to find other perspectives on how to think or solve a problem."

If you provide legal, accounting, technology, or other more specialized services, you're not going to be advising your client on the direction of the economy or on corporate strategy. But this doesn't mean you don't need to have a wide-ranging understanding of the forces that affect your client's business and, ultimately, influence the nature of the more specific issues and problems that you are asked to address. Think about broadening your understanding of your client's world at multiple levels: Your client as a person, their company, their industry, and the general business and economic environment that surrounds them. You need to know enough to ask intelligent questions, and to put the particular issue you are working on into a broader context.

The question that you have to ask yourself is, "Why would a top executive want to have a 'seat at the table' with *me*—either in the office discussing critical business issues, or over dinner at a restaurant?"

Value for Time

For senior corporate executives, value for time has become more important than value for money. Most clients can easily fill each day twice over with appointments and meetings, given the crushing demands on their schedules. For every request, they are asking, "Does this align with my most critical priorities? Can someone else handle this? Can it wait a few weeks?" They invest their time in relationships only where there is tangible value for them. Therefore, if you want to successfully build strong relationships with executives, you have to understand how to consistently add value for time.

How do you maximize your impact with clients whom you are trying to engage, given the limited access to their time? An executive is giving value—and therefore, feeling that their time is well-spent—when they are energizing an important initiative, making a key decision, shaping the direction of a program, meeting a key customer, or perhaps mentoring a direct report. They are feeling, "I really used the power of my office and my experience and judgment to have an impact here." On the other hand, they are also getting value when they are learning valuable new information, being pushed to rethink a problem, getting their perspectives broadened, or making a new personal connection. Examples of ways to add more value for time would therefore include the following:

- Always ensure that the focus of your conversation connects to and aligns with the executive's agenda of critical priorities.
- If it doesn't seem like you are connecting with the other person, consider redirecting the conversation. Ernst & Young Managing Partner Mike Hamilton, who is Chief Learning and Development Officer for the Americas, likes to ask clients a simple question: "What's the most important issue we should be discussing today?" This can powerfully focus your time together.
- Think about information you can contribute that the executive is not getting from his or her own organization. This could include insights drawn from customers, markets, employees, the capital markets, or other key constituencies.
- Lead into your conversation with a strong "hook," like a great pop song. Engage the other person's interest immediately, and get to the point very quickly.
- Push your client's thinking by posing thoughtful questions that others are not asking: "Why ... ?" "What are the implications ... ?" "Have you considered ..." "What if ... ?" And so on.

Remember, if your client is not thinking, "That was a really good use of my time," then you won't get a second chance.

Don't confuse quantity of time with quality of time. Most advisors would like to have more time with their clients, believing (correctly) that face time builds trust and familiarity. However, less is sometimes more. If you can use an executive's time sparingly but consistently add value during your encounters, you are doing them an important service. Finish a meeting in 45 minutes instead of an hour, and you'll be remembered as someone who uses time well.

Getting to Know Clients as People

The managing partner of a large professional services firm once pulled me aside just before I was to give a speech at an annual partners retreat. "Please don't tell them that they have to become *best friends* with their clients!" he told me, adding, "It'll terrify some of them and they may tune out right then and there." Lurking behind his comment is a common fear among some professionals of getting too personal with clients.

While no one has to become best friends—or even friends—with clients, you do have to get to know them *as people*. This means understanding their aspirations, personal values, risk tolerance, decision-making style, the key influences on their thinking, and other facets of their personality that might affect your professional interactions. If you don't understand these aspects of their character, it will be difficult to serve them effectively, reach correct judgments, and build a personal bond.

Here are some practices that will help you move from a purely professional, arms-length relationship to one that has a personal dimension to it:

- *Be human and accessible.* Sometimes we are too professional, too buttoned-down, or too flawless. It's very hard to become enamored of someone who has no imperfections or vices, and who has seemingly never made a mistake. It's okay—even necessary—to occasionally show your human side.

- *Offer praise and complement your client when it's appropriate to do so.* You can be sure that a lot of people certainly aren't patting them on the back. Even highly successful clients appreciate positive reinforcement. Just make sure that it's sincere!

- *Use humor.* Humor is a universal way of connecting to others and diffusing tensions. If you make fun of yourself, it also is a way of showing you are human (a client of mine recently got a promotion, and said to me, "You're one of the people that helped me get to this position." To which I replied, "Thank you for saying that, but I feel more like you had to cross the goal line while carrying *me* on your shoulders..." We both laughed.)

- *Ask your clients for advice.* They may in fact have some very good counsel for you on issues of importance, and it will certainly make them feel good to be asked.

- *Look for breakthrough moments.* In *Clients for Life*, I talk about "breakthrough moments" in the life of a relationship—moments that catapult your bond to a new level. These can include working through an extraordinarily difficult project or transaction together, dealing with a major crisis, or perhaps, when your client faces a daunting personal issue, providing support and advice.

- *Ask about their lives.* Most clients are quite happy to talk about their family and interests outside of work.

- *Follow your client's lead.* Move slowly and take small steps. If someone is very private and resistant to invitations to talk about family and personal interests, don't push them—gradually build familiarity.

Accelerating Trust

I am frequently asked, "How can I accelerate trust with this client?" This is a tough question. I wish there were a fast-forward button that, when pressed, would compress nine months of relationship-building

The partner that manages our relationship came to me and informed me of a mistake that his firm had made in handling a particular case they were working on for us. It's something that we might not have noticed for a long time, if at all, but he came to us and told us as soon as they knew about it. I trust him *more* now because I know that if there is ever another error or lapse that they will be immediately forthcoming.

—General Counsel

and quality delivery into a few weeks, with the resultant trust that you would expect from such earnest efforts. It's a bit like asking, "How can I accelerate the healing of my sprained ankle?" Well, do all the right things—ice it, elevate it, take an anti-inflammatory, have a positive attitude, and gradually flex and stretch it—and it will heal as rapidly as possible. However, the healing process still takes time. You cannot overturn your body's natural metabolic processes; and the same is true of client relationships.

The literature on trust has expanded greatly over the past decade, and some interesting frameworks have been developed to explain how and when trust will develop. But in the end, building trust is still rooted in the basics. Be authentic; focus on your client's agenda, not yours; help your clients with their issues; be consistent and reliable; and of course, demonstrate great professional competence. In a nutshell, try to:

- Add value early in the relationship—ideally in the first few meetings with a client.
- Occasionally say, "I don't know," or "I'm not sure how to answer that question right now."
- Answer every question from your client with refreshing honesty and candor.
- Occasionally say no to a client request for more work if you're not the best firm to do that kind of work.
- Make a recommendation that is clearly in your client's interest and clearly *not* in your own interest.
- Invest time to understand your client better—especially during moments of crisis or high anxiety (a merger, a board presentation, etc.).

- Spend more time together—at work and outside of work.
- Take an interest in your clients as people—in their interests, aspirations, and goals.
- Always keep promises and always be consistent, reliable, and discreet.
- Recognize unspoken issues and emotions, and try to bring them out into the open.
- Never criticize others who are not in the room.
- Tell your client, right away, if you've made a mistake.
- Set and review expectations.
- Use third-party endorsements.
- Be authentic and transparent.
- Always be prepared to meet the "light of day test" in your behavior. (Would you be embarrassed to tell your client which hotel you stayed in last night?)

Conclusion: Relationship-Building Principles

Mahatma Gandhi, the great Indian spiritual leader, once said: "Men want to have lots of laws so they don't have to be good." In a similar vein, I am sometimes asked by workshop participants to simply tell them "how to do it" (that is, how to build strong relationships). The problem is that when it comes to relationship building, there are many wrong answers, but also many right ones. There are definitely some best practices—which form the foundation of this book—but in any given client interaction, there are probably several different, acceptable alternatives that will work for people.

A set of implicit principles, however, does underlie these "best" ways to deal with different client interactions. For example, recall the story at the end of the last chapter about the woman who was promoted to general counsel. When law firms she had never heard from before suddenly starting calling her to solicit her company's legal work, she asked, "Where were you five years ago?" The principle that would have obviated this embarrassing situation for the law firm partners might be framed as "Follow the person, not the position." I would add: Build connections with interesting, ambitious, bright individuals and good things will eventually come of these relationships.

Here, then, are 12 relationship-building principles that I believe will be helpful as you build your network and engage with clients. I am sure that many readers have some of their own principles that they can add to this list—it is by no means exhaustive:

Relationship Principles

1. Build your network before you need it.
2. Become truly distinctive at something.
3. Be enthusiastic and passionate about your work.
4. Be generous with your time and wisdom, and help others without expecting to receive anything in return.
5. Start a relationship by having an interesting conversation together, not by showing how brilliant you are.
6. Ask yourself, "How can I help? Does this person have a particular interest, need, or goal that I can contribute to?"
7. Focus on the person—on following him or her throughout an entire career—not the position.
8. Be authentic. (Whoever you are—be that person! If you're introverted, be comfortable about it; if you're extroverted, be that way all the time.)
9. Cultivate your own interests so that you are interesting to others.
10. Be genuinely curious about the people around you.
11. Assume positive intentions in others' actions.
12. Exemplify integrity at all times: Be honest, consistent, reliable, and discreet.

You could do much worse than to embed these principles into your day-to-day relationship building efforts. Do they sound simple or obvious? They are, but I think that most of us may struggle to follow them consistently. Consider the following story about a famous

Chinese Zen master named Bird's Nest Roshi, which illustrates the dilemma of these basic principles. My wife's Zen teacher, Joan Sutherland, shared it with me:

> *Bird's Nest Roshi got his name because he often meditated in a tree. One day, an eminent man, who was the governor of the province, paid him a visit. When the governor found him, he said, "What a dangerous seat you have up there in the tree." Bird's Nest Roshi replied, "Yours is more dangerous than mine." The governor said, "I am the governor of this province and I don't see what danger there is in this." Bird's Nest Roshi responded, "Then, sir, you don't know yourself very well. When passions burn and the mind is unsteady, this is the greatest danger." The governor then asked, "What is the teaching of Buddhism?" and Bird's Nest Roshi said, "Not to commit wrong actions, but to do all good ones, and keep the heart pure." When the governor heard this, he was not impressed and exclaimed, "Any child of three years knows that!" Roshi responded, "Any three-year-old child may know it, but even an eighty-year-old man has a hard time doing it."*

6

Strategy Four: Institutionalizing Client Relationships

Growing Your Clients

Some years ago, one of my clients suffered a major loss when a senior partner left and took several major clients with him. Later, the CEO told me that he never wanted this to happen again. "We need to institutionalize our relationships so that they do not depend entirely on a single partner," he said. A few days later, one of the other partners in the firm pulled me aside and said, "I understand our CEO's sentiment—not wanting to lose clients—but it seems to me that, ironically, someone shouldn't be made a senior partner in the first place if they aren't capable of taking a client with them if they leave the firm!"

This story highlights the difficulties of moving from an individual relationship to a firm relationship. To cross the chasm from trusted advisor (Level 5) to trusted partner (Level 6), the individual who developed the relationship in the first place needs to gradually take on a new and different role and consciously make room for other colleagues—not always an easy step for someone who enjoys a trusted advisor relationship and the feeling of being indispensable to the client.

In Chapter 1, we looked at the examples of Citigroup and Booz Allen Hamilton and the strategies that they used to build deep, broad relationships with Shell and the U.S. Navy, respectively. Let's look at yet another case study, this time involving a major bank.

Towers Perrin, a leading human resources consulting firm, has had one of the top banks in the world as a client for many years. Today, this bank draws on a variety of Towers Perrin's consulting capabilities in areas such as compensation, talent management, and employee benefits. The bank's senior management has told me that they view the firm as a long-term partner in helping them achieve their most critical human resources strategies and goals.

Level 6 relationships are not always smooth and wrinkle free—you have to expect periodic crises or rough patches, and this example is no exception. About eight years ago, in fact, the relationship had waned somewhat, and the client felt that there was a lack of responsiveness on the part of the consultants. The senior client executive personally called the head of Towers Perrin to relay his concerns. Often, these stories end badly; but in this case, Towers Perrin responded vigorously. The firm put in one of their most senior and experienced relationship managers to manage the team and become the lead content expert for the client. She reaffirmed the firm's commitment to serving the client on the terms it required, made a number of changes in the composition of the team, and also negotiated a long-term pricing agreement that provided additional value for the client. After a year and half, the relationship was on a stable footing and whatever crisis had occurred was well over. For a variety of reasons, the firm decided to transition the account leadership to someone new, and after an extensive review and selection process in which the client participated, a new relationship manager was assigned.

This new client relationship manager spent the first year building relationships with the client and getting to know its business. He also began introducing his own management style to the team, one which—now that things were on a stronger footing—was appropriately more empowering and less hierarchical. He then used a variety of strategies to reinforce and grow the relationship. These included emphasizing an in-depth account planning process, which the client participated in; holding monthly calls with every consultant working for the client in any location around the world; putting on ad hoc team dinners; introducing subject matter experts from different practices and offices at Towers Perrin to provide perspectives on issues of interest to the client; and conducting a highly structured, independent review process using senior Towers Perrin executives not involved in the account. He also ramped up the team's responsiveness to new levels. One Friday he got a call from the client about a time-critical issue, and in response mobilized a team to work through the weekend in order to have an in-depth point of view ready for presentation on Monday morning. From that crisis eight years ago, this has been solidified as a true Level 6 trusted partner relationship, and one of Towers Perrin's top clients.

From Trusted Advisor to Trusted Partner

What do this and the other examples we have looked at in these early chapters have in common? I have studied the case histories of about 50 large institutional relationships that have been cultivated by a variety of professionals in many different markets. In these relationships, the client purchases a breadth of services, several or more trusted-advisor relationships are developed at multiple levels, and the service provider is well connected with key economic buyers in senior management. As noted in Chapter 1, these Level 6 relationships create significant benefits for both sides.

But how do you get there? How do take a small, narrow relationship—or one that may have languished—and grow and institutionalize it? Some would suggest that the secret is effective "cross-selling." But cross-selling as a strategy simply has not worked in practice. Worse, it is a self-centered view of how to interact with a client. What client, after all, wants to be "cross-sold" to?

Imagine that a plumber comes to your house and fixes a leaky pipe. Then, as he leaves, he says to you, "I'd like to schedule a meeting next week for you to meet my colleagues from our painting and flooring divisions because your house looks like it could use some sprucing up." My guess is that you wouldn't be very thrilled at this suggestion. But if the plumber observed your scratched floor tiles; and then spent time explaining different techniques to remove the scratches, which

FIGURE 6.1   Pathways to Growth

products work best, and how to prevent floor damage in the future, you might just get engaged in a dialogue about your home improvement needs. And who knows where that would lead.

The secret to relationship growth is more complex than just trying to sell a client other products and services, which may or may not fit its needs. In fact, my research shows that there are five fundamental pathways to creating a long-term, trusted client partnership, illustrated in Figure 6.1.

In almost every case I have seen, the professionals who have been able to chart a course from good to great—in my terms, from Levels 4 or 5 to Level 6—have significantly increased their effort and investment in each of the following five areas:

1. *Relationship expansion:* Strengthening and multiplying relationships, both externally and internally, by creating many-to-many relationships between your firm and the client, usually across multiple organizational levels and geographic locations; and augmenting your *internal* network within your firm.

2. *Capabilities expansion:* Identifying client problems and opportunities that can benefit from your firm's capabilities, exploring these with the client, educating them about your capabilities to address them, and building trust in your ability to deliver them.

3. *Client relationship management:* Engaging in a more sophisticated, systematic, and deliberate management of the relationship itself, and substantially increasing the flow of communications.

4. *Team leadership:* Taking a dynamic approach to selecting, managing, and developing team members; and learning to lead the team, not just manage it.

5. *Client account planning:* Undertaking a rigorous account planning process that drives the right strategies and tactics in the other four pathways.

Adding great value, of course, is also an essential ingredient in reaching Level 6. These five pathways help create the foundations for adding value, which I take up in the next chapter.

Let's look at specific best practices for activating each of these pathways.

Pathway 1: Relationship Expansion

External Network

The very first step in institutionalizing a client relationship is developing many-to-many relationships with the client's organization. A good number of firms put an almost exclusive emphasis on the relationship between the partner or principal who is the relationship manager, and the most senior client. But relationship building is the responsibility of the *entire* team of professionals. Each team member should have a specific mandate to develop one or more relationships with their counterparts in the client organization. Good team leaders keep and monitor a simple matrix, which has team members' names on the left and key client relationships across the top; and they coach their team on developing these connections.

> **Every Head Must Nod**
>
> Our best relationships with our bankers and consultants are characterized by strong individual relationships; not only at the top, but at all levels. When we have a major transaction, I'll talk to our entire staff about whom we are going to use as advisors. If we are gravitating toward a particular firm, it's critical that I see every head in the room nod, from junior staff right up through the treasurer. The really good firms build strong relationships throughout our organization.
>
> **—Chief Financial Officer**

Another aspect of the many-to-many approach is taking the time to cultivate relationships that are not necessarily critical for the *current* engagement, but which will be important down the road. You should build connections keeping in mind where you want to be with the client next year—and the year after. Don't limit yourself to only those required for today's business.

As you build many-to-many relationships with your client, keep in mind that there are at least five types of people in the client organization upon which you must focus:

1. *Economic buyers:* These are the executives who have the budgetary authority to approve the decision to hire you. Their main concern? Return-on-investment. They are asking: "Is this a good investment for our company?"

2. *Work-with clients:* These are the executives with whom you will work on a day-to-day basis. They are concerned about what it will be like to interact with you and your colleagues. They want to know: "Are they right for me, and can they help me get the job done?"

3. *Influencers:* There may be individuals, ranging from a board member to someone's trusted executive assistant, who can influence a decision to retain an outside firm—but who are otherwise uninvolved in the actual project.

4. *Technical buyers:* These are procurement managers who screen vendors and outside service providers. Their main concerns are, "Do their services meet our specifications? Is the price appropriate? Are we getting good value?"

5. *Coaches:* A coach is someone inside the client organization who wants you to succeed. It may be the CEO, or a relatively low-level manager; but regardless of their title or position, coaches are essential to helping you sell new work and expand the relationship. They can educate you about the ins and outs of the organization and the various agendas of different executives.

Relationship expansion requires discipline and accountability. One partner in a consulting firm described her approach as follows: "Each one of my client accounts has a relationship matrix. Every member of the team is assigned as *primary* and *other* for every client executive in the matrix. We're very disciplined about that. We ask regularly, 'How often are you meeting with them? What are you talking about? Are you deepening this relationship?' "

Internal Network

Expanding relationships with the client is an important first step, but strengthening your internal network is just as important. In fact, the most successful relationship managers whom I have studied consistently invest to build very strong connections with their colleagues across their organizations. How can you marshal your firm's people and resources, and bring the best that your firm has to offer to your client, if you don't have a strong network within your firm?

As you think about your internal network, consider the fact that you'll need strong relationships with five different types of people who represent important resources or capabilities necessary to develop a broad-based, institutional client relationship:

1. *Delivery capability:* You need access to and knowledge about the right delivery resources for your particular project or transaction.

2. *Practice leadership:* If you are to grow the relationship, you need connections with the leadership of the practice groups, departments, or product groups within your firm in order to access their know-how and people.

3. *Branded experts:* From time to time, you are going to want to engage the client by bringing in some of your firm's "branded experts"; that is, colleagues who have developed strong marketplace notoriety around a particular area of interest to the client. Often, these branded experts are widely published and speak frequently.

4. *Relationship management:* For particularly large client relationships, you may need and want help in relationship management. For example, you might ask one of your firm's most senior executives to meet with your client's CEO.

5. *Geographic capability:* If your client is multinational, it's important to have strong relationships with the heads of your geographic units (offices, countries, regions) around the world.

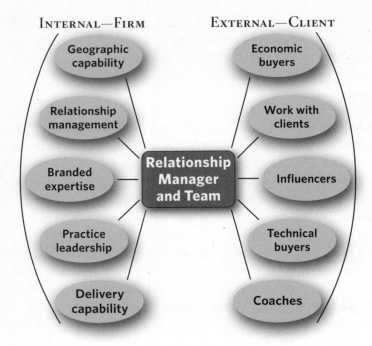

FIGURE 6.2 Relationship Expansion

If you have grown up in your firm, you may very well have developed strong internal connections over a period of many years. If you are a lateral hire, however, you're going to have to invest some serious time in getting to know individuals who can represent the capabilities you will need to grow and broaden your client affiliations.

Figure 6.2 summarizes the internal and external relationships that you will need to develop to evolve to a Level 6 trusted partner relationship.

Pathway 2: Capabilities Expansion

As you develop and strengthen your network of relationships with the client and within your firm, you need to also broaden the client's perception of your capabilities. This can be a difficult challenge, because we are often "pigeonholed" by clients. The CEO of one of my clients—a leading technology services company—told me that one of his frustrations as he goes around visiting the senior management of his company's major customers is that he often hears the comment, "I didn't know you did that!" in response to the mention of a particular service or capability.

In the eighteenth century, the compartments in writing cabinets used to sort and file documents became known as "pigeonholes," because of their resemblance to the nesting holes that domesticated pigeons lived in. The word eventually became a verb meaning "to classify or sort"—and this is exactly what clients do when they develop their perceptions of the different firms with whom they work. I've had clients describe a large, general management consulting firm to me as "the cost-cutting people," for example, even though it had as broad a set of capabilities as anyone in the business. Clients often develop a very specific view about a service provider that is based on a combination of the particular team they have worked with and the specific project or transaction that was completed. Changing this perception once it is formed takes time and effort; and sometimes it's not possible unless your old clients leave the company and you begin working with new ones. Other barriers can include a desire to hire different firms for different services based on the belief that no one firm is good at everything.

> One of our advisors had a very effective approach to growing their relationship with us. Several times a year, they would take a "deep dive" into a topic that we were concerned about. For example, I remember that at one point we were quite focused on asset productivity. They did an in-depth analysis of our performance, and put together an overview of best practices in a variety of industries. Then, they had a team of their experts come and spend a day with a group of my people. It was very effective. That was their ticket to broadening the relationship.
>
> **—Chief Executive Officer**

There are a number of things that have to fall into place from a capabilities expansion perspective in order for a client to feel comfortable about hiring you to do something that is outside your current focus. You must first present, in all of your conversations, a *deep generalist* mindset to the client. When you do this effectively, you are able to put your particular expertise into the client's total business context and discuss a broader set of business issues. In other words, it all starts with the relationship manager—if your conversations with your clients are narrow, then the relationship with them will probably remain narrow.

Second, you have to be tuned in to the client's problems and opportunities because these will drive the need for your services. This means regularly debriefing with your team to find out what they have been learning in the client's organization and holding periodic discussions with the client about their agenda of critical issues and goals.

Third, you need to expose the client to your capabilities. There are a number of well-tested strategies for doing this, such as the following:

- Have your client visit another client with whom you have had a very broad relationship. Let the second client implicitly sell your capabilities.
- From time to time, introduce colleagues—especially ones who are well known in their field—who can talk authoritatively about issues of interest to the client.
- Hold a "capabilities workshop" where you bring in your best experts in a particular area to spend an afternoon sharing their experiences with counterparts in the client's organization.
- Invest time to develop a point of view on an issue of importance to the client that is not part of your current assignment.
- Ask your client to participate in research that your firm is conducting and follow up afterward with a presentation on the results.
- Add *surprise value* by offering ideas and suggestions to address problems that you haven't been asked to solve.

Finally, have a candid discussion with your senior client during which you tell them that you value the relationship and are committed to investing time and resources to develop it further. Get their feedback about how you can improve current service levels, and the kinds of issues you should be thinking about on their behalf. Test out ideas with them, highlighting capability areas with examples that you think might be of interest. This discussion will communicate your intentions to your client and, importantly, help you to understand how they perceive you and your firm's capabilities.

Pathway 3: Client Relationship Management

It is difficult—if not impossible—to build and sustain a Level 6 institutional relationship without significantly increasing your capabilities at client relationship management. Just as a company cannot grow from being a startup to launching an initial public offering without organized leadership, a client relationship cannot go from good to great without strong, consistent relationship management—without what is essentially effective quarterbacking. We'll cover this subject in more depth in Chapter 9, and talk about the specific roles and responsibilities of relationship managers, and the kinds of firm-level support they need.

Next, I'm going to briefly outline some of the basics that need to be in place—the evolution that you must undergo in order to move from simply having a client and serving it with a small team to proactively growing and sustaining a large, institutional relationship. Each of these is characterized as a series of contrasts or shifts:

- *From informal to formal:* Every professional takes responsibility for his or her clients, but Level 6 relationships require a formally appointed relationship manager who is held publicly accountable for results. A light must be shined on this role in order to motivate the right set of behavioral changes.
- *From gatekeeper to door opener:* Most professionals are proud and somewhat protective of their client relationships. One of the biggest changes that must occur in order to evolve from trusted advisor to trusted partner is a mindset shift from feeling like you "own" the relationship, to considering yourself a steward who acts on behalf of the firm.
- *From expert selling to strategic selling:* Level 6 relationships cannot be built on the kind of individual, short-cycle, expert selling efforts that usually result in small projects. The relationship manager must lead a more complex, multiphase selling process, which links to the client's strategic agenda, takes into account a broad range of buying influences, and usually requires a significant investment of time and resources.
- *From content expert to business advisor:* In the early stages of a relationship, when it is still relatively small, the lead professional invariably acts as a content or subject matter expert. Within an

effective relationship management process, that person must move more into the role of strategist, big-picture thinker, and business advisor. He or she will still wear the "expert" hat some of the time, but that role must increasingly be taken over by other colleagues on the team.

Experian has made many acquisitions over the last five years, and as a result we have a much broader range of services than ever before. To institutionalize our client relationships we implemented a multifaceted strategic client program. First, we created teams around each key client, drawing the relevant resources from each product area. Second, I visited senior management at each client, and explained explicitly what we were doing and why. Third, we created new metrics, which include goals in areas such as relationship breadth. Finally, we have significantly increased the strength of the account planning process, and we now have our client teams develop a three-year strategy for relationship growth that will truly impact the client's business.

—Steve Thomas, Managing Director, Experian

- *From hands-on delivery to walking the halls:* Increasingly, a relationship manager must focus on the expansion of relationships—the first pathway, described previously—rather than purely delivery.

- *From narrowband to broadband communications:* The scope and frequency of communications between you and the client's organization have to increase dramatically. Periodic updates and the occasionally shared cup of coffee will no longer be sufficient.

- *From sitting across the table to sitting on the same side of the table:* This is an important change, which has to occur as you move to Level 5 (trusted advisor) and, even more so, Level 6 (trusted partner). The client must increasingly see the relationship manager as its advocate, someone who makes sure that it is getting the absolute best that the firm can offer.

An increased intensity of relationship management activities is critical to growing and institutionalizing a relationship. Remember that the way you implement relationship management must conform to the client's desires and needs. Some client executives, for example, have told me that while they value having a coordinating partner in a relationship, they prefer to go directly to individual specialists within the firm, and don't want to pay a lot for account oversight. Others have told me just the opposite—that they want a single point of contact who is also the main communications channel. You must take your cue from each individual client on how to proceed with this step in developing your client connections.

Pathway 4: Team Leadership

Institutional client relationships require team *leadership* as opposed to simple team *management*. Putting a team together to serve a large relationship is a complex task with many facets. Ultimately, your goal is to make your client relationship a magnet for talented professionals from all over your firm. Let's look at these in more detail.

First, you need to get the right skills on board, and in particular, calibrate the right mixture of specialists and deep generalists. Specialists are subject matter experts who are not expected to be big picture thinkers or manage relationships in the c-suite. They are asked, rather, to focus on doing a great job on delivery and bringing their particular skills to bear on the client problem. Deep generalists are also experts, but in addition they are individuals who—either through many years of experience or concentrated study—have acquired *breadth* around their depth. They will have well-developed powers of synthesis and excellent listening skills. They will excel at relationship building. I cannot tell you what the exact ratio should be of specialists to deep generalists because this will vary by firm. In most situations, however, you're going to field far more dedicated specialists than deep generalists.

Second, you need to spend far more time developing and nurturing the professionals on your team. Simply put, this means getting to know each individual in the same way you would aspire to understand each of your clients (see Figure 4.3 in Chapter 4, "How Well Do You Really Know Your Client?"). You need to act as a coach to help improve their performance and possibly serve as a mentor to help them navigate their careers within the firm and manage the usual pressures of work.

Third, just as communication with the client has to increase as you build a Level 6 relationship, communication with the team has to be augmented. At a minimum, you'll graduate to monthly or even weekly information-sharing sessions over lunch or by conference call, with more frequent dispatches sent by e-mail or memo to update team members on new events. Some firms, which have to field very large teams, systematize their communications even more. For example, they will store document libraries that are available to all team members on a secure, client-specific web site. They use a variety of means to stay in touch, including teleconferences, video conferences, e-mail, instant messaging, collaboration software, and increasingly, corporate versions of social networking programs (you'll read more about these in Chapter 10). With a large team, just remembering to say thank you for a job well done requires a more conscious effort.

Some clients are explicitly asking for the increased oversight and relationship management that is required to sustain successful Level 6 relationships. Shell in North America, for example, reduced the number of law firms it works with from hundreds to about 15. It then insisted that each of those 15 designate a relationship partner and a formal team, and it also assigned a Shell relationship manager for each of these major law firm relationships. This practice is increasingly common across a wide array of markets.

> My approach with this relationship is to give team members quite a bit of autonomy and freedom to pursue opportunities with the client. It's such a large organization that it's not feasible to control things too tightly. I'd rather err on the side of too much activity than too little. We do, however, meet monthly, discuss the opportunities that are developing, and decide as a group where to invest. You have to strike a balance between letting team members be entrepreneurial and imposing some top-down structure.
>
> **—Relationship Manager**

Strong team leadership is also essential for retaining and developing your young professionals. The client service team is in many ways the principal organizational unit in most services firms. Gen-Xers (born between 1963 and 1982) and Millenials (born after 1982) do not have the same workplace loyalty that the previous two generations did (Traditionalists and Baby Boomers). They change jobs more frequently, and demand opportunities to improve their skills and develop their careers in a way that balances professional achievement and personal freedom. The first 5 or 10 years in a professional services firm or investment bank can be extraordinarily intense for young associates, and if you don't create a positive, energizing experience for them on your client relationships, you're going to be in trouble. You won't attract people onto your teams, and worse, those who pass through your gristmill may be likely to leave your firm. So the question is, "How can you make *your* client team the most interesting, fulfilling experience that a young professional can get in your organization?"

Pathway 5: Client Account Planning

The central tool that you must utilize to make sure that you are constantly improving in each of the first four pathways is the *client account planning process.* Simply put, client account planning is a formal process designed to set a strategy for the client relationship, and then marshal the resources required to implement that strategy. To do this, you must periodically ask, and then answer, a series of important questions about the relationship. These five are perhaps the most critical ones:

1. What is this client's agenda? What are the most challenging issues that the client faces, and how can we help?
2. What are our aspirations for this relationship?
3. Which potential opportunities do we want to invest in, and what actions can we take to pursue them?
4. What individual relationships do we need to develop and/or deepen?
5. Do we have the right team in place to grow this client relationship? How can we best leverage the people, ideas, and resources of the firm to help this client achieve its goals?

The sixth question needs to be: "Who is responsible for following through on the steps that we've agreed to take?"

In working with many client teams on account planning, I've learned that there really is not a "one-size-fits-all" approach. The planning process and the tenor of your discussions for an existing multimillion-dollar, mature client relationship will be different from that for a relatively new client who you are trying to take from Level 2 (expert) to Level 3 (steady supplier).

Broadly speaking, most if not all of the following elements should be present in a good planning process:

- Upfront involvement of the client to provide input on key issues, needs, and goals for the coming year;
- Periodic meetings of the full team to reflect and strategize (at least once a year and probably two or three times a year);
- Development of a written account plan;
- Weekly or monthly update calls or meetings; and
- Individual follow-up between the relationship manager and individual team members.

For any client, the core of the client account planning process is a team planning session to reflect on the questions listed here and strategize how to improve and grow the relationship. A best-practice planning process, set against a calendar year, should reflect the kinds of activities listed in Figure 6.3.

You can download from my web site a free account planning toolkit that will help you in your own client planning efforts. It includes a guide for holding a client account planning session, key questions to ask about each of your client relationships, and an outline for an account plan. Go to www.andrewsobel.com and look for the "Tools" page.

No Client Plan Survives Contact with the Client

The famous nineteenth-century German military strategist Field Marshall Helmuth von Moltke wrote "No battle plan survives contact with the enemy." His point was that once the battle starts, the plan you devised beforehand will invariably have to change. The same is true of client plans; they are a good starting point, but as events unfold and you begin to interact with your client, you must dynamically adapt your strategy. That's why I generally don't advise client teams to produce long, detailed client plans. This may work well in some organizations,

4th Quarter	✓ Meet with client executives to discuss their needs and goals for the coming year.
	✓ Convene initial team planning session.
	✓ Draft client plan.
	✓ Meet with your client to test your ideas.
1st Quarter	✓ Finalize client plan at year-end or in early January.
	✓ Begin holding monthly update calls/meetings.
2nd Quarter	✓ Hold one-on-one meetings with each team member.
	✓ Hold monthly update calls/meetings.
3rd Quarter	✓ Convene second team planning session (if not sooner) to review progress and revise the plan.
	✓ Seek client feedback on team performance, evolving needs and goals for the year.
	✓ Continue monthly update calls/meetings.
4th Quarter	✓ Review progress against goals.
	✓ Begin planning cycle again.

FIGURE 6.3   The Client Account Planning Cycle

but because of the dynamic nature of most client relationships, a brief plan that is periodically revised and refocused is more effective and a better use of scarce time.

The CEO of one of my clients insisted that the new client planning process that I was helping his firm to implement incorporate a client plan that was no longer than two pages. Eventually, it stretched to three or four, but by keeping it brief, the firm's partners participated much more actively than they would have had we insisted on using a long, complex document. An in-depth analysis of a client's issues and of the competitors serving that client can be a very useful exercise to accompany a client plan, but there is no substitute for a brief outline of what you're going to do, how you're going to do it, and who is responsible for taking each specific action. And that information will usually fit in just a few pages.

Some firms base their budgeting process on the forecasts in individual client plans, and you need to separate this exercise from what should be your own more client-centered planning. *You* should be asking, "What needs does this client have that we can help with? How can we build a better, more mutually beneficial relationship?" At the firm level, quite naturally, the question is more like, "How much additional revenue can you get from the relationship we have entrusted you to manage on behalf of the firm?" It's not an unhealthy tension, but it is a tension.

Client Account Planning Best Practices

Here are 14 points you should keep in mind as you go about conducting your client planning:

1. Concentrate on the quality of your thinking, not the forms.
2. Involve your client in designing your account plan.
3. Constantly refine your understanding of your client's goals and strategy.
4. Find a colleague who can serve as a disinterested, honest broker to participate in the planning process.
5. Make sure you first deliver on what the client has asked you to do; don't overreach.
6. Focus on the executive relationships you need to build or strengthen.
7. Map all of the key buying influences.
8. For each key executive, understand both rational and personal agendas.
9. Map your competition.

10. Examine your share of wallet or your market share. (You may profitably enjoy 1 percent of a client's business, but how important will you be to the client?)

11. Conduct an independent client review.

12. If you're the relationship manager, ask yourself every year: "Am I still the right person to lead this account?"

13. Consistently track and assess value added, and ask: "What have we done to really help this client? How else can we add value?"

14. Always, always follow up and make sure each team member feels "on the hook" to accomplish his or her part of the plan.

Conclusion

Institutionalizing a relationship requires patience, investment, and the coordinated effort of many individuals. It also entails risk. You may make a large investment of time and money, and, after months or even

Growth Pathways	LEVELS 1–5	LEVEL 6 Trusted Partner
1. Relationships	▪ Client: one to one ▪ Personal network	▪ Clients: many to many ▪ Interconnected networks
2. Capabilities	▪ Deliver your expertise	▪ Deliver the firm's expertise
3. Relationship Management	▪ Manage your own relationship ▪ Communicate informally	▪ Manage a constellation of relationships ▪ Communicate systematically
4. Team Leadership	▪ Coordinate resources	▪ Lead and develop a team
5. Client Account Planning	▪ Ad-hoc, short-term focus	▪ Core process to grow and broaden the relationship

FIGURE 6.4 Key Challenges to Reaching Level 6

a year, have little to show for it. Getting your firm's support for your efforts is therefore critical. To do this, you'll need to demonstrate that you're taking the kinds of actions that are outlined in this chapter; and that you have a clear plan to sustain and grow your client relationship. To secure institutional support, you need to clearly articulate to the firm's leadership the investments you want to make in growing the relationship, the associated costs, and the potential benefits.

Figure 6.4 summarizes the key aspects of the institutionalization journey that we've discussed. Remember, though, that it starts with your attitude and mindset: You have to be able to "let go" psychologically, in order to turn an individual relationship into an institutional relationship.

7

Strategy Five: Adding Multiple Layers of Value

Creating More Value in Your Client Relationships

I recently conducted a survey asking 350 senior relationship managers at 18 major services firms about the most important trends affecting their ability to develop long-term client relationships. The number one trend that they cited was: "Client demands for more value for money." Client executives have been telling me this in interviews for several years. "We'd like to get more value out of our relationships" is their common refrain. This is not surprising. Most corporate executives are being asked to do more for less, and they must continually justify their spending. It's only natural that the pressure on corporate management to increase value for shareholders is being passed on to the firms that advise and provide services to them.

Client demands for more value have produced a great deal of frustration as well as dysfunction on the part of service providers. The frustration arises because it's not actually that easy to come up with new ways to add more value. The dysfunction occurs because a frequent response is simply to offer fee discounts—a path that can become a downward spiral of lower profits, decreased investment in intellectual capital, and a reduced ability to attract the best talent. Unfortunately, it is easier and more expedient for some to simply lower prices (the denominator of the value equation) than to increase benefits (the numerator).

What Is Value?

What is value, anyway? The following quotes from client executives whom I have interviewed illustrate how difficult it is to generalize about this subject:

> *Our consultants helped us make an important strategic shift to a customer-focused culture. That was their mandate, and they accomplished it well. But just as important was that they helped my team of senior executives to develop and grow. I did not think about this at the beginning of the assignment, but after several years of working together it emerged as a major benefit. It happened slowly, and was not noticeable until the end, but I now see major improvements in my team's ability to lead and manage change.*
>
> —Chief Executive, Healthcare Company

> *One of the most valuable things my lead bankers have done for me is to introduce me to other CFOs and influential individuals who are now part of my regular network.*
>
> —Chief Financial Officer,
> Telecommunications Company

> *This particular lawyer really understood how I am evaluated at the end of the year. He grasped what would help my team and me be successful with our internal business clients, how to help us accomplish our goals. Because of that, he and his firm provided superior legal advice that was based on a deep understanding of our business, of us as people, and the internal clients that we have to serve.*
>
> —General Counsel, Energy Company

A lot of it was about risk reduction. We could have done this program ourselves, but having some extra, experienced hands working side-by-side us took some of the risk out of it and allowed us to move faster than we could have without them.

—Division President, Consumer Products Company

So is value defined as solving a particular problem? Growing revenues? Reducing risk? Helping a client executive become more successful? Developing people? In truth, it can be any and all of these, and it will be somewhat different for each client. Your job, in short, is to *identify the most important elements of value for your client, and then work to deliver them.* But doing this is not so simple. There is some value that clients expect but may not be willing to pay for—ongoing counsel and advice, for example, which is provided alongside the delivery of a service or product. Next, there is the "contractual value" they expect at the outset, and will measure at the end—that's more straightforward. Finally, there is value that they will recognize only *after* you deliver it—benefits that they did not know they would end up valuing when they bought your services. In the case of the CEO who cited how his team had developed and grown, for example, it's unlikely he would have seen this as a major benefit in the original proposal phase; and he certainly wouldn't have paid more for it. Yet, after the fact, he was delighted with the result.

Although the formula for value is benefits minus price, there are a host of subtleties that we need to understand if we are to increase our ability to add more value. In this chapter, I set out several frameworks to help you think about value more effectively, and a number of best practices that will help you add multiple layers of value in your client relationships. Specifically, we're going to look at five different aspects of value within two specific areas:

Foundations of Value
- Factors that affect a client's perception of value
- Ways to identify what is most important to each client

Value Tools

- The *Value Positioning Process*, which describes the communications and timing challenge of delivering value
- The *Value Matrix*, which sets out the "what"
- The *Value Levers* framework, which sets out the "how"

Foundations of Value

Let's begin by examining six factors that *almost universally* influence a client's perception of value. Value, after all, is not absolute—it is what the client thinks it is. By addressing these factors, you can increase your client's perception of delivered value.

1. Profit and Loss Impact

Nearly all tangible, institutional benefits—for example, increased productivity, faster time-to-market, a reduction in lawsuits, and so on—will ultimately either help to increase revenues or reduce costs. Profitability and profit growth also ultimately drive stock price, another important factor for clients at public companies. Any proposal that can be specifically linked to revenue growth or cost containment—regardless of the particular focus of the project—is going to be perceived as more valuable.

2. Risk Reduction

Years ago, I damaged a tendon in my elbow while playing tennis, and it turned out I needed surgery to repair it. I discovered that no orthopedic surgeon in my hometown had done more than a half-dozen of what is a fairly specialized procedure. I ended up going to a hand surgeon in San Francisco who had completed over 200 of these operations; and today my elbow is as good as new. His vast experience extended a promise of reduced risk of failure. In business, risk reduction represents a powerful benefit. If you can convey a greater assurance of success, your client will perceive more value and be willing to pay you a premium over another riskier alternative.

3. Perceived Substitute

The old adage, "Don't just be the best at what you do, be the only one who does it" is rooted in solid economic theory. If clients believe there are many people or firms who can do exactly what you do, there will be a diminished perception of relative value and therefore downward pressure on your fees. You must develop and demonstrate a unique—if not differentiated—approach or expertise, which, combined with a trusting relationship, puts you in a market space where there is no competition. The more you look like everyone else, the more readily clients can shift demand to other alternatives.

4. Difficulty

Is this a run-of-the-mill assignment, or does it pose particular challenges in terms of the difficulty of the task, the speed with which it must be accomplished, or other possible pitfalls that must be overcome? Can you convincingly demonstrate a 360-degree understanding of the true complexities of an engagement—including what may go wrong—and communicate this to your client? There is obviously greater perceived value in solving a difficult problem than an easy one, but you may need to educate your client about just how hard it's going to be.

5. Personal Impact

As we'll see when I discuss the Value Matrix later in the chapter, personal value—not just institutional value, such as profit improvement and risk reduction—is always part of the equation. To the extent that your work helps your client improve his or her career prospects or achieve some personal goals, the value will be enhanced.

> Never forget that the executives you work with are people, and they care more about their careers than they do about return-on-investment or the next outsourcing project. You work for the institution, but you also have to think about how to help your individual client accomplish his or her particular personal goals.
>
> **—Relationship Manager**

6. Organizational Improvement or Knowledge Transfer

Almost all clients perceive significant value if you can improve their own capabilities while you deliver your services. Capability improvement could come from a variety of sources, including training, coaching, knowledge transfer of best practices and methodologies, new technology, and so on.

Whenever you are making a proposal to a client, think about each of these six factors, and how you can influence the client's thinking about them. As I point out next, some of these will carry more weight than others, but they all have tremendous potential to increase or decrease a client's perception of the value you offer.

Determining What Is Valuable for Each Client

A friend of mine has a terrific housekeeper whom she simply adores. Recently, the housekeeper told her that she was quitting. My friend sat down with her and began to renegotiate her salary, offering her significantly more money if she would stay. The housekeeper refused. My friend offered her even more money, but the answer was still no. Finally, she asked her, in frustration, "What do you want?" And the housekeeper's reply was, "I need more time off." Money, it turns out, had almost nothing to do with her desire to quit. My friend reduced her housekeeper's hours and kept her in the job—but at a higher hourly salary.

This story has what may seem to be an obvious twist; however, any one of us might have assumed that it was all about money, and missed the opportunity to explore what this employee really wanted. The same is true with clients: We often accept the specifications for an engagement at face value and don't take the time to really understand what's important and what is not.

There are several techniques you can use to gain a better sense of what the client values most. The first is simply to *ask*. You might consider questions such as these:

- "As you look at our proposal, which elements are the most critical for you?"
- "What are the principal benefits that you're hoping to reap from this project?"

- "As you've described this program, it seems to me that there are four different, distinct benefits that you are seeking [*list them*]. Is it possible to rank these? What's your number one priority?"
- "You've shared your specific goals for this program, which is very helpful. Are there any other *intangible* benefits or outcomes that you're hoping to achieve as well?"
- "We find that there are always some tradeoffs that have to be made between speed, quality, gaining organizational consensus, transferring knowledge and skills, and so on. What are your thoughts on this? What's most important to you?"

A second way to understand your clients' priorities in terms of what they value is to offer options with your proposal. There are two approaches to formulating these options. One is to offer a core solution, with two additional options that add increasing value in the form of additional activities or deliverables. Author and consultant Alan Weiss refers to this as a "menu of yeses" that offers growing amounts of total value as you go to options two and three. Human nature, he avers, is to gravitate toward more, not less, value; and clients will often choose options two or three, which generate more fees for the advisor and more value for the client. So, for example, your base option may consist of a reorganization plan for your client; option two might include implementation assistance; and option three could add skills training to make people more effective in their new roles.

A slightly different approach—espoused by Professor Vicky Medvec at Northwestern's Kellogg School of Business—is called "multiple equivalent simultaneous offers," or *"mesos."* Her method involves making three or four offers that contain equivalent value but that emphasize different elements or benefits. This allows you to be aggressive in the negotiation process while collecting valuable information about what is truly important to the other party. In other words, you learn about what your clients value by seeing their reaction to options that contain different combinations of benefits such as speed, scope of work, payment terms, and so on.

Value Tools

The Value Positioning Process

"Adding value" tends to sound like a one-off event: A client hires us to do some work, and there is a discrete period of time we have to deliver the value. In reality, it's not so simple. I believe there are four distinct stages of value creation, and the process starts before you even begin work (Figure 7.1).

The first stage has to do with the firm's brand positioning. Goldman Sachs in investment banking and McKinsey in consulting, for example, are perceived by clients to be premier firms that charge high fees and deliver equally high value. The truth is that a smaller, less well-known consulting firm or bank might very well be able to do as good as or even a better job at a particular assignment—but they will not be perceived as such. We tend to position suppliers on a brand ladder, and your individual rung will have strong connotations of expense and value. The point is this: To the extent you are able to position yourself as a high-value brand, you will be able to go into a sales situation with a client who is already prepared to pay higher fees, and who expects to receive commensurate value. The beauty of the psychology of

	1. Preengagement	2. First Sale	3. Delivery	4. Postengagement
Client Concerns	"Who is out there that can do the job? What should I expect?"	"Who is best for this particular task? Will they get the results we need?"	"Are we getting the desired impact? Is this working for me and my organization?"	"Are the results sticking? Was it worth it? Do we need to make a course correction?"
Challenge to Service Provider	POSITIONING FOR VALUE	BUILDING TRUST IN VALUE	CUSTOMIZING VALUE	REINFORCING VALUE

FIGURE 7.1 The Value Life Cycle

expectations is that they are often self-fulfilling: Clients of a premier provider will look hard for value everywhere they can.

You are probably familiar with the experiment involving grade school teachers and their perceptions of their young students. If a teacher is told a group of students are gifted and possess high IQs, then he will subtly alter his teaching approach. He will treat these children as though they are smart, challenge them more, and they will subsequently earn better grades compared to a control group being taught by a teacher who has been told that his students are normal. Client expectations work in similar ways. Achieving a status as a "premium services brand" is obviously a long and complex journey, which must involve brand development activities; careful client targeting and selection; service offering refocusing; extensive investment in intellectual capital development; publishing; and other strategies.

The second challenge in the Value Life Cycle is to build trust in your ability to *deliver* value during the sales process. This is one of the hardest hurdles to overcome in the early stages of a relationship. Existing clients are familiar with how you work and the value you can add, but a new client doesn't have this firsthand experience. Simply describing to a client how much value you will add is a bit like showing them a picture of a gourmet meal: It's just not the same as being there at the restaurant and tasting the food. Useful techniques for building trust—that actually *show* your client how you can add value—include:

- Employing references and testimonials from past clients;
- Organizing a client-to-client visit where a prospective client actually meets with an existing client who has been through a similar transaction or program;
- Investing time, up front, in getting to know the client's organization, thus making your value claims more compelling and realistic;
- Using value-based selling methods that focus on desired client *outcomes* as opposed to activities, methodologies, and features;
- Offering guarantees and/or fee arrangements linked to achieving specific goals;
- Quantifying the value you will add and associating it clearly to revenue growth or cost reduction;

- Emphasizing other factors that increase the perception of value, such as difficulty and risk reduction; and
- Getting key client executives (e.g., the CFO or head of human resources) to sign off on the benefits case you put together, which makes it far more believable to the economic buyer.

The third stage of positioning for value occurs during delivery. During this phase, the client will be asking, "Are we achieving the desired results? Is this working for *me*?" Obviously, it's critical to actually realize the results that were originally promised. That's your job, and I cannot tell you how to do this for your particular area of expertise. But there are many things you can do to ensure that the client understands and appreciates the value you are creating. First of all, you should revisit the six factors cited at the beginning of this chapter, which can heighten or reduce a client's sense of value—in particular, profit and loss impact, risk reduction, degree of difficulty, and capabilities enhancement—and emphasize these to the client. Second, you must communicate with the client frequently; when clients are kept in the dark, they often assume the worst. Finally, try to give the client transparency and control. When your work and the processes you use are clear to your clients—and when they feel that they have control over what is happening—their perception of value will be heightened.

One of the most important things to keep in mind is that value delivery—and the process of enhancing a client's perception of value—does not stop when the engagement is over. During the fourth stage set out in Figure 7.1, clients will be asking, "Are the results sticking? Was it really worth it?" There are very simple things that you can do to reassure clients at this point in time. The first is a postengagement audit or review. Between three and six months after you complete an assignment, take a few hours or a half a day to meet with the client and explore the aftermath of your work. How have things gone? What has worked out well? What would the client do differently next time? This type of meeting will reinforce the fact that you care and are willing to hear the good and the bad. It will enable you to get constructive feedback and have the opportunity to reinforce the positive things you accomplished with the client. In Chapter 12, I explore other types of client listening strategies that you can employ, above and beyond this type of postengagement audit.

A second way to reinforce value after you've finished is to follow up and continue to add value around the client's particular areas of interest. I do this in several ways. First, I send clients my newsletter, *Client Loyalty*, which features a new article each month on building client relationships. Second, I give a client articles, clippings, books; share interesting web links; or suggest personal introductions that relate in some way to the focus of our work together. I may also meet with the client just to talk about what's happening in the market, and share some of the most recent work I have been doing. If you can continue to add value after you've left—even in a very small way—your clients will greatly appreciate it.

The Value Matrix

During my research into successful Level 6 relationships, I have observed that as these relationships grow and prosper, the firm that is providing services to the client adds increasingly *diverse* types of value. When clients first hire a service provider or advisor, they are nearly always looking for tangible, institutional value; in other words, value that can be quantified in some way, with benefits that accrue to the company as a whole rather than to any one executive. So for example, growing revenues, reducing costs, implementing a successful audit, outsourcing a function, or completing an acquisition all deliver tangible value for the client's organization and shareholders.

Over time, however, a Level 6 client should perceive other types of value being added. The first evolution is from *institutional* value to *personal* value, and the second is from *tangible* to *intangible* value. Examples of personal value could include learning, network growth, wealth creation, career advancement, and many others. Examples of intangible value would be things like increased organizational effectiveness, better relationships, improved morale, and so on. Ultimately, intangible benefits will lead to quantifiable value such as profit improvement and growth; but it's hard to put a number on them.

Interestingly, I have found that while the tangible institutional benefits usually have the biggest bottom-line impact on a client, it is often the intangible, personal value that clients most remember and feel strongest about. Ironically, however—and especially if you are

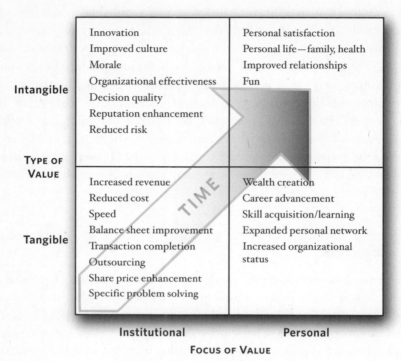

FIGURE 7.2   The Value Matrix

dealing with a new client who has never worked with you before—it's difficult to *sell* an engagement based on these latter benefits. You can tell a client that she will experience these intangibles; however, she will most likely focus on achieving a particular, quantifiable business goal. The "other stuff" will seem like something that's nice to have, but not essential. It is only *afterward*—once the clients actually experience these benefits—that they will grow in importance.

Figure 7.2 sets out these dimensions of value and gives examples of benefits that fall in each value quadrant.

You can use this matrix to push your thinking about the overall value you and your teams are adding in your client relationships. Don't be timid about asking clients about the benefits they have experienced from your work together, and then giving your candid views regarding the value you've seen. You don't have to frame this conversation as one where you discuss what *you've* done for the client, but rather what you have accomplished together.

The Value Levers

The *Value Positioning Process* helps us appreciate the timing and sequencing that are part of the value equation. The *Value Matrix* articulates the "what" of value—the different types of value that you need to add as you grow a relationship. Now, let's look at the "how."

As I've interviewed countless senior relationship managers— partners, managing directors, account executives, and others with related titles who fulfill the relationship management role—I've tried to understand exactly what they and their teams *do* to add these multiple layers of value. It's easy to say, "Bring your client new ideas," but where do you get them?

> One of the most effective ways to communicate value in advance is to arrange for a prospective client to visit an existing client. This is especially appealing if the existing client has gone through a similar transformation or confronted a challenge that is comparable to what your prospect is facing. A phone call is okay; but it's far more powerful when an executive actually meets with the individuals who have worked with you and your team, and experienced the intangible benefits first hand.
>
> **—Relationship Manager**

Based on these discussions—as well as hundreds of interviews with client executives—I have identified six value levers that any client-facing professional can and should draw on to deliver value to clients. These six types of leverage, illustrated in Figure 7.3, are:

1. Relationship Leverage
2. Organization Leverage
3. Network Leverage
4. Market Leverage
5. Innovation Leverage
6. Technology Leverage

I'll describe each of these and give specific examples to bring them to life.

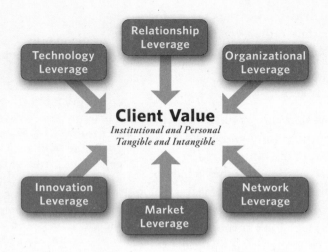

FIGURE 7.3 The Value Levers

Relationship Leverage

Relationship Leverage occurs when you add value through the relationship management experience itself and create multiple points of contact with senior-level advisors from your firm. There are several ways you can use Relationship Leverage. First, you have to elevate the quality and tenor *your own* individual relationships with senior clients. As I've mentioned, when you exemplify the advisor attributes and approach your relationships with the advisor mindset—rather than as a narrow expert—you can add far more value. By earning deep personal trust, you are able to influence your client to act on your recommendations. When you help a client see the big picture by synthesizing the most critical patterns and isolating the most important issues, you greatly improve his decision making. When you exercise selfless independence, you stand alone as someone who is willing to disagree with your client and say *no* when objective advice is most needed.

You can capture a second source of Relationship Leverage by getting help from other senior professionals in your organization. I have seen two models for doing this: One is systematic and the other is more ad hoc. Examples of a systematic approach can be seen at

Citigroup's global corporate bank and Parthenon Group in Boston, Massachusetts (see sidebar).

Citigroup utilizes a cadre of what it calls "Seniors" to help manage its most important global relationships. These are highly experienced bankers who have often occupied leadership positions in the organization, roles that they have sometimes relinquished in favor of younger, up-and-coming professionals. These Seniors may bring 25 or 30 years of deal-making experience to a client. Many of Citigroup's top 500 global corporate relationships have a Senior assigned to them, who then works closely with the full-time relationship banker for that client. The Senior might attend meetings with the client's top management; coach the relationship manager and her team behind the scenes; help get access to a higher level of management at the client; or perhaps use his clout to marshal Citigroup's global resources in the service of the relationship. The exact protocols for each relationship are arranged between the Senior and the relationship banker—for example, in some cases the Senior might visit a client alone; in other situations he'll go with the relationship manager. In addition to this group of around 50 Seniors who actively help to manage major client relationships, Citigroup's client strategy group organizes an extensive client visit program using the top 12 executives at the bank, from the chairman and CEO on down. They typically get the individuals from this senior group in front of 400 or 500 CEOs a year around the world. These programs create significant Relationship Leverage

> ## Two Partners for Every Client
>
> Every Parthenon consulting client is assigned two partners. One will take the lead and have primary responsibility for the relationship, but both are active in content development and relationship management—they both commit at least 25 percent of their time to the client. The second partner might challenge or disagree with his colleague, even in front of the client. It sends a couple of messages: First, that we're focused on putting the best ideas forward for confronting the client's issues and then allowing constructive debate and discussion to arrive at the best solution possible. Second, it demonstrates that we are committed to collaboration, both with our clients and internally with our colleagues.
>
> **—Bill Achtmeyer, Chairman and Managing Partner, Parthenon Group**

for individual bankers in charge of Citigroup's global corporate clients.

You can also draw on Relationship Leverage on an ad hoc basis by having other senior professionals from your firm meet periodically with your client. Don Lowman, who is a managing director and board member at Towers Perrin, the human resources (HR) consulting firm, has made it a personal priority to offer his client relationship managers as much Relationship Leverage as possible. Recently, for example, a Towers Perrin client hired a new head of HR, who had worked with Lowman at a different company. Lowman spoke to the relationship manager who managed this client for Towers, and offered to break the ice and help transition the relationship. He flew across the country to visit the new HR head, and met with him alone—a strategy he and the relationship manager had discussed and agreed on. In the first conversation, Lowman said to his former client, "Knowing both your old company and this new organization, here are some things I believe you absolutely must be thinking about as you settle into this new role." He then set out an agenda of possible issues for the executive to react to, including where he might get organizational resistance to change. Lowman offered to have Towers Perrin experts from each of the issue areas to meet with him, a suggestion that was accepted gratefully. Lowman subsequently introduced the relationship manager to his old client, and continued to periodically come back and visit. Lowman comments about the process, "I try to share my own relationship capital with the relationship managers and their teams. I'm not looking to get any sales credit—in fact, I'm not evaluated on sales. I go in and help, but I also get out quickly so that the relationshipmanager can develop his or her own relationship."

Organization Leverage

One of the biggest barriers to relationship growth is a relationship manager who tries to be all things to her client and is reluctant to introduce her colleagues. Organization Leverage, therefore, refers to adding value by drawing in different capabilities from across your firm. In a sense, you act as a broker to connect your client with the right resources at the right time. It sounds simple, but many relationship managers tend to act as *gatekeepers* rather than *door openers*.

One of my clients, for example, is a senior account executive with a leading technology services company. Historically, the company's main business has been software development, but over time it has also entered the outsourcing business. His firm had been engaged for over a year to help a Fortune 500 company transition a number of its legacy software applications. The client decided to outsource a major IT function, and began talking to the top three or four IT outsourcing companies around the world—huge organizations that handle billion-dollar contracts. My client urged the company to consider his firm for the outsourcing, even though it was a far smaller player than the behemoths with whom it was in active talks. His client demurred, however, and said it was not interested in a proposal. Nonetheless, my friend persisted. When the company decided to send a team of executives to India to meet with his competitors, he told them, "You're going to be in India anyway—I know you don't want to consider us for outsourcing, but why don't you at least meet some of my colleagues there who have extensive experience in this area? They will definitely give you an objective point of view about what you're doing; not least because we're not even in the running for this."

The company executives attended a dinner in India with my client's colleagues and were impressed with what they saw and heard. They set up a subsequent meeting with several other top executives at my client's firm, and the company began to slowly change its mind about considering the firm for the bid. After many introductions with their outsourcing experts in the United States and India, my client's firm was asked to prepare a proposal, and ended up winning the assignment against very stiff competition. It was the largest outsourcing job the firm had ever been awarded, and it propelled them on a significant growth trajectory in this burgeoning market. Without my friend's tenacity in trying to connect the client to the rest of his organization, the opportunity would have been lost.

Network Leverage

Whereas Organizational Leverage refers to tapping into your firm's internal resources, Network Leverage focuses on external connections that you can use to benefit your client. I also referred to this as "connection value" in Chapter 4. The main principle here is to consider not just whom *you* know, but whom your *firm* knows. You may recall the example in the introduction to this book where Citigroup's Sir Win Bischoff leveraged a connection he had with a former finance minister to help build a relationship with a major energy company. This is why large banks and some professional services firms will hire or retain well-known individuals not just to help with marketing, but also to enhance existing relationships. UBS, for example, hired former Senator Phil Gramm as a rainmaker in its investment bank, and Bain & Company retained former Vodafone CEO Christopher Ghent as a senior advisor. These individuals can delight an existing client when they show up at a meeting, can get access to meet with just about any business leader in the world, and they leverage their own networks to great effect.

Bringing in outsiders who are to be valued for their connections is a delicate process that must be handled carefully. These individuals contribute in a different way than other professionals, and you have to work with them to maximize their contacts and also translate their relationships into real business for your organization.

When you use your Network Leverage to connect clients to one another, the results can be unpredictable but powerful, and they have the potential to create both institutional and personal benefits. My old firm once organized a sumptuous party at the Savoy Hotel in London to celebrate the founding of our U.K. office five years earlier. It was, essentially, an excuse for our professional staff to have fun and for our clients to connect with each other. We sat the CEOs of a major bank and a large insurance company together at dinner. Based on the personal relationship they developed that night, they began to explore a business combination, and the two companies later merged.

Another example is the nonprofit mentoring network that my friend and colleague James Kelly—the former chairman of Gemini Consulting—set up. Kelly has enlisted a number of senior executives with whom he has worked over the years to participate in this organization, which pairs a top executive with a charity that is in need of management advice. A collateral benefit has been that many personal connections have been established or strengthened within the group of executives who serve as mentors.

My own clients have asked me on several occasions to make presentations or facilitate workshops for *their* clients on the subject of building long-term relationships—yet another way of using their network of external resources. In a similar vein, I recently asked a good friend of mine, a senior World Bank executive who is a leading expert on Africa and China, to host a lunch for a small group of interested executives to talk about economic development trends in those countries. They all found the experience invaluable.

You should periodically ask, "Whom do we know in our network who could be a valuable connection for this client?"

Market Leverage

Market Leverage simply means bringing your clients interesting, useful, and up-to-date information about their competition, their customers, and the markets within which they operate. These discussions are always valuable for clients. They can be quite informal and take place over a cup of coffee during a midmorning break—you don't need PowerPoint slides or a memo to engage in this type of dialogue.

I generally find that there are three different types of market information and insight that clients find valuable. These include:

1. *Information about the competition:* What new strategies and tactics are competitors implementing? What interesting management practices are they adopting? What's happening in the c-suite, in terms of the careers and movements of their peers at these other companies?

2. *Customer insights:* What are customers saying about your client's strengths and weaknesses? Do you have customer data you can share, either from your own primary research or from that conducted by others?

3. *Capital markets insights:* Investment bankers, for example, can be very effective at using capital markets insights by drawing on conversations with their trading desks about who is buying and selling a client's securities. With more and more executive compensation linked to stock price performance, it's important to become familiar with this type of market intelligence.

How do you gain access to Market Leverage? If you work with a large consulting firm, bank, or marketing communications company, you may very well conduct your own customer or investor research that you can bring to clients. When I was a partner at Gemini Consulting, I once led a study for a major bank client that entailed conducting interviews with 125 institutional investors around the world. Although it was not something one would do on a regular basis, that work yielded unique insights into their institutional investor marketplace. It's important, in short, to be in the flow of the markets in which your clients compete.

One of my clients, a partner at a large law firm, was working with a new general counsel who was looking at how to reorganize his legal staff to be more responsive to their internal business clients. He was not asked to opine on this task, but over the course of several long conversations, he shared a lot of valuable information about how the client's competition was organized, and he made a number of suggestions based on his work with dozens of general counsels over the years. The core value added was definitely the legal work he and his team completed for this client, but the advice he gave on the restructuring put him, in the client's mind, in a different category than other lawyers.

Innovation Leverage

When I interview client executives, they frequently express a desire to get more new ideas and perspectives from their advisors. While it is true that now more than ever, clients want help actually *implementing* the ideas or programs that they are pursuing, innovation is still the magical elixir for many clients. It is not an easy task to come up with a stream of good ideas, but it becomes more feasible if you take a systematic approach and focus serious time and attention on the innovation process. The ability to generate insight for clients is an increasingly fundamental capability that separates the market leaders from the average firms, and it's worth exploring how you can become more effective in this area. In this section, I highlight some of the Innovation Leverage best practices that I have observed.

Innovation Networks   Citigroup's Client Strategy Group established an innovation network aimed at identifying interesting ideas and practices that the relationship managers in Citigroup's global corporate bank could bring to clients. The network links about 50 up-and-coming Citigroup professionals, drawn from all parts of the global corporate bank and from many countries around the world. The Client Strategy Group—which helps oversee and manage Citigroup's client relationship management programs—hosts regular conference calls with the innovation network participants during which they discuss trends, issues, and ground-breaking banking practices they have seen or used in their individual markets. The most promising ideas are codified, documented, and distributed throughout the bank to client-facing bankers.

New Idea Capture   Cognizant, a leading technology services firm that is also one of the fastest growing companies on the Nasdaq stock exchange, uses a variety of strategies to put fresh ideas in front of clients. One of these is called the "10-10-10 program," which works as follows: On the tenth day of each month at 10 AM, all project team members (of which there could be dozens or even hundreds) pause for 10 minutes at their desks or wherever they are in the world. Using an electronic post-it system designed for collaboration, everyone lists ideas that might be helpful to the client in some way. These may have to do with the current project, or with some other aspect of the client's business. The team leadership collects, reviews, and screens these ideas, and the most promising ones are developed further for the client. The approach has had excellent success: One team, for example, came up with an inventive approach for helping a client in the consumer products business do a better job of capturing online customer feedback on its products around the world.

Big Ideas Programs   I have observed several companies—including IBM Global Services and Amdocs (a leading supplier of billing and CRM software)—successfully implement big ideas programs for clients. It is a bold approach, and you must be willing to back it up with time and resources. There are several variations on this strategy. One is to approach your senior client and say something like: "Every quarter we are going to come to you with three new ideas. We'll facilitate a one-day workshop to explore these with you. You will tell us at the end of that session if you think one or more of these ideas are promising, or you can reject them or put them on the shelf to reconsider at a later date. If you'd like to pursue one of the ideas, we'll invest time *that week* to meet with the executives who would be responsible for developing and implementing the idea in your organization. Those conversations will help to flesh out the idea and create an initial implementation plan for how the idea could be brought to life. At that point, you can pursue it on your own or ask us to continue helping you develop it."

This approach is gutsy because it puts you on the line to come up with new ideas on a regular basis for your client and forces you to invest in systematic idea generation. It positions you as a thought leader with the client and can potentially help you grow the relationship by broadening the playing field.

Idea Days   ZS Associates—a consulting firm that specializes in sales and marketing—has been one of the fastest growing major consulting firms over the past 10 years. ZS currently has 1,000 professionals and 17 offices around the world. ZS has systematized Innovation Leverage by creating the concept of an "Idea Day" for any partner who is managing a major client relationship. Once a year—and sometimes as often as once a quarter—the relationship partner, or the senior client, gets a "free" day to meet with several other experienced ZS partners. These colleagues don't just show up—they prepare thoroughly for the day, familiarizing themselves with the client, its issues, and the work ZS has been doing. The day is then devoted to providing new perspectives and ideas for adding value to the client's business.

Project Cross-Fertilization   This is the most basic means of achieving Innovation Leverage, and one that many firms could better utilize. When I first moved to Rome, Italy, to become country manager for Gemini Consulting, my first priority was to familiarize myself with the most interesting and leading-edge work that we had done in a variety of industries in North America. I spent one afternoon with several of our project teams that had been working with the U.S. telecommunications companies. At the time, Gemini's telecommunications practice was among the largest of any consulting firm in the world. Months later, I found myself in Rome in a meeting with the head of strategic planning for Telecom Italia, the Italian state telephone company. We talked for an hour, but nothing seemed to pique his interest. Before the meeting wrapped up, I mentioned in passing an interesting project that we had done for one of the U.S. telecommunications companies to help them prioritize their over 2,000 information technology investment projects with an innovative screening process. A week later, I got a phone call from the assistant to the senior vice president of IT, who wanted to meet with me. He was quite interested in the methodology we had used in the United States, and after checking some references, retained us to do a similar project. We ended up working with him for many years. All it took was investing some time to meet with our people in the United States, and then sharing a short description of an innovative project we had completed, at the right time, with the right person.

Ongoing Research and Development   This is the traditional route to innovation and thought leadership, aimed more at brand building than generating specific insights for individual clients. Some firms are very systematic about their research and publishing efforts—consultants McKinsey and Bain are two that come to mind—while others tend to be driven by the interests of individual professionals who may or may not be motivated to pursue such endeavors. The challenge is to make firm-sponsored innovation relevant to individual clients, a process that requires an investment of time to link the research conclusions to a client's particular set of issues. The playing field is also getting crowded, with dozens of major firms annually publishing hundreds of articles, white papers, briefs, industry outlooks, and newsletters—all of which compete for the attention of a relatively small pool of top executives. Your publication needs to be incisive, trenchant, and truly insightful, or else it may very well get lost in your clients' inbox.

Academic Intellectual Capital   My original firm, The MAC Group (which we eventually sold to Cap Gemini, where it became Gemini Consulting), was based on a network of over 200 of the world's leading business school academics. These professors—all leaders in their fields—provided introductions to clients and shared their rich intellectual capital with us. As a result, we had access to and utilized a wide variety of different methodologies for helping clients solve problems. Other examples of academically sourced innovation include ZS Associates (mentioned earlier), which was founded by two marketing professors at the Kellogg School of Management, Andris A. Zoltners and Prabhakant Sinha; and the consulting firm Monitor, founded by Harvard Business School professor Michael Porter. Some firms today tend to be closed systems; in other words, if they haven't developed the ideas themselves, they are not terribly interested in offering them to their clients. This is partly because some academics are, well, very academic and theory focused; their ideas have not yet been translated into actionable strategies. But more service firms could benefit from an open-idea architecture, and graduate schools have been and can be valuable sources of concepts and innovation.

Innovation Summits and Jams   Each year, IBM organizes a Global Innovation Outlook (GIO) session in seven key regions around the world. These sessions include more than 150 thought leaders from business, government, academia, nongovernmental organizations, and venture capital. They focus on identifying policy issues, investment strategies, and technology priorities that relate to innovation and economic development in the region. IBM has also pioneered the use of the online "innovation jam," the first of which was held in 2006. This online event involved 150,000 individuals, including IBM employees, clients, and external partners. Over a period of three days, the participants contributed ideas about everything from IBM's corporate strategy to product, technology, and process innovations. Using special software, IBM tracked the thousands of ideas that were submitted and linked them thematically. One hundred million dollars was later allocated to fund the most promising suggestions, many of which have since come to successful fruition.

The firm—rather than individual relationship managers—must clearly fund and drive some of these Innovation Leverage best practices. But individual professionals have to take responsibility for tapping into them, and using the ideas that they spin off. Most of the firms and companies I work with produce large amounts of intellectual capital that is there for their people to take advantage of—it just requires a little work. New ideas for clients usually materialize at the *intersection* of deep client knowledge and the fresh perspectives that these various Innovation Leverage practices can generate. It's up to you to combine them.

Technology Leverage

Technology Leverage means that you use technology to improve communications with clients in order to accelerate project delivery, capture new ideas, and generally make it easier for clients to do business with you. This is already old news in mass markets, and technology has clearly revolutionized the relationship between businesses and consumers. Today, it's normal for consumer products companies to use software agents to scour the "blogosphere" for customer feedback, or for an automobile insurance company (e.g., Progressive) to offer discounts to customers who install a monitoring chip in their engines.

Within the realm of high-end professional or advisory services, however, there has been only modest use of the Internet and other technologies to improve and enhance client relationships. Part of this has to do with the highly personal nature of many service businesses, but part is also generational. Most chief financial officers in their 40s and 50s are probably not going to invest the time to go to a web site to give real-time feedback to their investment bankers or consultants on how they did on the last transaction. Most CEOs are not going to participate in an online forum to give their ongoing views about the latest economic crisis. Few senior executives, anywhere, have put their profiles up on FaceBook. But as a younger generation moves into the c-suite—one that has grown up using social networking software and sites like TripAdvisor to rate the hotels they have stayed in—this will change.

But why wait? A more important question for service professionals is, "How can you actively *convince* your clients to participate in technology that can help add more value in the relationship and create switching barriers?"

A good example of using Technology Leverage in high-end services is the Ringtail litigation system used by Fulbright & Jaworski, an international law firm that is a global leader in litigation and dispute resolution. A major litigation case potentially involves hundreds of thousands of documents. Normally, the law firm defending the company being sued will store and manage all of these documents. When the client wants a particular deposition or brief, it will call the law firm, which will find it and send it to the client. Ringtail is a web-based technology that handles all aspects of electronic evidence discovery by helping the client and its outside counsel manage what could be thousands of cases and millions of documents at once. It creates a shared database that the client can access without having to go through the law firm and incur additional fees. It makes it easier for clients to do business with Fulbright, speeds up the document management and retrieval process, and reduces legal costs.

Another example of Technology Leverage is simply granting clients direct access to your internal databases. Several of the large human resources consulting firms, for example, allow clients to directly access compensation data for different management positions, instead of having to phone their consultant and request a report. Similarly, Grant Thornton, the accounting firm, has created secure, web-based "client portals" for several hundred of its largest clients. These allow the chief financial officer and other selected executives to rapidly access a wide range of financial and accounting data.

New entrants are also using Technology Leverage to bypass or disintermediate established firms who rely on traditional data collection methods. The Nasdaq stock exchange, for example, has created a web site and database called Boardrecruiting.com to help its member companies find directors for their boards. Companies pay between $10,000 and $20,000 for access to a database of candidates, and candidates pay a $350 annual fee to have their profile listed. This service competes directly with the high-end board search offerings of the major executive search firms such as Spencer Stuart and Heidrick & Struggles.

There is a world of value that you can bring to your clients. To do so, you need to make a concerted effort to connect with the rest of your firm and to draw in other relevant resources that may lie outside of it.

Conclusion

The teams that consistently develop Level 6 trusted client partnerships are able to deliver multiple layers of value. To do this, they first work to influence the factors that will increase the client's perception of value, such as financial impact, perceived substitutes, degree of difficulty, and risk. Second, they invest time to really understand what parts of their offering or solution are *most* valuable to the client. Third, they think about value broadly. They emphasize the delivery of both tangible and intangible benefits, and personal as well as institutional value. Finally, they regularly reach out and draw on six distinct sources of value leverage in their own companies.

Most of the organizations I am familiar with have significant, untapped opportunities to deliver more value to their clients, and they can do this without having to spend a lot more money. Don't restrict your thinking to something as narrow as "If only I had a great new idea; then I could really demonstrate more value to my client." Figuring out how to enhance the value you are delivering will, no doubt, require some hard work. Like Dorothy in the *Wizard of Oz*, however, I'm betting that the tools and resources you need to get there are already within your reach (in Dorothy's case, she just had to tap her shoes and say, "There's no place like home" three times—something she already knew, in effect, how to do).

In Chapter 12, we'll pick up the theme of value again, and explore how to create a more differentiated experience for your clients that will enhance value and, ideally, reduce costs for both of you.

PART III

The Five Institutional Strategies

8

Strategy Six: Targeting the Right Clients

Choosing the Right Client, the Right Executive,
and the Right Issue

After working for over a year with a large consumer products company, my client was at the end of her rope. Her main contact was a vice president who was enthusiastic about her firm, but who struggled to get budget approval for each successive assignment. Two other competitors worked directly with the CEO and the business unit heads, and it was impossible to get her work noticed at the senior management level—not least because the vice president did not feel confident enough about his own power base to push to get his ideas and proposals onto the table. The relationship generated modest fees—income which, on the one hand, represented a reassuring revenue stream, but which, on the other hand, was becoming a distraction from pursuing bigger fish. Her client had lots of ideas about changing the organization, but he lacked the authority and clout to actually do anything about them, and their wide-ranging discussions about how to improve the company's operations never went anywhere.

Does this story sound familiar? Most professionals have had a client like this. Once you are in the middle of this type of situation, however, it's very hard to fix it. By being more discerning at the beginning of the relationship about which client, executive, and issues you will engage with, you can dramatically reduce the odds that you'll end up stymied like this.

Effective client targeting is both the easiest and hardest of the 10 strategies illustrated in this book. It's easy because most of the readers of this book have a clear market: The top 500 or 1,000 corporations, and possibly major governmental organizations, in their home market. It's difficult because the factors that should influence whether you pursue a particular client or opportunity usually don't have much to do with obvious things like the client's size or revenue. Instead, they center around intangibles such as whether the executive you're dealing with sits at the right level in the organization, whether this is the right issue for you to be working on in the first place, and preexisting relationships that the client may have with your competitors—all factors that are difficult to assess using a spreadsheet full of quantitative market data. Undisciplined client targeting, however, leads to a lack of focus, underutilization of talent, and missed opportunities.

Not every lead will make a good client, and not every client can develop into a Level 6 trusted partner relationship. Therefore, careful screening of your new business opportunities—and your ongoing relationships—is essential. What works against many firms is the fact that their gross margins (revenue minus direct labor costs) are extremely high; which means that most client assignments are quite profitable and there is little economic incentive to turn down work unless it's truly terrible. Furthermore, individual professionals at most firms are fairly entrepreneurial and independent, and don't like to be told what clients to work with or turn down.

The intent of this chapter is to help you invest more of your time with the right clients, and to ensure that you are working with the right executives at those clients on the right issues. For our purposes, "right" means conducive to *mutually beneficial, rewarding, long-term relationships.*

The Right Client

Every firm has a particular market focus that may incorporate any number of factors such as industry type, company size, geographic location, IT-intensity, manufacturing versus services, and so on. I can't tell you what these should be for you. But there are other, more subtle considerations that you should be thinking about as you select and pursue specific client organizations (and in *this* chapter, when I say "client" I mean the *institution*—not the individual). Let's look at some of the factors that you should consider when deciding whether a client is the right fit for you:

- *The client has a history of building productive, long-term relationships with professional advisors and other service providers.* If it doesn't, you need to wonder why not. I have worked with several organizations, for example, which themselves provide high-end advice and other services to their clients; and it turned out they were highly intolerant of outside advisors. I simply could not be very effective with them because of their resistance to what I represented. In other cases, you may have a client that simply does not have a relationship culture and treats everyone like a vendor.

- *The client has strong leadership.* It doesn't matter if the client's problems are minor or major—the question is whether it has the leadership to take firm decisions and follow through. The worst situation is a client organization that is disorganized, politicized, and lacks coherent leadership at the top. On the other hand, a highly ambitious, well-led client is usually a pleasure to work with.

- *The client has a good reputation.* Your own reputation is strongly affected by your clients' standing in the marketplace. It's one thing if they are suffering financial woes but are developing a plan to come

> Here is an infallible rule: A prince who is not himself wise cannot be well advised.
>
> **—Niccolò Machiavelli,**
> *The Prince*

back. It's quite another, however, if they have a reputation for poor quality, lack integrity, take shortcuts, badmouth their competition, or create a hostile workplace for minorities.

- *The client is large enough to support your ambitions.* Small clients can be valuable in a number of ways. They can be fun to work with, they can give younger professionals valuable experience in the c-suite, and you might get in on the ground floor of what could become the next Microsoft or Google. But a small client with limited growth potential can also represent a poor use of your time, and you may be better off working with a company that has the economic base to support a broad-based relationship with you and your firm.

- *The client is a user of your services—it is used to dealing with your type of firm.* It's one thing if a client regularly uses consulting services but treats its consultants like a vendor. Here, I'm talking about a slightly different case in which the client has no experience using consultants (just to give one example). For instance, one of the companies I advise took on a large client that seemed very promising. However, it turned out that the client had always done the work in-house, and had almost no experience with using an external provider. The relationship was fraught with difficulties that included mismatched expectations, jealousy between the internal staff and the outside advisors, disagreements about fees, and many other frictions. This doesn't necessarily have to disqualify a client, but it should be a warning sign that you need to proceed slowly and carefully.

If a client or potential client demonstrates these characteristics, then you probably have an excellent candidate for a Level 6 relationship.

The Right Executive

Working with the right executive in the client organization can make up for many other shortcomings. It's akin to the advice my father gave me when I headed off to college over 30 years ago: "Pick courses that have great professors. Don't worry about the actual subject—it won't matter because anything will be fascinating if you've got an excellent teacher." There are two aspects to picking the right executive: The first has to do with organizational clout and decision making; the second with chemistry and interpersonal compatibility.

From the organizational perspective, the right executive is someone who has the organization's respect and the authority to support and sponsor the work you are doing. Ideally, he is the economic buyer—the person who makes the final decision to buy your services—but he can be someone else if you also have a strong connection to the ultimate economic buyer. The right executive is also someone who is a competent manager and strong leader, who knows how to connect her project to the organization's broader strategic agenda, thus elevating its importance.

It's also critical to have the right personal chemistry with the individual. This does not necessarily mean sharing the same interests and hobbies, or growing up in the same city. Rather, it has to do with whether you "get along" together. Do you have a similar way of looking at the world? Are you both curious and inquisitive? Do you have compatible communications styles? Do you enjoy each other's company? I don't know what all the ingredients are—I'm not sure anyone does—but you'll know pretty quickly whether it's working. If you don't hit it off, but the client is otherwise important to your firm,

> In order to build a broad-based, institutional relationship, you have to have a client who is intent on accomplishing his goals but who also sees himself as part of a larger mission. The client has to realize he is on a bigger stage. One of my early clients was a three-star general who ran two different national agencies. One of them really did not have a strong profile with key government leaders, and he earnestly believed that it should. He worked hard, over a long period of time, to get it onto the president's agenda and elevate its stature. We became his partner in helping to accomplish this, and as a result this became a long-term, institutional relationship.
>
> **—Ralph Shrader, Chairman and CEO, Booz Allen Hamilton**

you always have the option of finding a colleague who might be more compatible with the executive.

The Right Issue

Many services firms have very broad offerings, and they are hard-pressed to find an issue that they don't think they can add value to or a service they don't offer. This attitude can lead them into a trap, however, when they find themselves working on an issue that may not be very important to the client or that they are not the best equipped to handle. Below, I have set out some of the characteristics that you should look for as you decide whether or not an issue is right for you. Many of these criteria are aimed at determining just how important the issue is to the client:

1. *The client has already tried to address the issue internally.* If not, what is the motivation to hire someone to fix it? A client usually goes outside when it finds that it lacks the skills to successfully deal with the problem or doesn't have the capacity to do so. A simple question—"What efforts have you already made to address this?"—can tease this out.

2. *The issue is either causing pain or represents an unfulfilled opportunity.* If your engagement is not going to address a significant problem or a growth opportunity, why would the client pay a lot of money to you? You'll also need this information to start thinking about a benefits case and the potential value to the client, when and

> If you think about why a client relationship doesn't grow and broaden, it often has to do with how you have defined the issue going in. If you go along with a very narrow definition of the problem at hand, then you may consign yourself to a pigeonhole. If instead you invest the time and are able to influence the client to think more expansively about the issue, you can create the foundation for a bigger relationship.
>
> **—Relationship Manager**

if you write a proposal. There are a number of questions that you can employ to probe this—for example, "How much do you think this is costing you?" or, "How is this affecting (costs, productivity, morale, sales, etc.)?" Or, "What do you think it would be worth to fix this/to successfully exploit this opportunity?"

3. *The issue is complex, requires sophisticated judgment, and/or affects multiple functions.* If so, then it's going to really leverage your and your firm's capabilities, and command a premium fee. It it's none of the above, chances are the client will buy on price and think of the solution as a commodity. Law firms, for example, face this dilemma in some of their work with insurance companies or in handling plain-vanilla employment law cases. The work isn't very complicated, the issues are fairly clear-cut, and you don't need 30 years of experience to handle it. As a result, clients balk at paying the same hourly rates that law firms ask for their other high-end services.

4. *The issue plays to your "sweet spot" as a firm.* The bedrock of Level 6 relationships is superb quality work, and if the issue at hand is not one you are well equipped to handle, you should take a pass. It's a different situation if a long-standing client asks you to do something that you know you can handle competently, but that might not be a core strength. In this case, factors such as mutual trust and a deep knowledge of your client's organization may tip the scale toward accepting the task.

5. *The issue is owned by the executive you are dealing with.* I once met with a prospective client

> A number of our younger partners are spending far too much of their time going after competitive bids because they have not made the effort to build their own networks or establish their brand in the marketplace. They aren't getting enough of their own leads, so they go after the RFPs. But that's a tough business with a very uncertain payoff. If they were more focused on the clients which already know them, and if we were more discerning about which RFPs to really go after and which ones to reject, we'd be far better off.
>
> **—Relationship Manager**

who was quite excited about the need to revamp his company's strategy. He was very senior, and it seemed like a natural topic for us to discuss. After spending many hours exploring this issue with him, however, I learned that he had no ownership at all of the company's strategy or planning process, which was firmly in the bailiwick of the CEO and his director of strategic planning. In fact, it turned out that everyone else in senior management thought the strategy was working beautifully and had no motivation to even question it. In other words, it's always important to find out if the executive you are dealing with can actually do something about the issue at hand. People like to complain about a lot of things, many of which they have no control over whatsoever.

Being disciplined about working with the right clients, the right issues, and the right executives can have a significant financial impact. A case-in-point is the New York law firm Milbank Tweed. About seven years ago, Milbank went through an extensive internal debate about its strategy. Rather than straining its resources through overly ambitious global expansion—or the pursuit of revenue for its own sake—it decided to refocus around a handful of core practice areas and be far more selective about the type of clients and legal work that it undertook. A not-insignificant side effect of this refocusing was a greater ability to raise rates each year because of the higher perceived value of its services. During the next five years, Milbank went from being a firm with slightly above-average profitability to being the seventh most profitable law firm in the United States. It has achieved this by concentrating on profit growth rather than headcount or revenue growth. It eschews commodity-type legal work and has focused on the most difficult and sophisticated corporate transactions. Milbank has 550 lawyers—only about 10 or 15 percent more than it had five years ago. Yet, it is far more profitable, probably has a more prestigious client list, and is able to attract a very high caliber of law school graduate.

Value to You

If you have the right client, executive, and issue, then the engagement will be—almost by definition—of value to you. There are a couple of other factors, however, that you need to think about as you carry out your selection process. These are:

- *Short- and long-term financial returns:* How acceptable are the fees and profitability of the engagement? Is this a one-off transaction, or do you think it will become a long-term relationship?
- *Intellectual capital creation:* In executing this assignment, will you develop valuable new intellectual capital or add to an existing body of know-how?
- *Risk:* Are you putting yourself and your firm at risk by taking this client on? Are you being asked to accomplish something that is fraught with difficulties and uncertainties that you can't control?
- *Fun and novelty:* Will you truly enjoy this work? Is it with a client you particularly like or in a location (e.g., the Caribbean or Paris!) that is attractive to you?
- *Alternatives:* What alternative uses for your own time exist right now? Are there other, more attractive client opportunities at hand?

Figure 8.1 takes two of the fundamental dimensions we've been discussing—value to the client and value to you—and looks at four different positions that you may find yourself in.

Inevitably there will be tension between the X and the Y axis on this matrix, with the most stable quadrant being Key Clients in the upper right. Here, you are doing work that is highly valuable both to you and your client. But invariably, most firms will have engagements in the other three quadrants as well. Bread and Butter might include routine but important activities like audit or compensation analysis. Question Marks seem attractive at the start, but they will quickly move down into the matrix and turn into Ball and Chain assignments that are commodities for both parties. Services in this quadrant, by the way, are the ones getting sent offshore to India and other countries—things like routine contract reviews, back-up research for consultants, and software development. The question you must answer is, "Is there client work that we should restructure or redefine, or that we should just stop doing?"

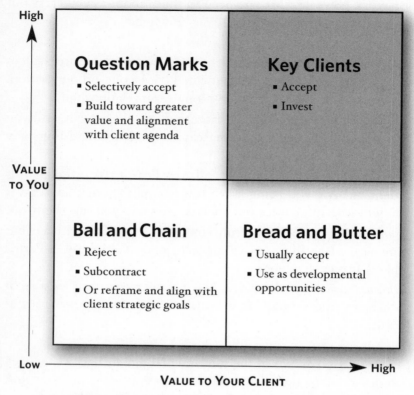

FIGURE 8.1 Focusing on the Highest Value Engagements

Improving Client Targeting across the Organization

It's great to have guidelines for determining which clients to accept, but how do you enforce them in what may be a far-flung, entrepreneurial organization full of independent-minded partners and managing directors? Step one is to actually *have* guidelines about the types of companies you work with, the executives you are targeting, and the issues that really make sense for you. These need to be carefully discussed, thought through, and agreed on; they should be straightforward, and fit on one or two pages.

Step two is to implement a client intake process that goes beyond simply checking for conflicts or ascertaining whether or not the gross margin on the proposal meets a certain benchmark. This intake process should compare the opportunity to the guidelines that have been established, and it should involve a member of senior management who is willing to take the time to really understand whether the client makes sense for the organization. Some large firms do have several levels of approval, depending on the size of the deal or program. However, even in these cases, it's not clear to me that the more intangible factors we have discussed are being considered.

Step three is for senior management and experienced client relationship managers to model these behaviors and put resources behind the client opportunities that are the best match. For example, if a request for a proposal (RFP) opportunity comes in the door that is a long shot and a poor fit with your guidelines, then the practice manager or office head needs to sit down with his team and say: "This is not the right client profile for us. We don't have any preexisting relationships that would help us during the RFP. It's not at the right executive level. We should pass." You need to allocate investment funds toward high-potential opportunities, and share the risk that individuals take by investing time in them.

Client-facing professionals need to be actively discouraged from pursuing small, unattractive opportunities that may provide some short-term fees but which have little long-term potential. It's not easy to do this, particularly when economic conditions are difficult; but to *not* do so results in a lack of leverage across the organization. I have seen partners in professional service firms blossom and take on vastly increased client responsibilities when they stop spreading themselves thin across six or seven small relationships, and start to focus on a few truly valuable ones. The secret is to take a long-term view of the business that allows you to make the right decisions, despite short-term pressures to make the wrong ones. If you are scrambling from month to month or quarter to quarter, there will be endless exceptions, and client screening guidelines will go out the window.

Conclusion

If you want to successfully build Level 6 trusted client partnerships, it is essential to pick the right clients. I've been happily married to

Right Client

✓ Meets specific firm criteria
✓ History of long-term relationships
✓ Strong leadership
✓ Positive reputation
✓ Sufficient size
✓ Experienced user of your services

Right Issue

✓ Have tried to address internally
✓ Significant payoff
✓ Complex, multifaceted
✓ Plays to your strengths
✓ Your contact owns the issue

Right Executive

✓ Respected in the organization
✓ Ambitous
✓ Economic buyer
✓ Good personal chemistry

Other Factors

✓ Acceptable financial returns
✓ Acceptable risk
✓ Intellectual capital creation
✓ Fun/variety

FIGURE 8.2   Client Acceptance Criteria

the same person for over 25 years, and when people ask me what has made the relationship work, I will often just say, "I married the right woman." Of course, it's more than just that, but the initial choice of partner is nonetheless critical. Take a long, hard look at your client base today—at the kinds of clients, executives, and issues you work with. In Chapter 4, I asked you to identify your most important "relationship hubs," across many categories of relationships, and create a plan to develop them further. Now, with regard to your current clients, I'm challenging you to think about whether you are working with the right raw material to begin with. The summary checklist in Figure 8.2 sets out the various screening criteria that I've suggested that you incorporate in your targeting efforts. Use it to assess where you stand today, and whether you'd like to make some changes.

9

Strategy Seven: Building a Client Leadership Pipeline

Developing and Supporting Client Relationship Managers

How many of your client relationship managers do you think are currently performing at a level necessary to support your future strategy? What percentage is capable of developing and sustaining Level 6 trusted client partnerships where you are working with senior management on the client's most important agenda? When I ask my clients these questions, the answer I am consistently given is that between 20 and 30 percent of their relationship managers can successfully develop and manage Level 6 relationships today; around half can do a solid but not spectacular job; and 20 to 30 percent are underperforming. Yet, most of these same clients will add that many of their relationship managers have the *potential* to lead Level 6 relationships. Your proportions may be slightly different, but I bet one thing is for sure: You can never have enough of the senior, experienced professionals who are capable of becoming trusted advisors to c-level executives—and then growing that individual relationship into an institutional partnership.

How valuable is a good relationship manager? Assigning an experienced relationship manager to lead and coordinate a client

173

relationship can double the rate of your fee growth. Several of my clients have studied this in their own organizations, and tracked revenue growth in client relationships with and without a dedicated relationship manager and supporting team. In the studies I have seen, the average year-on-year fee growth for clients who have a well-supported relationship manager ranges between 25 and 30 percent—which is usually at least double the growth rate of the average relationship in the same organization. Is some of this growth due to the fact that the clients picked to have a relationship manager were better bets in the first place? Maybe; but the data still stand, and there is no doubt that a skilled relationship manager can make a huge difference.

Why is there a chronic shortage of these individuals, who will have different titles in different organizations (relationship partner, client relationship manager, key account executive, client service officer, managing director, coverage officer, and so on)? Frankly, it is because it's a very difficult job to do well. Great relationship managers combine a variety of hard and soft skills, of technical knowledge and emotional intelligence. They must be able to connect with top executives in the c-suite and be accepted as their peer. Most firms, however, hire for the technical skills and quantitative talents that enable young professionals to excel in the early part of their careers, instead of looking for more intangible capabilities—such as empathy or big picture thinking—that are necessary to succeed in the executive suite.

The relationship manager, in short, occupies *the pivotal role* when it comes to developing Level 6 trusted client partnerships, and in this chapter I set out a series of best practices for developing and supporting these key professionals throughout their careers—for creating a client leadership pipeline of individuals capable of the highest levels of relationship management. Specifically, I address the role of the relationship manager, recruiting, professional development, ongoing support, and measurement and rewards.

Role of the Relationship Manager

The precise role of the relationship manager varies from firm to firm. However, I have found that there are six main areas of focus for any professional who has responsibility for a significant client relationship. Let's briefly review each of these.

1. Aspiration Setting

The relationship manager has to articulate aspirations for both the client's business and for the relationship itself. First, she needs to have a deep understanding of the client's agenda, and a vision for how to accomplish it. A good relationship manager develops this by investing time to understand the client's strategy and organization, walking the halls, and having explicit agenda-setting discussions with the client. Second, the relationship manager needs to set aspirations for her firm's relationship with the client. Diana Brightmore-Armour, CEO of Corporate Banking for Lloyds Banking Group, told me an inspiring story about this. She had just started work at the bank and found herself at Wimbledon with several major clients. As they walked through the corridor to enter the tennis stadium, she asked one of the CFOs where Lloyds ranked among the banks he used. "Eighteenth" was his blunt answer. She stopped dead in her tracks, shocked, nearly blockading the entrance. But then she boldly told the CFO that within a year her bank would be in his top three. She later sat down with the client team, and they set an even further aspiration: To be number one in two years. That ambitious goal galvanized the account team and helped transform the client into a Level 6 relationship.

> My client is a large, multinational energy company that has dozens of economic buying units around the world. I'm the overall coordinator of the relationship, but I don't manage people too tightly—it's more of an open network. I encourage colleagues to explore opportunities throughout the organization. They keep me informed, I give them advice, and ultimately I make judgments about where we should really invest. This loose approach, which suits this particular client, results in far more opportunities than would develop from tight, centralized control.
>
> **—Relationship Partner**

2. Relationship Strategy

The relationship manager has to lead the decisions about which issues to focus on, which opportunities to actively pursue, and which executives to build relationships with. In any large company, you could flail away for years and never get anywhere if you're not discerning about where and how you invest your firm's resources. Some clients must be approached centrally, and the relationship manager has to exercise a great deal of control and discipline in terms of managing the senior contacts at the client. Others give wide budget latitude to multiple buying units throughout the organization.

3. Client Leadership

The degree of a relationship manager's specific content expertise will vary; but in any case, the client must perceive you to be a thought leader. You must come across as someone who has a deep knowledge of the client's business and people, a thorough understanding of its agenda, and a point of view on how it can achieve its goals. You cannot be an "empty suit" who is just there to coordinate delivery resources and sell more work; today's clients are just too sophisticated and demanding for that role to have much value for them. You don't have to be *the* content expert—indeed, your expertise can and will limit the growth of your relationships if you cannot step back from it—but you do have to exercise *thought leadership*.

4. Team Leadership

One of the five growth pathways for institutionalizing a relationship that I discussed in Chapter 6 focuses on more effective team leadership. Effective relationship managers spend a great deal of time ensuring that their teams have the right mix of skills and experiences. They actively coach and mentor team members, set goals for them, and follow up. They create client teams that are magnets for talent in the organization—exciting, fun places to work that attract other professionals.

5. Ambassadorship

The relationship manager should be the client's window into the rest of the firm's capabilities. Clients should view this lead professional as someone who knows exactly where to go to get the right skills for a given issue, but who will also say, "We're not the best at that"—and recommend someone else. Good relationship managers are door openers, not gate keepers. They build strong networks within their firms, and invest time to fully understand their firm's complete capabilities and resources. As simple as this may seem, it doesn't always happen as it should. One client commented to me, "Surprisingly, I still see e-mails shooting around with questions like: Does anybody know if we do X or Y? For some of our relationship partners, a lack of understanding of our service offerings is still a barrier to relationship growth."

6. Commercial Management

In most organizations, relationship managers are responsible for the financial aspects of a client relationship; including negotiating contracts, ensuring that profitability targets are met, managing overruns, and so on. They also have the overall task of ensuring quality control.

This list of roles represents the *high-level* functions of the relationship manager. I have not included things like "building client knowledge," "selling additional services to the client," "problem solving," or "hard work." Although these are certainly part of the job, they can all be found as a component one of the six roles outlined previously.

Part of the relationship manager's role is external (or "client-facing"), and part is internal. Usually relationship managers combine both facets; however, I have seen situations where there are co-relationship managers. In these cases, one person takes on the external client leadership role, while the other focuses more closely on internal roles like team leadership, commercial management, and coordinating the firm's resources. Sometimes, an arrangement like this makes sense because every relationship manager is not equally proficient at every role.

Capabilities of the Relationship Manager

There are specific capabilities that relationship managers need in order to *fulfill* the six roles outlined previously. *Capabilities* refer to a combination of skills, talents, and behaviors. What are the differences between these three? A skill is the *how-to* for accomplishing something; a talent is a *natural ability* you are born with; a behavior is how you *react to* other people or situations.

These distinctions are important because great relationship managers are successful due to a combination of all three, and you select for and develop these in different ways. Because skills, talents, and behaviors are so closely related and at times bound up with each other, I use capabilities, and sometimes skills, as catch-alls to describe the overall set of abilities that relationship managers need to possess and display. Certain processes—such as building trust—are clearly part talent, part skill, and part behavior. There are six major, underlying capabilities that relationship managers need to accomplish their mission—to fulfill the roles that I just outlined:

1. *Relationship building skills:* Relationship managers must master the core skills required to form meaningful interpersonal relationships. These include empathy, social skills, self-awareness, self-control, and the ability to build trust.

2. *Thought leadership:* Relationship managers must be recognized by clients and peers as thought leaders who offer keen judgment and big picture thinking. Thought leadership is based on many different skills and talents, one of which is big picture thinking—the ability to see patterns, prioritize the most important issues, make knowledge connections, and draw insights from data. It also requires that relationship managers have a strong "point of view" and general business savvy.

3. *Network development:* Relationship managers need to be able to develop and maintain a vibrant, long-term network of relationships with key individuals in the client's organization, across their firms, and with other key constituencies. For example, relationship managers must systematically build a multilevel network of many-to-many relationships with their clients. They also need strong internal relationships within their firms, so they understand and have access to a wide range of capabilities.

4. *People leadership:* Relationship managers must be able to assemble, manage, and lead successful teams whose members learn and grow from the experience. They need to form strong, trusted relationships with delivery team leaders and members; set clear goals; and coach and delegate effectively.

5. *Relationship management:* Relationship managers must be able to develop, manage, grow, and institutionalize complex relationships on behalf of their firms. A number of abilities fall under this topic, including using solution-selling strategies to win the sale, account planning, communications, expectation setting, and communicating value.

6. *Personal leadership:* Relationship managers must engage in continual personal development. The personal leadership task for individual delivery experts is more straightforward than for a relationship manager, who must possess a breadth of knowledge and a wide range of skills in order to perform a very complex job. Personal leadership would include such things as setting priorities, time management, personal renewal, and career management.

> In *Clients for Life,* I introduced, with my co-author Jagdish Sheth, a framework of seven attributes that differentiate the client advisor from the expert for hire. Nearly 10 years later, this model has been thoroughly validated and reinforced by tens of thousands of service professionals. The seven attributes highlighted in this model can be characterized as follows: Experts are for hire; advisors have *Selfless Independence*—they balance dedication with objectivity. Experts tell; whereas advisors ask great questions and listen—they have *Empathy.* Experts are narrow specialists; advisors are *Deep Generalists.* Experts analyze; advisors analyze and *Synthesize*—they bring *Big Picture Thinking* to their clients. Experts make decisions based singularly on the evidence, while advisors offer *Judgment* that incorporates the client's values and organizational capabilities. Experts have credibility based on their facts; advisors have *Conviction* rooted in deeply held beliefs and values. Experts build professional trust; advisors also develop deep *Personal Trust* with their clients.
>
> **—Andrew Sobel**

Figure 9.1 summarizes these relationship manager roles and capabilities.

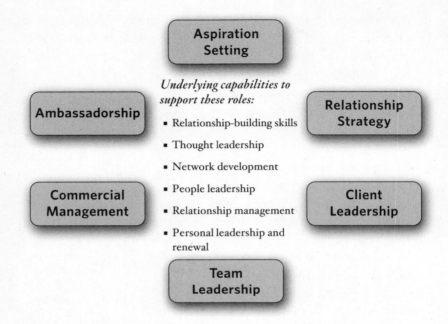

FIGURE 9.1 Key Roles of the Relationship Manager

Recruiting Potential Relationship Managers

Most services firms look for a wide variety of skills, talents, and experiences when they recruit young professionals, but they aren't necessarily thinking about whether a candidate will be able to relate to CEOs 15 years down the road. This is partly because of short-term needs; they want someone who can do the job tomorrow, not in the distant future. It's also due to the fact that—given the huge turnover among young professionals—it's no sure thing that this person will even be around in 5 or 10 years. Analytical and technical skills are thus highly sought after, and they have the advantage of being much easier to measure and assess than emotional intelligence. Many organizations reject highly promising candidates who have broad intellects and strong interpersonal skills, but who are not perceived as having "good enough" analytical skills.

Creating a pipeline of client leaders, in short, starts with the hiring decision. Here are some of the qualities you ought to look for in hiring young professionals if you'd like to create a better gene pool of individuals capable of leading Level 6 relationships:

- *Emotional intelligence:* Are they self-aware? Can they control their emotions and impulses, and adapt to changing circumstances? Do they possess social awareness and empathy? Can they inspire and influence others?

- *A relationship orientation:* Do they have a genuine interest in other people? Are they interested in how decisions may affect others? Do they invest in building their own networks?

- *The ability to both be a team player and lead teams:* Do they have a track record of successfully working in a team environment? Do they talk about "I" all the time, or "We"? What philosophy and strategies did they use as a team leader?

- *Curiosity and intellectual breadth:* Do they ask good questions? Are they motivated to learn? Do they read widely? What outside interests do they have? Are they fluent in current events and business issues? Are they able to make knowledge connections between disparate topics?

- *Conviction and persuasion:* Do they communicate effectively? Are they articulate? Are they passionate and enthusiastic when they talk about their interests and experiences?

Most organizations have their own competency model that they use when hiring young professionals, but to the extent you are looking for specific potential to become a leader of Level 6 relationships, these are some of the qualities you ought to seek.

Developing Relationship Managers

I am often asked if you can teach someone to become a trusted client advisor who is capable of building relationships with top executives. The short answer is that it's hard to *teach* this, but professionals can *learn* to do it. In other words, traditional training methods can instill some of these qualities, but many of them must be acquired through experience. There is no question that some individuals who have a strong natural talent for relationship building are innately better at this role than others. But at the same time, most professionals can significantly improve their game—if they are *motivated to do so*.

This last point represents a major caveat about developing relationship managers: Because of the behavioral changes that are usually required, people have to be highly motivated to learn and improve. The problem with this topic is that most professionals think they already know a lot about it. They are usually already making good money and enjoying healthy professional success, and—to top things off—they sometimes falsely attribute their success to habits that they *think* are effective but which *don't* represent anything near best practice. If you combine this with the natural self-confidence (cockiness or even arrogance, in some cases) that many highly educated professionals possess, you have a formula for a difficult learning challenge.

Another issue that affects services firms' ability to develop client relationship managers nowadays is their sheer size and the consequent weakening of the apprenticeship system. When I started with the MAC Group right out of business school, the firm had about 100 consultants; when I left Gemini Consulting (its later incarnation) 15 years later, we had several thousand professionals. Today, the largest firms are bigger than most of their clients: Ernst & Young now has 130,000 employees, and Accenture 180,000. Even law firms, which represent a very fragmented industry, have gotten large; Clifford Chance leads the way with nearly 4,000 lawyers. Historically, most of us learned how to build client relationships by watching and doing—as one of my clients told me, by "sitting at the feet of the masters." Today, a young consultant may be part of a team of 25 or 50 serving a client, and get little or no exposure to the partners; and a law firm associate may scarcely meet a client in his or her first five years of work in a large law firm.

Because of these changes, you have to take a more institutional and systematic approach to developing the next generation of client leaders. But what's the best way to go about doing this? In the rest of this section, I describe a number of developmental activities and programs that can be effective in improving the capabilities of relationship managers, including:

- Career management
- Coaching and mentoring

- Formal training
- Senior forums
- Experience sharing
- Fast track programs
- E-learning programs

Let's look at each of these.

Career Management

Great client relationship managers possess both knowledge *breadth* and *depth*—they are, as I say in *Clients for Life*, "Deep Generalists" (see previous sidebar). Deep Generalists are able to connect to senior executives' business issues more readily than narrow specialists, and they consistently put their expert knowledge in the context of their client's overall goals and strategy. Deep Generalists tend to be naturally curious people who ask a lot of questions and read widely. You can encourage the development of this type of breadth by giving professionals a rich and varied set of career experiences during their first 5 or 10 years of work.

The career of Steve Pfeiffer—current chair of the executive committee for international law firm Fulbright & Jaworski—is a terrific example of how these experiences can prepare a professional to develop and lead Level 6 client relationships. After graduating with a Bachelor's degree from Wesleyan University, Pfeiffer went to England, where he studied as a Rhodes scholar at Oxford University. He subsequently earned a Masters degree in African studies at the University of London. Having won a Thomas J. Watson fellowship during his senior year at Wesleyan, he was able to travel extensively in Europe and Africa while studying at Oxford. He then served as an officer in the U.S. Navy, where his final active duty assignment was special assistant to the Secretary of the Navy. He eventually retired as a Commander in the Naval Reserve nearly 20 years later. After graduating from law school in the mid-1970s, Pfeiffer went to work as a young attorney in Fulbright & Jaworski's main office in Houston, Texas. After a few years, he moved to Fulbright's nascent London office, where he spent seven formative years encountering a wide variety of international corporate transactions and developing important client relationships that would endure for many years to come. Pfeiffer then transferred to Fulbright's Washington office, and later became its partner in charge.

Interestingly—and not coincidentally—each experience that Pfeiffer accumulated helped create a foundation, not only for his ability to lead major client relationships, but also for his eventual leadership of the firm. The internal relationships that he developed during stints in Houston, London, and finally Washington gave him a deep knowledge of the firm's people and service offerings, and a base of support to both marshal resources into his client relationships and assume leadership positions within the firm. His broad knowledge of international law and cross-border business transactions gave him a leg up in a fast-growing area of legal practice that has increased in importance over the years. His non-legal experiences have also been invaluable to his career: His time in the U.S. Navy, for example, provided him with valuable contacts in Washington, and his extensive involvement in non-profit organizations, such as Wesleyan University's Board of Trustees, expanded his network in the business community. Even his degree in African studies figured into his rainmaking capabilities: While in London, Fulbright pitched a major South African company; and Pfeiffer's keen understanding of the history and culture of that region turned out to be a deciding factor in winning the business. Twenty years later, this major, publicly held company is still a client of the firm, and Pfeiffer sits on its board of directors.

> An artist has to be careful to never think that he's arrived somewhere. He has to be in a constant state of becoming.
>
> **—Bob Dylan**

While Pfeiffer's resume is unusually impressive, it's not untypical—in its variety and diversity—of many of the hundreds of successful client leaders I have studied in dozens of firms. As you look at your own high-potential professionals, think about how you can systematically give them a wide diversity of experiences as they mature and grow. These might include things such as:

- Spending time abroad
- Working in different offices
- Being involved in a start-up (e.g., of a new service offering or office)
- Moving to a new practice area or subspecialty
- Working for a variety of senior professionals

Coaching and Mentoring

Coaching and mentoring young professionals should be an important task for every partner or senior executive in a services firm. Changing a relationship manager's behavior is often best accomplished through the intimate, one-on-one feedback and follow-up that expert coaching affords. Unfortunately, crushing time demands on most service professionals have made it harder for them to make room for this job in their schedules. I remember as a young associate debriefing with the relationship partner after a client presentation. I listened to him talk about what went well, what we could have done better, why different client executives had reacted the way they did to our materials, and what our next steps ought to be. Today, I see partners rushing off to the next meeting and catching up the next day with a cursory e-mail, or delegating these discussions to junior managers. Learning by "sitting at the feet of masters" has become, all too frequently, a catch-as-catch-can jumble of late-night e-mails and sporadic feedback. However, there are several steps you can take to remedy this situation.

The first step is to reinforce a culture of mentorship among your senior professionals, and you start this process by leading by example. There is no better exemplar of this than the chairman of Citigroup, Sir Win Bischoff. He will always

> ### A Great Mentor
>
> When I lived in London and worked for The MAC Group in the 1980s, one of our senior partners was Dean Berry, a former business school professor who had also been one of the early heads of INSEAD, the international business school. Dean was a big bear of a man who loved ideas, relationships, good food, and wine. He was also well connected to many CEOs across Europe. I was a young partner struggling to master my new role, and Dean was always available to talk to me, no matter how busy he was. I would pull my chair over next to his leather-topped partners desk and ask him about a client dilemma I faced or perhaps even a personal issue. Dean would listen deeply, ask thoughtful questions, and help synthesize the critical issues for me. It was nothing for him to take an hour out of his hectic day to just talk with me. At the end, he would usually offer one or two incisive observations or suggestions, but always in the spirit of, 'Here's something you might think about …' Dean knew what mentorship was, and took time for it. I don't see enough of that today.
>
> **—Andrew Sobel**

make time in his demanding schedule to talk with one of Citigroup's relationship managers about a key client relationship. He sponsored a mentoring program at Citigroup called "Passing Down the Wisdom," where he spent entire evenings sitting down with younger professionals and sharing his 40 years of experience in developing long-term clients.

You also need to embed these values in the performance review process, and ask your senior professionals pointed questions about their mentoring activities. Office heads and practice leaders should shift some of the focus of management meetings from administrative affairs to client relationship reviews, and spend time with their teams to reflect and strategize how to develop and sustain more Level 6 client relationships.

The second step you can take is to institute a formal relationship manager coaching program. As I mentioned earlier, Citigroup does this through a cadre of "Seniors"—highly experienced senior bankers who are assigned to work with the relationship managers for each of their largest corporate clients. Environmental consulting firm ERM started a highly effective coaching program aimed at helping partners who were still individual "experts" become more skilled at working with senior executives and bringing a firmwide perspective to their client's issues. A handful of ERM's most experienced partners, all of whom had a strong track record in building Level 6 client relationships, were each asked to coach five junior partners. The coaches talk to the relationship partners they are coaching at least once a month, and perform several roles. First, they help the partner think more broadly and holistically about the client they are serving. Second, they act as a bridge between the partner and the rest of ERM, which has 3,500 professionals in 41 countries around the world. It's very hard for any one partner to fully appreciate all of the service offerings and resources that are potentially available to ERM's clients, so having a coach who has a broad knowledge of the organization is extremely helpful.

You can also use external coaches in your company to supplement your own internal mentoring efforts, but you need to be careful about whom you ask to do the coaching. Most executive coaches focus on either behavioral change (e.g., getting rid of bad habits that are holding someone back) or on general performance improvement (e.g., taking one's career to the next level), whereas the kind of coaching that relationship managers need is usually more specific and narrowly focused. I am leery about "quick-hit" business development coaching sessions that last 20 or 30 minutes, or one-month coaching programs that purport to incite lasting change. In my experience, you need to work with a relationship manager for six or eight months to get her to adopt new tools and techniques, learn new skills and behaviors, and therefore to have a meaningful impact on her performance.

Training

I agree with author David Maister's contention that training is usually the last thing that you want to rely on to achieve your strategic goals. This is because training is helpful only *after* you have made all of the other organizational and systems changes that are needed to support the development of Level 6 trusted client partnerships.

I was approached several years ago by a large global services company about creating a training program for their key account managers. The company had recently instituted a key account manager organization and wanted to "train" these professionals to build trusted CEO relationships. However, after interviewing a number of its senior executives and reviewing its strategic plans, I concluded that a training program would be a disaster at that time. This company had not put into place any of the infrastructure that is needed to support a group of relationship managers. All of the client relationships were still controlled by local office heads and practice leaders, who were resentful of the new key account management structure; the roles and responsibilities for these individuals had not been clearly defined; the measurement and reward system had not been adapted to reflect the particular goals and challenges of a relationship manager; and so on. Unfortunately, the client was fixated on a training program as the solution, and my assessment was received rather coolly.

This said, training—especially when combined with other approaches such as coaching and supervisory follow-up—can be quite effective. But what exactly do you train relationship managers *in*? Relationship building is such a large topic that it can be intimidating. Can you really cover all of it in a one- or two-day training session?

After working with numerous service firms on a wide variety of training initiatives, I have developed a fairly straightforward model for what needs to be taught to relationship managers to help them build their capabilities. There are three buckets that you need to think about: *Principles, Skills and Behaviors,* and *Best Practices.*

Principles are those underlying assumptions or beliefs that drive your behavior as a relationship manager (I included my own list of these at the end of Chapter 5). Examples include statements like, "Build your network before you need it," "Follow the person, not the position," and "Great relationships start with great conversations, not one person trying to show the other how brilliant they are." You teach and instill these principles by sharing them, encouraging people to think of some of their own, telling stories that illustrate them, and so on. You sprinkle them throughout a training session, as opposed to creating a special module entitled "principles."

Skills and behaviors refer to, among others, the core trusted advisor attributes described earlier, along with characteristics like self-awareness, interpersonal skills, and social awareness. These soft skills reside in your brain's primitive limbic system, which controls emotions and impulses, as opposed to your neocortex, where logical thinking occurs. Because of this, soft skills are very difficult to learn from a lecture or PowerPoint slide; you won't become more empathetic by reading a series of bullet points. Rather, you need to use case studies, personal exercises, self-assessments, videos, small group discussions, individual feedback, and role plays to help people improve these aptitudes.

Best practices focus on effective ways of handling the different client situations and issues you encounter as you move from Level 1 (contact) to Level 6 (trusted client partner). What's the best way to handle a first meeting? How do you defuse a client crisis? How do you connect with a c-level executive? How can you gain access to the economic buyer? What are effective strategies to broaden a narrow relationship? How do you build relationships with clients who are much older than you? Obviously, as you resolve these challenges, you will use the principles, skills, and behaviors from the other two buckets.

In short, you need to emphasize all three of these capability enablers in any kind of training initiative, as summarized in Figure 9.2.

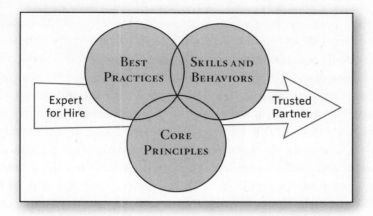

FIGURE 9.2 Developing Relationship Managers

What about psychological profiling or personality preference systems like Myers-Briggs? These personality-typing frameworks can help you better understand how your clients think and make decisions, and even how to best tailor a sales presentation. Myers-Briggs, for example, has been used by millions of professionals around the world. Furthermore, participants routinely give very high ratings to sessions where they explore their own personalities and preferences; we definitely like to dwell on ourselves and explore our own psyche. However, these systems are often of limited utility. A year after such programs, when I ask people who have been through them what their Myers-Briggs type is (e.g., ENTJ versus INFP), most of them cannot remember. Furthermore, while you can guess what type your client is, unless they take the assessment, you really don't know for sure. Unless you plan to use these systems thoroughly, and spend the time necessary to acquire real expertise (which takes a few days, not hours), I'm not sure they make sense for a limited-duration relationship training program. However, if you have a particular interest in these approaches, do explore them because they can only enhance your awareness of yourself and others.

It's important to bring the voice of the client into a training session of this nature, and there are two main ways to do this: Through an in-person client panel and with videos. Having several senior client executives participate in a panel discussion on what it's like to walk in the client's shoes—and what they look for in working with outside service providers—can be a valuable experience for your group. This format is not very scalable; however, and so an alternative is to use video. For a number of programs, I have videotaped in-depth interviews with a cross section of clients, and then edited these conversations into topical compilations that reflect the key subjects being taught in the training program. The trick is to ask very specific questions during the video interviews and probe for examples. If a client says "trust is essential," you have to go deeper and ask "Can you describe what a state of trust feels like to you as the client?" or, "Can you give me an example of the specific behaviors that instill trust in you and your team?"

What's the best way to structure and deliver a program like this? First, you need to employ a variety of teaching methods (lecture, case studies, exercises, role plays) in order to capture everyone's attention and do justice to the content, which as we've seen varies from left-brain, logical skills to right-brain, emotional intelligence capabilities. Second, you need to consider it an ongoing program, rather than just a one-time event. For example, a prework exercise followed by two one-day sessions spaced two months apart—with individual coaching and assignments in-between—can be a very effective format. Finally, you have to involve some of your best and most experienced relationship managers in the training. These senior professionals can either be seeded into the main group, where they take a leading role in sharing their experiences and underscoring key points; or they can be part of the faculty for the session, serving on a discussion panel that is set up for a question-and-answer session with the participants. You cannot outsource this type of professional development. Your own senior management must be involved to help motivate, teach, and put the imprint of your own culture and values on the approach that is being proposed.

Senior Forums

Another positive approach is the use of senior forums. Quite simply, this format requires that a couple of your most senior professionals sit down with a group of relationship managers for two or three hours to talk about their own experiences in developing trusted client partnerships. A good example of this is a program I mentioned earlier at Citigroup, which is sponsored by Sir Win Bischoff. It is called "Passing down the Wisdom," and it usually takes place over an evening, after work. Highly experienced bankers share their stories—both good and bad—and facilitate a conversation about the tough client issues that the relationship managers are facing in the marketplace. In some ways, Citigroup's "Passing Down the Wisdom" program tries to emulate the traditional mentorship process where you listen to stories from the grey-haired eminences in your firm and, hopefully, watch them in action.

Experience Sharing Summits

It can be extremely valuable for relationship managers to simply gather to share experiences and brainstorm common issues. A good example of this is the client service officer experience-sharing summits organized by Booz Allen Hamilton (now two separate firms, Booz Allen Hamilton and Booz & Co.). The summits last one day and usually involve about 20 experienced partners who are all managing major client relationships. The format varies, but the core of the session revolves around individual partners who each take about 20 minutes to present and discuss a case study of their relationship, which is summarized on a *single* slide. The slide highlights the client's background and key issues, the consulting work Booz has done, and five or six bullet points summarizing lessons learned. Client confidentialities are carefully respected

Refocusing on the Client

Each of our major practice and industry groups has a quarterly business review meeting. Unfortunately, these sessions became increasingly focused internally, on administrative issues. We made a conscious shift to devote a chunk of each business review to discussing our most important existing and potential clients. We now have a completely open, give-and-take discussion about how to take each relationship to the next level, how to address potential problems, and how the rest of the partner group can help the relationship partner. It's a kind of group coaching process. These quarterly reviews have gone from being dreaded and contentious to refreshing and helpful.

—Relationship Manager

during this session—client details are disguised when appropriate, and relationships with competitive companies are not considered on the same day. Other partners get to ask questions, and there is usually some very vibrant discussion about how some of the lessons learned can be used to improve other relationships. Participants in these workshops say that they are the most valuable internal meetings that they ever go to.

Fast-Track or High-Potential Programs

Several of my clients have created fast-track or high-potential programs for up-and-coming relationship managers. Sometimes the participants are existing relationship managers who have the potential to raise their game and go to the next level; in other cases, they are younger professionals (in their late 20s or 30s, possibly early 40s) who are managing small relationships and need additional experience and training to be qualified to take on a major client. These programs usually last anywhere from nine months to two years, and they are invariably sponsored by senior management. They usually cover a broader array of subjects than just relationship building, including the role of the relationship manager and the firm's service offerings.

A fast-track program must be tailored to your particular needs and goals. For example, human resources consulting firm Towers Perrin has a holistic fast-track program that is aimed at creating well-rounded relationship managers. It puts equal emphasis on tools and techniques to perform the client relationship management role, understanding the firm's service offerings and capabilities, teaching relationship managers how to build senior-level client relationships, and developing business acumen. It lasts over a year, and incorporates many different learning approaches. Executive search firm Heidrick & Struggles has implemented a somewhat different version of this fast-track approach. Its program is intended to help implement a strategic shift from transactional search services to a more integrated talent management model, where the firm provides both search and leadership consulting to help grow talent internally. It was rolled out regionally and comprises three workshops over a nine-month period, each of which focuses heavily on understanding the firm's complete offering of consulting services, how to identify client needs for them, and how to take a more integrated approach to talent management. A different but also very effective approach has been implemented by another leading human resources consultancy, Hewitt Associates. This program exposes Hewitt's high-potential professionals to a series of well-known academic thought leaders in different aspects of human resource management and practice, and also to the top management of the firm.

E-Learning and Other Approaches

It's difficult to learn how to become a relationship manager from an online learning program, but e-learning and digitized resource libraries can play an important support role for other initiatives. Several firms have created online resource centers to which relationship managers and their teams can turn for a variety of content about relationship-building strategies, including case examples, best practices compilations, tools, articles, videos, and so on.

Other distribution channels that can work well include short teleconferences, webcasts, weekly or monthly e-mails with a short case example or lesson learned, and other similar "short bursts" of content. Ernst & Young, for example, has long used a format called the "19 Minutes," where outside guest speakers are asked to lead a 19-minute conference call with several hundred or more interested E&Y professionals who sign up for the teleconference. E&Y found that when the calls were scheduled for a full hour, there was limited participation; when the calls were compressed to 19 minutes, however, the number of participants grew enormously.

For one client, we videotaped interviews that I conducted with 20 of their most accomplished senior relationship managers. We then edited these conversations down to short (5 to 10 minutes) compilations organized around eight important topics such as listening, building your network, developing c-suite relationships, and so on. Interviews with a few outside experts were also incorporated into the videos. These video clips, which captured the lessons learned from some 400 years of experience, were then loaded onto video iPods and distributed to every relationship manager in the firm, and also made available online. The client's professionals began enthusiastically using the iPods to watch this material on airplane trips or during other downtime.

Supporting Relationship Managers

Relationship managers need to be supported on an ongoing basis. First, they must have the backing of senior management. If relationship managers are viewed as "third wheels" or interlopers by practice and geographic leaders, they will never be very effective. They must have the power to lead key relationships, marshal resources, and have tie-breaking votes on relationship strategy.

Second, relationship managers need to be connected to each other. This can happen in person or virtually through collaboration technologies and online forums. Towers Perrin, for example, has created a very well-developed support network for its 400 client relationship managers. They organize a once-monthly 90-minute conference call (held twice to accommodate different time zones around the world) in which all relationship managers participate. Written materials are circulated in electronic form two days prior to the conference call. During the call, managing partners provide an update on the state of the firm, a win-loss analysis that reviews two recent client successes and one loss, and a report on new intellectual capital that the firm is developing. The calls are taped, so even if people miss one, they have access to the full content. Towers Perrin also supports its network of relationship managers with a highly sophisticated online knowledge management system called TP World, which provides a vast array of resources about the firm's service offerings, research and publishing, best practices, and client case studies.

Measuring and Assessing Relationship Managers

Relationship managers need to be assessed against a balanced score-card of measures that reflect their fundamental goals. As discussed in

Chapter 10 on collaboration, it is difficult, if not impossible, to assign precise sales or origination credit in a professional services firm. To base a relationship manager's compensation purely on client revenue is to discount the efforts of everyone else involved in the relationship. Many people—delivery professionals, other ad hoc experts who are introduced to the client, and senior colleagues who may assist in relationship management—contribute to sustaining the revenue stream from a client. You also need to adjust expectations based on the particular client situation. In a law firm, for example, client revenue might spike upwards during a year when there is a large litigation case that the firm handles for the client, but then decline back down to a base level the next year. This certainly doesn't mean that the responsible partner was a hero one year and incompetent the next. Similarly, a banker could see client revenues jump due to a major acquisition, or wither because the client had no financing activity in a particular year. For a small client with potential, it's reasonable to expect significant revenue and profit growth, whereas in other situations, even the best relationship manager might struggle to keep revenues at the same level as the previous year.

In assessing relationship managers, you need to consider both quantitative and qualitative measures, as well as short- versus long-term impact. If you get the balance right, you'll be able to create a very robust snapshot of a professional's performance. Here are some of the questions you should ask a relationship manager about each client relationship at the end of the year:

Quantitative
- Have we grown our revenues with this client? If not, are we satisfied with the trend in revenues relative to our expectations for this particular client situation?
- Is the relationship meeting our benchmarks in terms of profitability measures and overall commercial management?
- Have we broadened this relationship over time? Have we increased the range of issues we are addressing and the services we are providing?

- Have we deepened this relationship? Do we have a greater share of wallet for our given services?

Qualitative

- Has the relationship manager set clear aspirations and goals for this client relationship?
- Is there a relationship-building strategy in place?
- Are we working with the right level of management for this client? Have we built relationships with key economic buyers?
- Is the relationship manager considered a leader in the eyes of the client? Does the client believe that the relationship manager adds value, is a thought leader, and is the go-to person for issues, concerns, and needs that they may have in regards to the overall relationship?
- Has the relationship manager built a team and been an effective team leader? Is this a client relationship that other professionals want to work on?
- Has the relationship manager been an effective ambassador for the firm, in terms of bringing the best the firm can offer to this client? Is he a door opener or a gate keeper?
- If the relationship manager had to be moved elsewhere, or were unable to continue working, who could take her place?
- Has this relationship created intellectual capital for the firm?

Striking a balance between short- and long-term measures is essential but difficult, because of the intense quarterly and yearly focus on financial results that characterizes many firms. In Chapter 10 on collaboration, we'll look in more detail at how some firms have handled this delicate balance. ERM, for example, uses two separate balanced scorecards for a key group of 50 partners. One scorecard focuses on achievement of short-term financial results, and it drives cash bonuses. A second set of measures focuses on long-term developmental goals, such as recruiting, new skill development, and building long-term client relationships, and it drives stock awards. Together, these scorecards help create a balanced focus on both the short- and long-term needs of the firm.

Conclusion

The relationship manager plays a fundamental role in developing and sustaining Level 6 trusted client partnerships, and you need to create

Hire Them

- Emotional intelligence
- Relationship orientation
- Team player *and* leader
- Curiosity and breadth

Develop Them

- Career management
- Coaching and mentoring
- Professional development

Support Them

- Senior management backing
- Decision-making authority
- Strong internal connections
- Tools and systems

Assess and Reward Them

- Short term—financial
- Long term—growth
- Team based

FIGURE 9.3 **The Client Leadership Pipeline**

a systematic client leadership talent pipeline to ensure you will have a sufficient number of these individuals available to drive your future revenue growth. Some professionals undoubtedly have more natural talent for the role than others, but just about everyone can improve their skills and become more effective in leading client relationships. This entire development process is summarized in Figure 9.3.

Ultimately, you have to go beyond developing capable client relationship managers and create a cultural ethos where the relationship management role is one that the *most talented* professionals in your organization aspire to. Managing a firm's most important client relationships should, in terms of organizational status and compensation, be on par with other senior, internal leadership positions. It should be seen as a prized role, not a stepping-stone to something better.

10

Strategy Eight: Promoting Collaboration

Creating a Whole That Is Greater Than the Sum of the Parts

A Tale of Two Firms

When Lou Gerstner became IBM's CEO in 1993, he took the helm of an iconic American company that had lost its way. It had become internally focused, its business units did not collaborate with each other, and customers were crying out for help to run the complex equipment and systems that IBM sold them. Gerstner oversaw a dramatic shift in the strategy and culture of the company, instilling a client-centered, collaborative ethos throughout its ranks. IBM has subsequently thrived, and today it is a leader in using collaborative technologies to connect employees with each other and with clients. Many of its most innovative ideas, from outsourcing to on-demand consulting, have been inspired directly by clients.

Goldman Sachs, as famous in finance as IBM is in technology, presents an instructive counterpoint to IBM's story. Historically, Goldman Sachs has assiduously cultivated and reinforced a culture of collaboration, unlike competitors such as Morgan Stanley, which has emphasized a "star system" and business units that compete with each other. Goldman's strategy has been to grow organically rather than through lateral hires or by acquisition. Its compelling value proposition—tremendous financial rewards combined with a teamwork environment—is the glue that draws people to the firm and keeps them there. It has a transparent performance evaluation and compensation system that values collaboration and is based on extensive 360-degree reviews. In recent years, however, Goldman has focused more and more of its best people and resources on trading for its own account. In fact, in 2006, when it had a record year and paid many traders and bankers sums in excess of $25 million each, it derived *70 percent of its revenue and profits* from its "Trading" revenue category, which is trading and M&A activity conducted on its own behalf.

While Goldman steadfastly maintains that it puts its clients' interests first, one must believe that this refocusing of intellect and resources toward making money for itself has created a truly conflict-prone landscape. Goldman's famously collaborative culture has shifted focus over the years, from collaborating to serve clients to collaborating to serve . . . well, its partners and its clients. Allegations in the media that Goldman and other investment banks were getting rid of toxic debt from their proprietary trading accounts, while selling the same paper to clients, would—if true—reinforce this notion. Goldman survived the 2008 financial crisis and has converted to a bank holding company in order to be eligible for government bailout money and create a more stable balance sheet. This move may well force the pendulum in the other direction, towards once again being client-centered; only time will tell.

In his book, *The Accidental Investment Banker*, Jonathan Knee—who worked at both Morgan Stanley and Goldman Sachs—puts it this way:

> *My experience . . . made me realize why my romanticized notion of being an old-fashioned relationship banker was so unrealistic. . . . The insurmountable problem . . . was that the fundamental premise of relationship banking was that the banker could deliver the firm for the client. The banker was trusted . . . because there was no question the firm was behind*

him. The RHD experience [a recent deal] *made me realize that neither I nor anyone else could claim that ability anymore. There were simply too many other clients, too many other products, too many other external and internal constituencies.*

IBM, in short, emerged from its crisis by refocusing on the market and using collaboration to better serve its clients. Goldman Sachs' fabled teamwork and collaboration, in contrast, has gradually been channeled more toward creating profits directly for the partnership. While Goldman has emerged battered but intact from the subprime financial crisis, one can argue that the investment banking industry as a whole has suffered from an excessive internal focus that has short-changed clients, and, ultimately damaged or destroyed some major financial institutions. Collaboration must be based on shared values and a shared purpose. That purpose, I believe, has to be helping clients and creating a great institution.

Without an underlying culture of collaboration, it is difficult if not impossible to develop Level 6 client relationships on a consistent basis. You can still become an individual trusted advisor, but you won't be able to identify, coordinate, and deliver your firm's resources and people to the extent that these trusted partnerships demand; nor share information in ways that are essential to firmwide collaboration.

Consequences of Not Collaborating: Feral Children

What do you think would happen if a small child were abandoned in a forest and was able to survive by scavenging fruits, vegetables, and nuts? Suppose you found the child, 5 or 10 years later, still alive. Do you think the child would speak English, or some other language? Would he have constructed shelter for himself and fashioned basic tools? Would he have learned to start a fire to keep warm at night? There are documented cases of so-called feral children who have grown up in the woods without any contact with other humans. Guess what? They resemble animals in their behavior. They sometimes walk on all fours and have a tremendous fear of people. They cannot speak and are usually unable to learn a language even after they are taken back into civilization. They eat with their mouths, not their hands. Their cognitive development is at a preschool level.

In an organization without collaboration and the social networks that foster learning, a newly hired graduate risks becoming a bit like a feral child, forced to grow up on her own without the benefit of all of the accumulated knowledge of the firm. She won't speak the firm's language, properly understand its culture, or have the requisite skills in softer subjects like relationship building. It is our social interaction and collaboration that allows each generation to learn and build on the knowledge of the previous one. Without this, we become like animals in the forest who are reliant solely on primitive instincts, rather than the evolved human beings that represent our potential.

Collaboration sounds like a simple idea, but in practice many things get in the way. A firm's professionals may not know each other well or at all, they may be geographically distant from one another, and they may reside in different practice or industry groups that have their own goals and profit targets. Some firms do a great job of collaborating to serve clients, however, and have overcome the challenges of fostering teamwork in a large, global organization with multiple service offerings.

The Power of Collective Cognition

When you look at apes and children in situations requiring them to put their heads together, a subtle but significant difference emerges. We have observed that children, but not chimpanzees, expect and even demand that others who have committed themselves to a joint activity stay involved and not shirk their duties. Human infants ... gesture and talk in order to share information with others—they want to be helpful. This unprompted sharing of information and attitudes ... ensures that members of a group can pool their knowledge and know who is or is not behaving cooperatively. The free sharing of information also creates the possibility of pedagogy—in which adults impart information by telling and showing. Our nearest primate ancestors do not learn in this manner.

—Michael Tomasello, Co-Director of the Max Planck Institute for Evolutionary Anthropology

Roots of Collaboration

Firmwide collaboration is such an essential ingredient of the *All for One* approach that it's worth briefly exploring the evolutionary origins of collaborative groups. What we're going to find out is intriguing, and it has powerful implications for promoting collaboration in modern services organizations.

During the past million years, the human brain has tripled in size. Humans now have, relative to their body size, the largest and most sophisticated brains of any species on the planet. It has been estimated, for example, that our brains require 20 to 25 percent of our body's energy production.

Why did this breathtaking growth in brain capacity take place? One leading explanation, the ecological dominance/social competition hypothesis (EDSC), posits that human brains grew in order to develop the capabilities required to overcome a hostile environment and form collaborative social groups. By collaborating in a variety of tasks such as hunting, food gathering, defense, construction of shelter, and childcare, humans enhanced their ability to survive and reproduce. In order to live in these sophisticated social groups, we developed a variety of capabilities such as language and advanced reasoning skills. And this is the key point: The imperative to collaborate, and the skills to do so, are hardwired into our brains. We may admire rugged individualism, but we fundamentally have a collaborative nature.

Reciprocal Altruism

Early on, humans learned to practice what scientists call *reciprocal altruism*. In other words, the attitude was "I'll share my deer meat with you this week, if you share yours with me next week." People who shared resources were able to outproduce and outlive those who didn't.

Reciprocal altruism, while critical for survival, presented a number of dilemmas. Cheaters and freeloaders, for example, seriously undermine a system of reciprocal altruism. Primitive humans thus had to evolve mechanisms to deal with some very vexing questions: How do you make sure cheaters are detected and punished? How can you know if someone is being honest when they take from you today and promise to give back next week? How do you keep track of transactions so you know what the score is?

Do these issues sound familiar? They should, because modern services organizations have the same problems. We all benefit if we help each other develop our respective client relationships. But at bonus time, what if someone claims to have contributed far more than his share? These "cheaters" disrupt the organization and pollute the delicate web of relationships that exist between colleagues.

Going back to the dawn of humanity: Humans developed a number of very specialized capabilities to deal with these dilemmas. These included:

- *Advanced facial recognition abilities:* We can consistently remember faces we have not seen for over 30 years, and distinguish between millions of individual faces.
- *The ability to detect cheaters and to identify real altruists:* Research has shown that we can intuitively distinguish between someone who is faking altruism and someone who is sincere. Interestingly, we have a better recall of known cheaters' faces than of altruists' faces—a tribute to the extreme necessity of ferreting out freeloaders.
- *The ability to communicate our values and intentions:* These provide reassurance of our intent to collaborate.
- *Skill at remembering transactions and understanding costs and benefits:* The development of double-entry bookkeeping by the Venetians was no doubt the result of the growth of commerce and greater social complexity.

Cheaters and Altruists

In a collaborative group, it is so important to accurately detect cheaters and altruists that our brains have developed distinct abilities for each. As mentioned, we are particularly good at remembering known cheaters. This is true today as it was a million years ago. One of the worst things you can call someone in any group or organization is a freeloader or a cheat. Studies have shown that when members of a group are administering punishment to cheaters, the reward centers of their brains are activated—no doubt an evolutionary adaptation to encourage the persecution of cheaters. Furthermore, individuals who *stringently* punish cheaters are perceived as being especially strong leaders, and high levels of cooperation emerge in a group when severe punishment is meted out to freeloaders. The implication of this research for service firm leaders is that it's essential to deal forcibly and openly with people who try to cheat the system or exaggerate their contributions.

The last piece of evolutionary science that I'll mention concerns something called Hamilton's Rule. Developed in 1964 by W. D. Hamilton, this rule basically states that our willingness to help or save someone else is a function of how *related* we are to them. Hamilton's Rule was demonstrated through studies of ground squirrels that whistle—and in the process put themselves at risk—to warn other squirrels of danger. Researchers found that the squirrels were far more likely to whistle in order to warn immediate family members than more distant relatives. The challenge in modern services organizations is to create extended "squirrel families," as it were, substituting mutual trust for genetic relatedness.

Implications of Evolutionary Psychology for Modern Organizations

So what does all this mean for building relationships in a modern business community? There are four clear lessons:

1. Humans are by nature collaborative, and firm leadership needs to appeal to and develop this side of its employees' innate character. Demonstrations of reciprocity and selflessness will evoke more of the same behavior in others.
2. It's absolutely critical to recognize and reward those professionals who collaborate, and publicly sanction those who do not. Freeloading undermines the entire culture and cannot be tolerated. Firms need to do a better job of tracking and measuring reciprocity and collaboration.
3. Building trust with a prospective client is an inherently difficult process because we are *hardwired* to be on the lookout for people

trying to take advantage of the system. You have to go out of your way to disprove and belie your client's natural instincts.

4. A key responsibility of management is, metaphorically, to increase the size and loyalty of the firm's "squirrel families" whose members will stick up for each other.

What Gets in the Way: Survey Results

Over the past two years, I have conducted a collaboration survey, entitled "Collaborating to Serve Clients" that has been filled out by 400 client-facing professionals in dozens of different service firms in the United States and Europe. The survey asks participants to rate 14 factors on a scale of 1 to 5, where 1 = This factor impedes collaboration to serve clients, 5 = This factor encourages collaboration, and 3 is neutral. (The public version of this survey is on my web site at www.andrewsobel.com under "Tools").

The four most important factors that respondents cite as *encouraging* collaboration were, in order:

1. Our culture—our underlying values and beliefs (the willingness to help others develop their relationships because it's "the right thing to do")
2. The example top management sets
3. Client account leadership to drive collaboration around key relationships
4. Our organization structure

The ratings were consistent across service firms. The only exception to this list was observed among several very large financial institutions, where "Our organization structure" was rated as something that *impeded* collaboration to serve clients, rather than encouraged it. This is not surprising: A large global bank, for example, might have 100 offices and 10 or 15 major product groups around the world, and their organization structures are very complex and often unwieldy.

The four most important factors that *impede* collaboration were:

1. The availability of a budget to support other professionals in the relationship.
2. Measurement and rewards: The extent to which our people feel that if they spend time on someone else's client and are team players, they will be recognized and rewarded.
3. The availability of time to invest in colleagues' relationships.
4. The availability of shared information about client relationships.

> We constantly try to reinforce a culture of collaboration. At partner meetings, we emphasize how people have collaborated to win clients, and we identify and celebrate "heroes" who have built effective teams and role-modeled strong collaboration. Every one of our principals must develop an annual plan that includes a section on collaboration and what they have specifically done to collaborate with others. We ask them, "Who are the main people you've impacted and made a difference to?" The plan has a values section which includes things like integrity, collaboration, commitment, and respect.
>
> **—Jaideep Bajaj, CEO, ZS Associates**

I find these results intriguing although not entirely surprising. People recognize the strong role culture has in driving collaboration; however, I think they tend to overestimate how collaborative and client-focused their own cultures really are. In fact, if they had a truly collaborative culture and if helping others in their relationships was "the right thing to do," then I don't believe the first two barriers—lack of budget and insufficient rewards—would matter much. The other positives—the example management sets and client account leadership—also make sense because these are powerful drivers of collaborative behavior.

Measurement and rewards, which we'll discuss later in this chapter, is a troublesome subject when it comes to collaboration. Many professionals tell me that their management says that *teamwork* is important, but then at the end of the year the rewards go to the individual contributors who have *sold the most business*, and teamwork goes out the window. I believe the best organizations are able to balance the rewards for teamwork versus those for individual performance. It is essential to a healthy culture to recognize and reward teamwork, compensate the best individual contributors, and also ferret out the freeloaders—people who claim more credit than they deserve.

Strategies to Build a Collaborative Culture

The strategies and actions that encourage collaboration fall into three categories—*Inculcation*, *Institutionalization*, and *Infrastructure:*

1. *Inculcation* refers to activities that allow you to set an example for others and impart collaborative values. To inculcate means "to teach and impress by frequent repetitions or admonitions." There are key moments in the life of your organization when you have the chance to role-model, reinforce, and even directly teach the values and beliefs that underpin collaborative behavior and teamwork.

2. *Institutionalization* refers to the development of management systems and processes that support collaboration—things like recruiting, measurement and rewards, and formal organization structure.

3. *Infrastructure* comprises collaboration technologies, knowledge management systems, and even office space—the hard-wired elements of a firm that are increasingly helpful in enabling collaboration. The ubiquity of the Internet and the rapid development of collaborative software tools have opened up a whole new world of possibilities for engaging and connecting professionals who may be spread around the globe.

Grouped under these three headings, I have set out a number of best practices and ideas for how you can encourage and support a client-focused, collaborative culture.

Inculcation Strategies

Senior Management Example

When leaders of the firm set the example and model the collaboration they seek, it sends a powerful message about expected behaviors. James Bardrick, for example, is co-head of the Global Industrials banking group for Citigroup. Certain clients in countries like Japan and India are not within his P&L, even though the interconnections between the largest industrial conglomerates around the world beg for an integrated approach to marketing and service delivery. So although he doesn't benefit from the revenue that is generated through these clients, Bardrick still expends invaluable personal time to make marketing trips to these countries and help his colleagues there develop their local client relationships. Here's his practical view about how firm leaders can role-model a collaborative culture:

> *What doesn't work very well is what I call the "state visit." Under this scenario, one of the bank's top executives makes his annual visit to Japan. He calls up our local office and says, "I'd really like to visit some of our most important clients while I'm there." This immediately creates a burden on both the local relationship manager and on the client, who now has to find room in his schedule for a high-level meeting that he may not actually perceive as adding much value or helping him with his short-term priorities. The client feels pressured to say nice things, and the local bankers are worried about whether or not the client will say them. A better approach is to put yourself in the relationship manager's shoes and think about their needs. I ask myself, "Based on the work we're doing today here in EMEA, which client of theirs could we really add value to? Can we share some valuable perspectives gleaned from our conversations with politicians, investors, customers, and so on?" I like to call the local coverage officer and say, "I believe we can help with this particular client of yours. We've got some interesting messages and insights we can share with them. What do you think?" It's all about showing an interest in them and their clients, and bringing value to their relationships. Of course, you have to come across as someone who is representing the whole firm, who is an ambassador—not someone focused on his or her own special interests. Finally, there has to be a commitment to follow up. Are you going to actually do the three or four things you agreed on at the end of your visit?*

Sir Win Bischoff, Citigroup's chairman and Bardrick's ultimate boss, has reinforced the messages of client focus and collaboration across boundaries by making himself freely available to visit Citigroup clients around the world. He tells us, "I have made it clear to the organization that I am available to meet with our clients anywhere in the world, at any time. In particular I want to be brought in to help in the most *difficult* situations, not the easy ones where the client is completely happy." Recently, Bardrick was able to use Sir Win to finally get a meeting—after many unsuccessful tries over the last year—with the chief executive of one of the largest companies in Europe.

At Bain & Company, Worldwide Managing Director John Ellis always describes major client proposal wins by talking about the members of the team—not the individual partner who led the sales effort. Through Ellis' communications, he constantly reinforces the importance of teamwork, and in particular of a maxim that permeates the Bain organization: "A Bain partner never lets another Bain partner down." It's a simple phrase that is in truth a deeply held cultural value at the firm. It is reinforced through inculcation—through constant role-modeling by Ellis and other senior partners. For Bain, it starts with the recruiting process. Wendy Miller, a Bain director and head of marketing, tells us "The consultants we hire have invariably been at the top of their class academically. But once at Bain, they cannot try to outshine their peers. During our recruiting, we ask a lot of questions about working on teams and teamwork. Does the candidate say 'I' all the time or 'we'? Can they cite specific examples of being able to work effectively on teams?"

At Lloyds Banking Group, which is one of the top 25 banks in the world in terms of assets, Corporate Banking CEO Diana Brightmore-Armour (introduced in Chapter 1) leads the bank's efforts with clients that range from middle-market, local companies to large multinationals. Since joining the bank, she and her team have dramatically grown their corporate business, and U.K. finance directors have consistently voted Lloyds as "Bank of the Year." One of her main strategies has been to promote teamwork and collaboration across the bank's various product groups and account management organizations, a real challenge because of the wide array of products and services that the bank offers and the geographic dispersion of the thousands of employees who service its corporate clients. One of the programs Brightmore-Armour has developed is called "Delivering Deals Together." Every quarter there is a major recognition event called Deal of the Quarter, culminating in the Deal of the Year at the end of the year. For each of these, the bank's top management is present, and the entire team that worked on the deal, including the account manager and every specialist who may have been part of the effort, comes up on stage in front of an audience of hundreds of corporate bankers. These and other programs have reinforced the teamwork and client focus that Brightmore-Armour has been trying to inculcate in the Lloyds Banking Group organization.

When I first joined Booz Allen Hamilton in 1975, client relationships were much simpler. We had a few CEO relationships, and you worked these by having lunch, setting priorities, bringing in a few expert colleagues, and solving problems. If you were my client, I *owned* you from the firm perspective. Now, clients are wrestling with huge strategic problems that combine elements of strategy, IT, operations, and change management. My first step was convincing our partners that no one individual has the talent to fully serve a client's needs—that we needed a team approach. In 1995, we made a very conscious decision to build a team-based culture. We recommitted to a compensation system based on a common bonus structure for each partner level, to avoid driving individualistic behavior. We also had to change some partners—five years later, one-half of the original partners from our government business in 1995 had left or been asked to leave. Some of them were just too attuned to the old culture. I personally have to constantly role-model our collaborative cultural values, to hold myself above reproach. At every forum, I talk about our core values. At partners meetings, I will sometimes have partners give testimonials about how our culture has supported the development of major client relationships. I try to demonstrate our values every day in my own behavior.

—Ralph Shrader, Chairman and CEO, Booz Allen Hamilton

Senior management role-modeling is a phrase we hear often, but it only can be brought to life when the firm's leaders are willing to consistently communicate and demonstrate the collaborative, client-centered behaviors that are needed to underpin the development of long-term, institutional client relationships.

Other Opportunities for Inculcation

The inculcation process starts when new hires come aboard. The nature and quality of their experiences in the first months of working with the firm will have a strong influence on the values and beliefs they ultimately adopt and live out as employees. Accenture, for example, is famous for its lengthy and comprehensive onboarding process. Historically, Accenture has hired a large number of college graduates who have no prior work experience, rather than MBAs who have already worked at other organizations. Every new Accenture consultant spends several months going through a comprehensive training and acculturation program held at training campuses Accenture has created around the world. Many of these sessions focus on learning technical skills, but there is also a strong emphasis on teaching teamwork and collaboration through exercises, case studies, and role plays.

Ongoing training and professional development events are also important opportunities to reinforce the collaborative values and practices that you first teach during onboarding. I find that experience sharing around client relationships, either through formal case studies or possibly a panel discussion, are excellent vehicles to showcase a firm's best practices for collaborating to serve clients and to inculcate younger professionals with important values like teamwork.

One of the mistakes some firms make is to outsource their training to external companies, or at least not to have their partners participate when outsiders conduct it. It's hard to "teach" your cultural values, but people can learn them by listening to stories and examples and hearing how different situations would be handled by more experienced professionals.

Institutionalization Strategies

The firm's leaders are the starting point for a collaborative, client-centered culture, and have to actively role model the values by being team players themselves and reinforcing the preeminence of clients. Next, you have to institutionalize collaboration through the organization's formal processes, systems, and structures. I have found four of these are particularly important and sometimes contentious: Measurement and reward, team management, firm organization structure, and recruiting.

Measurement and Reward

One of the most frequent laments I hear from client-facing professionals is that they would like to focus *more* on long-term relationship building, but their firm's compensation system does not sufficiently recognize and reward such investment. The measurement and reward system is indeed important as an enabler of collaborative behavior, but at the same time its impact must be put in context. Other researchers have reported that compensation that is strongly individually driven gets in the way of teamwork, although compensation that is calibrated to foster teamwork has only a mildly positive effect. People collaborate with each other for many reasons, in short, and most of them probably have little to do with money; but money can pit them against one another.

In a professional services firm or a financial services institution, there are invariably two different tensions that a compensation system must recognize and balance:

1. *The short-term versus the long-term:* For example, achieving short-term financial results versus investing to build long-term client relationships that may not pay off for a year or two.
2. *The individual versus the team (or the firm):* For example, focusing on one's own billability or individual sales versus taking steps to keep others busy or to help colleagues with their relationships.

Measurement and reward in a services firm is more problematic than in an industrial corporation because most professionals are seller-doers—the typical partner in a professional firm, for example, spends time on many different activities, including recruiting, business development, and project delivery. Don Lowman, a managing director at Towers Perrin and leading expert on executive compensation, puts it this way: "In a professional firm, it's impossible to attribute sales,

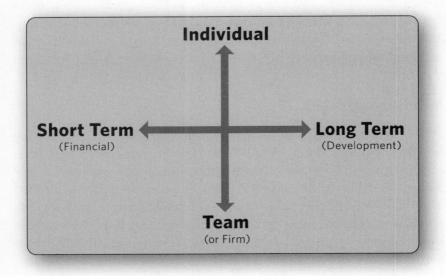

FIGURE 10.1   Compensation Tensions

in any kind of precise manner, to an individual. How do you account for the legacy you may have inherited from previous consultants who built up the relationship you are now managing? How do you accurately divide credit up among a large team of individuals who all made a contribution to a new sale?"

If you look at services firms in general, they tend to fall into three broad groups when it comes to how they address these different tensions (see Figure 10.1):

1. *Team-based with a common bonus pool:* Firms like Booz Allen Hamilton and Egon Zehnder, for example, pay partners at similar levels (or tenure, in Zehnder's case) exactly the same. Law firms, traditionally, have also had fairly lock-step compensation systems. The argument is that this approach maximizes teamwork and collaboration.

2. *Short-term, individually driven:* Despite the example of Egon Zehnder, some executive search firms pay 50 percent of each search fee to the individual partner. Business development professionals are often paid on a straight, individual production basis.

3. *Balanced between short/long term and individual/team:* Many firms are moving toward a balanced approach, which takes into account quantitative and qualitative accomplishments as well as individual and team success.

ERM's Balanced Scorecard

A very successful and innovative example of a compensation approach that balances the short term and the long term has been developed by ERM, the world's leading environmental consulting firm. In the Introduction, I mentioned that I have found excellent best practices in both large and small firms—ERM is an example of the latter, not just in this area but also in using collaboration technologies. ERM has 3,500 staff, including 400 partners, and the firm operates in 41 countries around the world. Over the past several years, ERM has grown at a much faster rate than either the consulting industry as a whole or its direct competitors—a tribute to a focused change effort by senior management. Pete Regan, ERM's chairman and former CEO, has personally led, together with current CEO John Alexander, the firm's efforts to become a client-focused, collaborative firm.

Several years ago, ERM embarked on a journey of strategic transformation. Its goal was to substantially increase revenue and profit growth by improving collaboration among its offices and practice areas, driving service excellence into every client engagement, and building broad-based, institutional client relationships anchored in senior management. To give impetus to the new strategy, a guiding coalition of 50 senior partners was established. Each of these partners is evaluated on the basis of a two-part balanced scorecard, which I briefly mentioned in Chapter 9. The first page of the balanced scorecard contains three to five goals, which are focused on operations and delivering this year's budget. Everyone's sales goals add up to ERM's overall revenue budget. This part of the scorecard is highly quantitative, and partners are scored individually, based on 100 points, on how well they achieve their goals.

The second page of the scorecard focuses on growth and development. It is tailored to each partner's own challenges and development needs, and lists qualitative goals in five areas: operations, service excellence, key clients, practices and innovation, and people. Each of these areas represents a firmwide theme that has a champion assigned at

> As we mapped out our growth strategy, we identified a group of 50 senior partners who we felt could be instrumental in leading the changes we knew we had to make in the organization. We were very clear and direct with this group about their responsibilities: They would have to both deliver on this year's results *and* build the business for the long term. It was an absolute requirement to grapple with both. When we recruited partners into this group, this was a condition of joining—it was not negotiable to not accomplish both of these goals. This led to the creation of a balanced scorecard for each of these 50 partners, as a means to focus them equally on the short and long term.
>
> **—Pete Regan, Executive Chairman, ERM**

the firm level. Each partner's growth and development scorecard, in other words, ties in to key institutional initiatives just as the financial goals from the first page link to ERM's overall budget. This second page is directly relevant to the issue of collaboration because many of the growth and development goals can only be achieved by working with and through others in the ERM organization.

An extensive process is undertaken to evaluate each partner's scorecard. First, individuals score themselves. Then, page one is reviewed by his or her boss, by the relevant business unit head, and the regional CEO. Regan and Alexander, the chairman and CEO, then also go through them. There may be modifications along the way as the scorecard goes up and down the organization. The five "theme" leaders at the firm level review page two, which contains the growth and development goals. Again, Regan and Alexander also review these. There is an extremely high degree of transparency to this process: Everyone's completed balanced scorecard, including the evaluations, is posted online and can be read by anyone in the group of 50.

Achievement against page one goals is the basis for the partners' cash bonus, whereas achievement against the growth and development goals drives the distribution of stock. If the stock is held for several years, it will equal the amount of the cash bonus, or possibly exceed it over time. Partners may have quite divergent results based on this balanced scorecard: Several, for example, have had poor years in terms of financial results, and gotten a lousy cash bonus; but they have done well against their growth and development goals and received a generous stock grant.

ERM's compensation system for this key group of partners is effective for many reasons. It clearly and separately addresses the short term and the long term. It differentiates between cash bonuses and stock grants, which can grow in value over time. It forces each partner to have a balanced focus on meeting this year's budget but also building for the future. Management is very involved in the process itself and the system is highly transparent, both of which contribute to trust in the outcomes.

ERM has also implemented an innovative approach to *measuring* collaboration in the organization, using a modified version of Net Promoter Score (NPS). NPS, which I discuss in detail in Chapter 11, asks your clients one simple question: "On a scale of 0 to 10, how likely are you to recommend our firm to a colleague or friend?" ERM uses this same methodology *internally* to gauge how collaborative and effective individual offices and partners are. Each year, ERM surveys its partners and asks them how likely it is that they would recommend each of their major offices to a colleague or friend. This process has had a huge impact on the organization. It turned out that ERM's partners would recommend some offices very enthusiastically—but were somewhat negative about others. ERM management quietly shared these "net promoter scores" with each office head around the world, and the results were *dramatic*. These data have cut through the clutter and caused the heads of the low-rated offices to reflect on why their colleagues would not promote them to others; and they have actively reached out to other office heads to understand what they can do to be better partners and collaborators.

Team Structure and Management

There are a number of excellent books on how to build strong teams, and I'm not going to repeat all of that wisdom here. I will, however, highlight a couple of my own key findings about team effectiveness that are particularly relevant to a services firm environment:

1. *Differences spark creativity*. Just as John Lennon's and Paul McCartney's radical personality differences combined to produce

an unparalleled creative explosion in pop music, a diversity of experiences, skills, and temperaments will greatly enhance a team's creativity and innovation.

2. *You need the right mix of deep generalists and specialists.* Deep generalists are those professionals who have added breadth to their depth. They have broad business knowledge, strong interpersonal skills, and a deep understanding of the client organization. Specialists are more narrow, "branded experts" in a particular service, function, or industry. When you get the mix right between these two types, you can build a powerful, value-adding team. Mixed teams always beat homogenous ones.

3. *The best brains don't make the best team members.* Professor Lynda Gratton's research shows that the higher the level of education among team members, the more likely the team is to disintegrate into unproductive conflicts. Dr. Meredith Belbin conducted the original studies on this phenomenon in the 1970s, finding that so-called "Apollo" teams with the smartest individuals on them almost always came in last during team competitions. Members of these teams spent most of their time trying to convince others of their point of view while failing to listen to their colleagues' ideas and perspectives.

4. *Team members need face time to build trust.* Virtual teams can be quite effective in tackling R&D or engineering tasks. However, client-facing teams need to build up a reservoir of trust and familiarity that requires real, live face time, especially if they have to make a live presentation to a client. By the time the young Beatles made their first U.S. appearance on the Ed Sullivan show in February 1964, for example, they had played together onstage in Hamburg's red light district for well over 1,500 hours, and performed 293 live shows at the Cavern Club in Liverpool.

The Beatles Principles

The Beatles sold over one billion records and forever changed the face of pop music. As a team, they were able to create a *whole* that was greater than *the sum of the parts:* Together, they created better music than they ever could have or did as solo artists. What did they do to accomplish this? We can draw a number of important principles from the way they worked as a team and collaborated to write their chart-topping songs:

Principle 1: *Face Time.* When the Beatles appeared on the Ed Sullivan show in early 1964, they seemed like an overnight success. But in fact three of the four Beatles had met in 1957, and by the time of their historic appearance they had spent thousands of hours playing together in clubs in the United Kingdom and Germany.

Principle 2: *Evolving Your Songs.* Every new record the Beatles released represented a dramatic evolution of their music, and as a result their fan base grew ever larger. They explored new themes, musical styles, unorthodox instruments (e.g., the Sitar), and new arrangements, producing an extraordinary variety of songs. The band managed to embrace and integrate each member's unique musical interests into their recordings.

Principle 3: *Brands within a Brand.* The Beatles were never a lead singer with a backing band but rather an ensemble of four equal (at least publicly) musicians. As a group, they were a world-renowned brand, but each individual Beatle also had a public persona and reputation. They worked at this: On almost every Beatles record, for example, John and Paul wrote a song for Ringo to perform, so that he could have his own platform with the public.

Principle 4: *Put Opposites Together to Spur Creativity.* John Lennon and Paul McCartney together wrote most of the Beatles' songs, and you could not have found two individuals who had a more different temperament and character. Paul was optimistic, a perfectionist, and loved the Beatles' fame; John was equally creative but also cynical and angry, and he grew to hate their notoriety. Their strengths and weaknesses were complementary, often creating sparks, but the result is the most valuable song catalog in the world.

(*Note:* For an in-depth article on The Beatles Principles, go to http://andrewsobel.com/articles.)

A Client Team Approach

Law firms have to overcome some particular barriers in trying to build Level 6 client relationships. Historically, they have usually operated as a series of loosely connected practice areas or departments; and even within those practices, individual partners have run their own fiefdoms.

Given this balkanization, creating a whole that is greater than the sum of the parts is a real challenge for most law firms. Fulbright & Jaworski, an international law firm that is a market leader in litigation and energy, has developed a strong client team approach and process that has yielded significant results. Large consulting and accounting firms have generally been ahead of law firms in having a systematic approach to client relationship management, but Fulbright & Jaworski's experience holds some lessons for everyone.

About five years ago, Fulbright & Jaworski implemented a formal client team approach to serving its largest clients. Initially, it selected 25 clients to be the focus of the program. The firm provided training and some planning tools to each relationship partner and gave the client teams a fairly broad mandate to develop and grow each relationship. The client team program was successful in its first year, and it created a focus on serving these clients with renewed vigor and bringing the entire firm's expertise and resources to bear on them.

Several issues, however, prevented the client team program from reaching its full potential. First, data about each client was spread all over the firm's information systems. It took a long time for each relationship partner to even discover which lawyers, across the firm's many offices, were working for the client or a distant subsidiary because legal work can be notoriously fragmented.

A second issue was commitment, on the part of the relationship partners, to execute an agreed program of activities such as holding monthly team meetings, creating a formal client plan, and involving other practice areas in the relationship. Some partners signed up for the client team program, but then didn't follow through because they didn't make the time for it or perhaps were not clear about what they were supposed to do differently.

Fulbright & Jaworski developed several solutions to address these problems and bring the program to yet another level. First, they created an online information portal, called "MySite," for use by the relationship partners and team members that participate in the client team program. This portal aggregates a wide array of information about each client. It includes extensive, historical financial information, the names of every lawyer—in any location in the world—who is billing to the client or any of its subsidiaries, fees by practice area and office, and much more. It also aggregates up-to-date company, market, and competitive information about the client. MySite, which is now being upgraded to provide a whole new level of knowledge management support to client teams, solved the problem of information flows.

Second, Executive Committee Chair Steve Pfeiffer began to regularly highlight the client team program, and the collaboration that it promotes, at every possible opportunity—at partners' meetings, in firmwide communications, and also with clients.

Third, to create more mentorship and learning, Fulbright & Jaworski assigned a senior partner to become the "coach" of each relationship partner in the program. This approach is analogous to the "Seniors" program started by Citigroup. These coaches typically will speak with the relationship partner once or twice a month, and provide advice and ideas on how to grow the relationship and draw in the right resources from across the firm.

The final change that the firm made was to create a more formal screening process for entry into the client team program, including a written compact that each new relationship partner has to agree to. This compact clearly sets out the roles and responsibilities for both the firm and the individual partner. There is a degree of self-selection, and partners are therefore more motivated to follow through.

Fulbright & Jaworski's client team program has developed into an effective vehicle to promote cross-office and cross-departmental collaboration. Today, it embraces over 50 major clients, and by almost any metric you choose—total revenues, revenue growth, referrals, level of relationships with senior decision makers, and so on—it has been a major success. The firm has also noticed that if a relationship partner retires or leaves the firm, the client's relationship with Fulbright & Jaworski doesn't end precipitously but rather will continue on, supported by a broad web of connections that have been developed with a variety of the firm's lawyers.

Organization Structure

Most services firms, in formulating their organization structure, have to balance three essential focal points: geography, industry, and practice groups or service offerings. Overlaid against these may be functions such as business development or training. It's safe to say that many firms have expended a huge amount of time and energy trying to figure out the right balance between these different dimensions. Office heads argue that a local geographic presence is essential to serve as a home base for professionals and to drive local marketing and networking initiatives. Service offering leaders want to have direct access to clients and drive their own business development efforts, because they feel that only *their* people have the specialist knowledge required to effectively sell their services. Industry practice heads think that everyone should be in an industry group, because these days, deep industry knowledge is essential in order to be able to sell and deliver any type of service. Of course, they are all right, and the balancing act that firm leadership faces is to create an organization that respects all of these perspectives.

In calibrating your organization structure, two central dilemmas must be overcome. First, most senior executives don't think about their business problems using the organizational constructs of their outside advisors. If I am the head of human resources (HR) for a large corporation, I may be thinking about how to get greater employee alignment around my company's strategy, how to increase employee engagement and loyalty, or how to create a more flexible workforce. These problems don't line up easily against typical HR consulting offerings. So whoever is acting for the firm in these discussions must—regardless of their background or role—represent the entire firm's capabilities and take a client-centered, solutions-oriented perspective on the client's issues.

This is a difficult shift, and to be successful you need a cadre of Deep Generalists who are broad, strategic thinkers. You also need to have the mindset that when you have early stage, issues-based conversations with clients, you must represent the firm and not just a particular practice area. This concept was an early focus of James O. McKinsey, the founder of McKinsey & Company. He believed it was essential for every McKinsey consultant to take the "top management perspective," and he obsessively drilled this into all of his up-and-coming young professionals. Not surprisingly, McKinsey consultants tend to think about the client service team as their most elemental organizational unit.

The second dilemma is that the client service team as an ad hoc organizational unit gets lost in the discussion about geography versus industry, and a culture develops where professionals aspire to "manage" an office or practice as opposed to leading the firm's most important client relationships. I am familiar with some professional services firms whose senior management spends almost no time with clients, and where partners aspire to join "firm management" and essentially get out of the business of serving clients. This is a formula for slow growth and stagnation. The most vibrant firms I know are ones where senior partners and firm leaders spend large amounts of time with their clients and therefore always have their finger on the pulse of the marketplace.

In summary, here are some considerations to reflect on if you want your organization structure to support firmwide collaboration and client focus:

- Think of the client delivery team as the most fundamental organizational unit at your firm.
- Set the expectation that professionals at every level—including those in firm leadership—have to spend a significant amount of time with clients.
- Establish an ethos where leading major client relationships is hierarchically on par with, if not more desirable than, other senior leadership positions in the organization.
- Try to separate organizational units (e.g., an office or industry group) with permeable membranes, not brick walls. Accountability is good, but you must ensure that there are incentives—not disincentives—to moving people and resources to where they can most benefit clients.

Recruiting

Southwest Airlines is renowned for a business model that combines excellent customer service with low fares. I was curious about why Southwest's flight crews seem to have so much fun at their jobs, and so I recently decided to do some research of my own. I began my quest on an evening flight from Albuquerque to Los Angeles. I asked one of the upbeat flight attendants the following question: "I'm curious. You're all so friendly. You seem to genuinely enjoy working together.

How do you do it? Do you have some kind of special training program that teaches this to your people? Do you get extra pay based on the number of jokes you tell or how well you collaborate together?"

Her answer was simple: "Oh, none of that. It's really simple: We just hire people who are like this. We have a very extensive recruitment process, and we look for people who are outgoing, funny, and are team players."

I have asked the same question on other Southwest flights, and the answer is always the same: "We hire people who are friendly and outgoing."

In his article, "The One-Firm Firm," author David Maister cites a highly selective recruitment process and a grow-your-own people strategy as two of the characteristics of firms that maximize the trust and loyalty that their people feel toward each other and the firm (*Sloan Management Review*, October 15, 1985). Today, many firms are also employing a lateral hiring strategy, and so the search for cultural fit has become even more important. Firms that have very cohesive cultures, like McKinsey, Goldman Sachs, Booz Allen Hamilton, and Egon Zehnder, don't hire a lot of lateral partners, and at any level of recruitment they will often subject candidates to 15, 20, or even 25 interviews to ensure the right fit.

Infrastructure

There are several different types of infrastructure that can be used to support a culture of collaboration, including, for example, office space and telecommunications services. My main focus in this section, however, is on Web-based platforms, applications, and technologies that enable knowledge sharing and collaboration to serve clients. It is in this area that I think the most dramatic change is occurring.

A new generation of collaboration and knowledge-sharing technologies are transforming the way professionals learn, interact with each other, and collaborate on a variety of critical tasks. They are going to influence how people develop and set firm strategies, create intellectual capital, build their internal networks, deliver services, and manage client relationships. No one can predict exactly how these changes will evolve, but I am convinced that firms that do not embrace these new collaboration tools will be left behind.

Many of these platforms leverage what is often described as Web 2.0. Broadly speaking, Web 2.0 refers to a new generation of Web applications that allow people to collaborate and share information online and that encourage user interaction and communication. Another term being used for these applications inside of a company is Enterprise 2.0.

What are we talking about? The following examples give you an idea of the range of innovative applications that have emerged to facilitate different types of collaboration:

- *Community crowd sourcing:* Kluster.com is a Web-based service that helps to organize communities of interest, which then collaborate to solve specific problems and come up with new ideas in areas such as product development, education, and advertising and marketing.
- *Online Innovation:* Mystarbucksidea.com is a web site created by Starbucks to capture the ideas and opinions of its employees and customers. The site also allows employees and customers to vote on proposed new products and services. A similar example is Dell IdeaStorm, a Dell community web site that gathers opinions and ideas and also has become a portal for individual customer forums.
- *Interactive communication:* Comcast, for example, now monitors online complaints that appear on blogs, message boards, and social networks, and responds directly to the customer.
- *Co-creating strategy:* The Paris public transportation authority, called RATP, set up a web site called "You-and-the-RATP." It began as a site to collect customer complaints, but evolved into a discussion forum about RATP operations and strategy. It resulted in a three-year strategic plan, which was based on over 3,000 proposals from RATP employees and passengers.
- *Crowd sourced R&D:* Cisco, for example, has started the "Cisco I-Prize," which is a contest to come up with a new, marketable business concept for Cisco. The winning team can be hired by

Cisco and share a $250,000 signing bonus, and it promises to invest $10 million over three years to develop the idea. More than 1,100 new ideas have been submitted to Cisco. GoldCorp, a Canadian mining company, first made this practice famous when it put all of its geological data into the public domain and offered substantial rewards to anyone who could help it identify gold deposits on its properties. Called "The Challenge," the effort was hugely successful, and outsiders have successfully identified the location of huge quantities of gold in locations where Goldcorp's own engineers had failed to find anything.

- *Prediction markets:* Companies are finding that the wisdom of the crowd can indeed be more acute than a small group of experts. BestBuy, for example, has started to poll employees about the chances for success of new product launches. It has found that its rank-and-file employees are better able to forecast sales for a new product than its own internal forecasting unit staffed by marketing specialists.

Chapter 12 cites further instances of these innovative uses of collaboration technologies as they pertain in particular to creating a unique client experience. Many of these examples have been identified by my friend and colleague Francis Gouillart, who heads the Experience Co-Creation Partnership and teaches at the University of Michigan Business School.

The possible uses of these new applications are unlimited, and their potential to facilitate collaboration is huge. They can allow a firm to:

- Facilitate rapid communications and collaboration between members of a geographically dispersed, client-facing team.
- Gain widespread input into the design of new service offerings, and even forecast their chances of success.
- Involve clients in previously hidden internal processes like service innovation and client account planning.
- Build vibrant internal networks that enhance the flow of information and ideas.

How are services firms using these new applications? I have already mentioned several examples, including Towers Perrin's knowledge management system, TP World, that aggregates a huge amount of easily accessible information for its client relationship managers; Fulbright & Jaworski's MySite, which is a similar tool for client teams; and ZS Associates' use of social networking technology to create communities of interest around its growing practice areas. But the best example of a true Enterprise 2.0 approach, which combines many different elements of these innovative applications, is ERM's new Minerva knowledge management system. Minerva has already won several awards, and it has quickly become the central artery of communications and collaboration within the geographically far-flung ERM organization.

Like many global services firms, ERM's employees are spread around the globe in 145 offices, and it offers clients a number of distinct environmental consulting services, ranging from strategy development to cleaning up contaminated sites. Minerva, which was developed over a nine-month period, is based on information science expert Brenda Dervin's Sense-Making Methodology. The system has four main goals:

1. Increase social networking of staff worldwide and reduce their feeling of separation and isolation by linking practitioners working in similar areas.

2. Leverage the firm's collective knowledge and make resources, tools, methodologies, proposals, and documents available on a global basis.

3. Improve cross-office collaboration to serve the needs of global clients.

4. Support internal communications and integrate new hires into the organization by making corporate resources and messages easily accessible.

Before I describe what Minerva does, let me give you a practical example of how it has transformed the ability of ERM's client teams to collaborate as they serve their clients. A relationship manager in charge of a major, global client came to Bonnie Cheuk, the head of Knowledge and Information for ERM, and lamented how difficult it was for her client team to work effectively together, given that the team members were spread around the world in five different time zones. "It's hard to have meetings together, it's difficult to collaborate on reports and proposals, and even day-to-day communications are awkward," she told Cheuk.

Minerva has allowed this client team to exploit a "Wiki" collaboration tool to jointly collaborate on client reports from remote locations. All of the client documents are now stored online and available to any team member at any time. Consultants can instant message each other for rapid-fire communications. The relationship manager can hold virtual meetings online and team members can post questions for each other. They can also instantly access ERM intellectual capital and the names of relevant experts when they are discussing new issues with the client or need access to specialist knowledge. Every team member has a personal site and can start a blog if they so desire. Client successes can be shared on a "Client Wins" section of the Minerva homepage. And, when and if the project closes down, the relationship manager decides which documents can and should be shared globally and these are then made accessible to other ERM staff. Minerva has unequivocally increased the effectiveness of this client team and transformed the ability of its members to collaborate anytime, anywhere.

A listing of Minerva's main features may be helpful to you. They are:

- *My Site:* a personal site for all employees containing contact and expertise information, photos, a resume, and, optionally, personal blog.
- *Integration with instant messaging:* An employee can initiate an online conversation simply by clicking on his or her name.
- *Operating company sites:* Each of ERM's 40 main operating units around the world has a portal for practitioners to share news, resources, and collaborate with each other.
- *A document library:* This enables any employee to share local work globally (after being cleared with appropriate communities of practice).

- *An unmoderated "Global Announcement" feature*: This enables employees to easily share news, introduce new hires, and send out global announcements (these replace "global e-mails" to all staff).
- *Online project sites:* These enable team members to collaborate with colleagues from other offices by sharing news, managing project documentation, assigning tasks, and discussing business issues.
- *An ERM Wiki Wiki:* This enables rapid collaboration around writing projects and other tasks that benefit from group involvement.
- *The CEO's blog:* This is prominently linked on the Minerva home-page and enables him to communicate directly with employees. Posts and comments are not moderated or screened.
- *Urgent requests:* Anyone can submit an urgent request for information about expertise or experience that they are trying to find within ERM. Most requests will first go through the consultant's practice group or community of practice, leaving only the most urgent ones for public posting on Minerva. About three to five of these a day appear on the Minerva home page for all to see, and they all receive at least three replies within 24 hours.

Minerva launches as the home page on the PC of every ERM employee. It also includes a global ERM calendar that lists all major company events happening in different parts of the world.

Do ERM staff actually use this system? Absolutely. In fact, it is starting to transform the ERM culture and organization. After less than a year in operation, Minerva has 500,000 visits per month. ERM has used Minerva, IBM-style, to hold online strategy jams to provide input into its strategy. Client relationship managers and project managers use it on a daily basis, as described in the previous example, to collaborate around clients. New consultants use its e-learning features to learn about the firm and its culture. It has become a platform for the CEO to communicate with members of the firm on a daily basis.

Why has Minerva been so successful when so many other knowledge management efforts have either been expensive failures or ended up totally underutilized? Minerva definitely has strong functionality, but the one thing that absolutely jumps out in this example is leadership commitment, involvement, and support. I am familiar with quite a few systems that aspire to do what Minerva has done, but which have remained sterile and static because the firm's leadership doesn't care and doesn't use the system themselves. The original impetus for Minerva came from the then-CEO Pete Regan, and throughout its design, development, and launch, Regan was steadfastly involved. He and the current ERM CEO use Minerva daily, they both blog for their employees, and they reinforce its benefits in communications with employees. The value in collaboration technologies can only be realized once you have a critical mass of participants, and you need strong support from firm leadership to achieve that.

Collaboration Infrastructure in the 2008 Presidential Election Campaign

Best practices in the use of technology to enable large-scale collaboration would be incomplete without some mention of Barack Obama's 2008 presidential election campaign, lauded by famed Republican strategist Ed Rollins as the most effective political campaign in history. Political ideology aside, it's an impressive story.

The Obama presidential campaign, which attracted millions of volunteers, combined intensive, face-to-face neighborhood canvassing with state-of-the-art, online collaboration. They integrated their campaign efforts into the social networking sites MySpace and Facebook; and used e-mail, text messaging, Twitter, and old-fashioned phone calls to great effect. During the campaign, they accumulated over three million cell phone numbers. On Election Day, for example, I received an e-mail urging me to vote, with a link to identify the nearest polling location. On that page, I could click to see a list of nearby neighbors who were willing to drive me to the polls if I didn't have transportation (one of them lived 200 feet down the road from me!). That afternoon, I received a text message on my cell phone also encouraging me to go vote. Throughout the campaign the online donation process was punctuated with opportunities to connect with other like-minded donors and exchange messages with them. You could even upload your contact database and automatically send everyone you knew a message saying that you had donated and explaining why.

Collaboration in Complex Services Organizations: The U.S. Joint Forces Command

In 1987, during the U.S. invasion of Grenada, an army unit became pinned down by enemy fire. However, the unit was unable to contact a Navy ship offshore to call in fire support because the army and navy did not share radio codes. With bullets flying, a member of the unit crawled to a pay phone, and used a credit card to make a call to his home base in Georgia, which in turn called the navy at the Pentagon, which then called the ship in Grenada.

The U.S. military has come a long way since that famous phone booth debacle, and it has invested significant resources in trying to increase the collaboration between different service branches in highly complex settings. Its example can serve as a useful analogy for the collaboration strategies that you need to consider in a large, global services company, while at the same time illustrating how difficult collaboration can become in a far-flung organization.

During the fall of 2001, a small task force composed mostly of U.S. Special Forces arrived in Afghanistan. Called Task Force Dagger, its mission was to work with the Northern Alliance to overthrow the Taliban. It was an extraordinary success at the time. With only around 400 personnel, Task Force Dagger managed to lead the ouster of nearly 100,000 entrenched al-Qaida and Taliban forces in just a few months. To the casual observer who simply read the newspaper accounts, the early months of the Afghan war seemed like a spectacular and almost effortless victory. What wasn't apparent, however, was the extraordinary degree of collaboration that was needed to pull it off, and the months of work that had gone into ensuring that dozens of different military and civilian constituencies could work together seamlessly. Colonel Wesley Rehorn, who now heads the U.S. Joint Forces Special Operations Command, led the team that helped to prepare the Fifth Special Forces Group to perform as a joint task force with the aforementioned name of Dagger. He and 17 other trainers from his command subsequently spent several months on the ground in Afghanistan with the team they had trained. He tells us,

> *In an operation like this, you have to coordinate and collaborate on many different levels. First, you have multiple special operations forces which must work together seamlessly, and these may include Army Green Berets, Navy Seals, and Air Force Combat Controllers. They in turn have to be able to work with conventional service members, who are often unfamiliar with special operations terminology and practices. We also had a total of 14 functional elements to coordinate, including aviation, intelligence, operations, communications, and others. When we were on the ground and pushing toward the northern city of Mazar-e-Sharif, for example, we encountered all kinds of explosive situations that we were able to successfully confront because of the joint training and preparation that the teams had undergone. We encountered villages, for example, which, in the space of several hours, changed sides multiple times, causing us to repeatedly order and rescind an air strike. A high degree of cooperation and communication are necessary to deal with these rapidly changing circumstances. The training that we went through before the operation ensured that we shared the same goals and expectations, were using the same language, could communicate rapidly, and understood everyone's capabilities.*

The U.S. Joint Forces Command, based in Norfolk, Virginia, is charged with preparing military teams from all services to operate effectively on the field of battle. Many major U.S. military operations are now joint, meaning they encompass all the service branches—the army, navy, air force, and marines—as well as special operations and conventional forces. The Joint Warfighting Center, headed by Major General Jason Kamiya, uses three main strategies to instill the necessary levels of collaboration between formerly competitive service branches. First, they offer extensive distributed learning programs—275 in total—through a network of servers in key locations. Second, his group puts on in-depth training exercises for major U.S. military commands around the world, prior to their deployment into combat zones. Third, they provide ongoing support services to the various branches of the military.

The training exercises, called Mission Rehearsal Exercises (MRXs), may involve several thousand officers and last 10 days. Although they represent an investment of time and resources that most private firms could not afford, the sophistication of their design and the impact they have on their participants are noteworthy. An MRX might be developed, for example, to prepare a new headquarters to take over command of all military operations in a war zone such as Afghanistan. During the exercise, every aspect of the future mission is simulated. Story lines are developed and presented to the participants, who must then react and make decisions. For example, what if the weather deteriorates, and air operations are not possible? What if an aircraft crashes? What is the right response to a sudden increase in insurgent activity? An MRX even has a media room where simulated news programs are broadcast to the participants, who have to react and then hold a press conference themselves. A key aspect of an MRX is teaching the joint mission participants to handle information flows effectively. General Kamiya tells us, "One of the most important lessons that emerges from these exercises is how critical it is to get the right information to the commanders who have to make decisions. There is always a huge amount of information around—the issue is understanding what is important and what's not, and ensuring it gets to the right people at the right time."

Not surprisingly, this is also essential for managers in private sector services firms. A June 2008 *Harvard Business Review* article titled "The Secrets to Successful Strategy Execution," for example, reported on a study of 26,743 managers in 31 companies. According to authors Gary Neilson, Karla Martin, and Elizabeth Powers, there are four key organizational traits that support effective strategy execution, and *two* of these involve information flows. These two are:

- "Important information about the competitive environment gets to headquarters quickly"
- "Information flows freely across organizational boundaries"

Finally, in complex services organizations—such as the U.S. military or a global financial services institution—effective collaboration

We can no longer take a purely military view of how to accomplish our mission. Early on in Afghanistan, for example, our first question was, "With whom do we need to collaborate to be successful?" One of our first stops was the United States Agency for International Development, because reconstruction of the Afghan civilian infrastructure was of critical importance. I worked hard to develop relationships with other key constituents as well, such as the Deputy Chief of Mission at the U.S. embassy; the governors of the 12 Afghan provinces; and our many coalition partners. I now think about collaboration in three important spheres: defense, development, and diplomacy.

—**Major General Jason Kamiya, Commander, Joint Warfighting Center**

must now extend well beyond the boundaries of the firm itself (see sidebar). To be successful, for example, a large accounting firm or global bank has to develop collaborative relationships with law firms and other financial institutions; nongovernmental organizations (NGOs) and nonprofits; government agencies and regulators; and internationally, with local governments. Taking this a step further, a new book titled *Megacommunities* written by Mark Gerencser, Reginald Van Lee, Fernando Napolitano, and Christopher Kelly advocates that our most intractable problems, such as the AIDS crisis or Global Warming, can only be solved by partnerships between the private sector, governments, and NGOs. One small example: In 2002, in Afghanistan's Khost province, where one million people live, there were 13 schools. Today, there are 205. The United States built 53 of these, and 30 other were funded by other donors including NGOs, the World Bank, and foreign governments.

As we have seen, however, whether we're talking about a large global bank or the far-flung military, engendering effective collaboration among multiple constituencies—in a complex environment—is no easy chore.

There are several points to remember about this discussion on collaboration in complex organizations:

- *Leadership drives collaboration.* When training for and running joint missions, military commanders must set the example by "leaving their uniforms at the door" and no longer thinking about whether they belong to the army, navy, or air force. Similarly, a partner in a professional firm has to lead a team or walk into a client's office thinking of himself as a representative of the *firm*, not an IT partner or litigation partner.

- *Face time builds familiarity, which in turn builds trust.* There is simply no substitute for spending time together prior to facing live fire, whether that fire is live bullets or just a client asking intimidating questions during a sales presentation.

- *Communications fail without a common vocabulary and common systems.* Each military service branch used to have its own terminology and incompatible radio and telecommunications systems, a situation which completely undermined collaboration. That's why having a common knowledge management and collaboration technology platform has become so important.

- *One-off events are insufficient.* The leadership of joint military missions are not just given a few days of training and then sent off to a war zone. They are put through a comprehensive process, which includes achieving alignment around strategy; building mutual trust and understanding through extensive joint exercises and training; and onsite, postexercise debriefs that ensure organizational learning. Similarly, many services firms are now realizing that a one-day training offsite alone will not change deeply ingrained behaviors.

- *Collaboration starts within your own organization, but it will most definitely include external constituencies.* To paraphrase English author John Donne, no firm is an island. The most successful organizations will be those that adopt an open architecture to developing their intellectual capital, building networks, and creating service offerings for clients.

Conclusion

In order to succeed, the strategies in this book need to take root in a culture of collaboration and client focus. It's easy to say, "We're going to change our culture," but remember that the values, beliefs, and

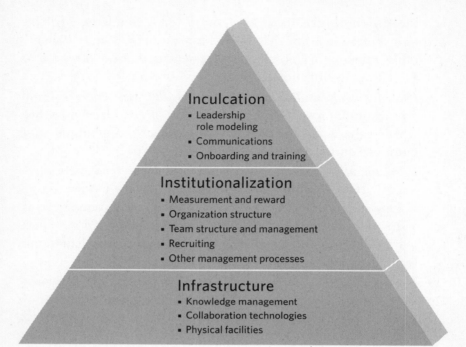

FIGURE 10.2 Developing a Culture of Collaboration

behaviors that constitute an organizational culture take many years to develop. You need to first understand what barriers may be getting in the way of collaboration, and then identify concrete steps you can take in each of the three areas of leverage that we've discussed—Inculcation, Institutionalization, and Infrastructure. Figure 10.2 summarizes this overall framework.

11

Strategy Nine: Listening to Clients

Using Multiple Channels to Connect with Clients

The chairman of a large professional service firm went to visit one of his firm's most important clients. Before the meeting, he debriefed with the partner who managed the relationship and became familiar with the work his firm had been doing for the client. The partner gave a rosy appraisal of the situation, indicating that the client was very comfortable having him as the go-to person for all of their various needs. During the actual meeting, the chairman began the conversation by thanking the client for his company's business, and then launched into a discussion about the executive's most critical issues and concerns. They spent a productive hour together, and as the chairman was leaving, he paused and asked one final question—a question he was sure he knew the answer to: "If there is ever an issue with our relationship that needs attention, or a particular expertise you're looking for, are you clear about whom you should first speak to at our firm?" The client thought for a moment, and a quizzical look passed over his face.

"Actually," he replied, "no. I'm really not certain who I would turn to in your organization in those situations." The chairman sighed quietly to himself and realized he had his work cut out for him.

A candid discussion with the client can upend even the most basic assumptions about a relationship. Do you think things are going swimmingly? Maybe they are—but maybe they aren't. Alternatively, you may feel that you're not exactly lighting up the sky with a client, but you might discover they love your work and would like to expand the relationship. One of my clients was recently implementing a client survey based on the Net Promoter Score methodology—which I'll discuss later in this chapter—and during a follow-up phone call, a senior client executive said to him, "I'm glad you called. We'd like to do more business with your firm."

Ironically, effective client listening is an extraordinarily valuable activity that always provides a strong return on investment—but sometimes it's a subject that generates more talk than action. Getting feedback from clients does take time, and as long as business is going well, many firms don't make the effort.

There are a number of reasons to talk to clients on a regular basis. Client conversations can give you ideas for new service offerings; suggestions for how to improve the relationship; a better understanding of the competition; and insights into your own particular strengths and weaknesses as a firm. They are also a good opportunity to show that you care and to thank clients for their business. Done well, these interactions serve to enhance the relationship.

In this chapter, I'm going to describe five different, complementary types of client listening activities. These are:

1. Surveys
2. Relationship manager reviews
3. Independent reviews
4. Senior management visits
5. Client events and forums

Let's look briefly at each one of these.

Surveys

Surveys are useful for obtaining certain types of information. They can be used on a recurring basis, which enables you to get trend data about client satisfaction and attitudes; or on a one-off basis, to get periodic data on things like brand positioning and competitive trends. They also allow you to reach a large number of clients at a relatively low cost. I find that there are several significant problems in using surveys with clients, however. First, most senior executives are not very keen on spending lots of time filling out a written questionnaire. There is not much value in it for them, and you just are not going to get many c-level executives—CEOs, CFOs, business unit heads, and so on—to respond. So it tends to be a very low value-added interaction.

Second, it is often difficult to know exactly what to do with the survey data. I have several clients who spend quite a bit of money on surveys, but the reports tend to get buried in someone's bottom desk drawer. The senior partner with oversight of marketing at one firm told me, "We get the survey data back, but we never really do anything with it. I want to know, is it actionable?" Finally, there is not a high correlation between survey ratings and economic performance. Just because clients say they are "satisfied" with their relationship may simply mean that they are not upset about anything. It does not necessarily mean they will buy more services from you or recommend you to someone else.

The one survey approach that I am particularly impressed with, and which overcomes most of these traditional objections, is the Net Promoter Score methodology (NPS) that I first mentioned in Chapter 10. NPS was developed by Bain & Company and was featured in Fred Reichheld's book, *The Ultimate Question*. NPS is based on asking one question: "On a scale of 0 to 10, how likely is it that you would recommend our firm to a friend or colleague?" The premise is that a *willingness to recommend you* is the most meaningful indicator of client loyalty and repurchase intention. In fact, companies that achieve long-term profitable growth have NPS scores that are double the average for their industries. To me, this is common sense. Most professional firms or financial institutions rely heavily on word-of-mouth to promote their services and develop new clients. All the studies I have seen show that the most effective way for senior executives to learn about you and your firm is through a referral from a trusted colleague or friend. It's not through brochures, advertising, or contest sponsorship, or because they received an unsolicited letter pitching your services.

NPS isn't just a survey. If implemented properly, it is a tool to create more dialogue with your clients. I will warn you up front, however: Most market research companies don't like NPS. They have produced some very academic articles attacking it as not being much better than satisfaction surveys. I don't share their opinion and I suspect that they have a vested interest in discrediting a very simple but powerful methodology that can put them out of business. Who needs long surveys when you can ask just one question?

To bring NPS to life, let me give you a brief description of how it actually works in practice, based on the case of a client who recently implemented NPS with its clients.

Within the NPS framework, there are three types of clients, depending on how they answer the "would you recommend" question:

1. *Promoters* are clients who score you a 9 or 10. They will actively promote you and your firm through word-of-mouth.
2. *Passives* are clients who score you a 7 or 8. They are satisfied, but not very enthusiastic.
3. *Detractors* are clients who rate you a 6 or less. They are unhappy clients who are essentially stuck in what they perceive to be a bad relationship. They will actively say negative things about you to their friends and colleagues.

Your net promoter score is the percentage of promoters minus the percentage of detractors. Companies with strong client loyalty generally have an NPS of 50 percent or better.

One of my clients recently implemented an NPS pilot to test the methodology. My client selected about 100 executives from 20 major clients. When you survey a client, you try to include every client executive who has had any meaningful interaction with your firm. NPS is not just aimed at the top; rather, it gives you a broad-based understanding of your overall client relationship across many individual relationships. In my client's case, each participant was sent an e-mail from the relationship partner asking him or her to answer a couple of short questions. Question one was the main NPS question: "On a scale of 0 to 10, how likely is it that you would recommend . . ." Question two was: "Can you give us the main reason behind your rating?" Certain selected clients—mainly those giving a score of less than 7 and those considered key economic buyers—were asked a third question: "Could a senior representative of our firm contact you to discuss your experience with us?" The survey took clients only a few minutes to fill out.

Because the participants had been given a heads up by my client before the surveys were e-mailed, there was a 50 percent response rate. Two partners followed up with phone calls to the economic buyers who had responded, as well as to the detractors who had scored less than a 7. These calls were extremely productive. My client was able to better understand why some executives had given them a low rating, and they were able to strengthen the relationship with some of their most senior clients. The most productive conversations, actually, were with the clients who had given them a very high rating. Most of these were interested in exploring ways to expand their relationship with my client, a very pleasant discovery indeed. This very low-cost survey effort, in short, enabled this firm to identify some unhappy clients; strengthen its relationship with senior economic buyers; and establish tracking data on the health of its key client relationships.

Relationship Manager Reviews

Relationship managers cannot wait for management to conduct client surveys or independent client reviews—they have to sit down with their client at least several times a year and have an informal conversation about the relationship. Don't assume that everything is great. Here are some questions you might consider asking during these sessions:

- In thinking about how things have gone over the past six months—can you share with me your overall assessment of our relationship?
- What have we done that has been particularly valuable for you?

- Is there anything you would change about how we work together?
- How effective a job have we done at listening to you and your colleagues?
- Are there any other issues that we ought to be aware of or thinking about for you?
- Do you feel we need to strengthen or augment our team in any way?
- Are there other people in your organization whom you think we ought to connect with in order to support the work we're doing with you?
- Are there any concerns you'd like to put on the table?

Independent Client Reviews

The gold standard for client listening and quality assurance is the independent review. During an independent client review, a partner or managing director who is *not* involved in the relationship meets with the client to gain feedback on a variety of issues. These can include things such as the client's key business issues and priorities; satisfaction with the work that's been delivered; feedback about specific team members; and general suggestions for improving the relationship. Independent client reviews are a time-consuming but very worthwhile investment in making sure your best relationships are on the right course.

Some firms give the responsibility for client reviews to their geographic office heads, or, in a smaller organization, their managing partner. Towers Perrin's office heads, for example, spend up to 40 percent of their time conducting these types of client visits, often interviewing 5 or even 10 executives at a large client. At Osler, a leading Canadian law firm, Dale Ponder—the managing partner—usually conducts 30 to 40 of these reviews a year with Osler's major clients.

A truly systematic approach to conducting independent client reviews is exemplified by Ernst & Young's (E&Y) Assessment of Service Quality (ASQ) process. The ASQ process is implemented for nearly all of E&Y's principal client relationships. In North America, for example, 3,000 to 4,000 ASQ visits are completed in any given year (there are usually multiple visits per client). ASQs are conducted by active and some retired E&Y partners. The overall ASQ process for a very large "office of the chairman" account might involve two dozen interviews with individual client executives. There are typically around 15 questions that are asked, and the interviewee gives an overall satisfaction rating from 1 to 5. If the rating is under 4, the relationship is flagged to receive additional attention and focus. These scores are not, by the way, incorporated into a partner's year-end review because to do otherwise would risk distorting the process (e.g., a relationship manager might become hesitant to collaborate in the ASQ process). Ed Beanland, a recently retired E&Y partner who conducts ASQs, says this about the process:

> *I always emphasize to the client that I want to hear the unvarnished truth, that I don't want anything sugarcoated. I start by asking "Can you tell me about your relationship with Ernst & Young?" I'll go on to other questions such as, "What's most valuable about what we do for you? Least valuable? What is really working well in the relationship? What should we do more of? What should we stop doing? What are your top three expectations of the firm in serving you? Would you recommend us to a colleague?" Sometimes I'll go back to the team with my report, and they'll say "Wow, we really had no idea this particular thing was so important to them!" It's rare—but it does happen—that a client is upset or dissatisfied. I'm then in perfect position to ask, "What can we do to fix this? How can we recover in your eyes?" That's a conversation that is difficult for the coordinating partner to have with the client. The ASQ process strengthens relationships that are already good, and it can also represent the start of a process to recoup a client relationship that is having difficulties.*

Senior Management Visits

Your firm's top executives can represent a powerful force in building and sustaining top-level client relationships. I have already mentioned Citigroup's *Seniors Program*, which connects the top 50 executives in Citigroup with hundreds of major corporate clients around the world. IBM developed a similar approach, called the *Partnership Executive Program*. The program started with the top 20 executives at IBM, but was later expanded to include several hundred of IBM's most senior leaders (keep in mind that IBM has over 350,000 employees world-wide). Each executive takes responsibility for up to five key client relationships, and works with the account executive for each client to help build stronger relationships at the most senior levels of the organization. In a large, global services firm, these types of programs also provide the opportunity to add value by exchanging ideas about shared company issues. Your firm may very well be grappling with many of the same business issues that your clients are confronting—everything from globalization to talent management—and when one of your firm's top executives sits down with her counterpart at your client, there is an opportunity to add value around a shared challenge.

Don't underestimate the work required to organize these senior management visits for your own leadership. You need dedicated staff resources to drive the process forward; otherwise, it will get bogged down in the daily demands of the business.

Client Events and Forums

Client listening can take place anytime, anywhere—it doesn't have to occur within the context of a formal visit or survey. Some of the most profound insights into client needs and issues can be discerned in an informal setting where people are relaxed and open. ERM, for example, the large environmental consulting firm, holds client forums that bring together an intimate group of senior clients at a three-day off-site conference. At these events, which I describe in more detail in the next chapter, top environmental officers from a variety of companies share their most pressing issues with each other and with ERM. E&Y's version of this is its CFO network, which brings together groups of 12 CFOs—by industry—on a quarterly basis. These meetings give E&Y a much deeper understanding of what's keeping CFOs awake at night, and they add tremendous value for the participants, who are able to have vibrant conversations with their peers in a relaxed atmosphere.

Client events such as these require persistence, organization, a long-term perspective, and someone from management who is willing to doggedly champion the effort. It's not easy getting a group of senior executives together away from their offices, and there is usually no immediate financial payoff. I've observed a number of these programs, however, and if done well and consistently over time, they produce a very strong return on investment.

Conclusion

Since I began my consulting career over 25 years ago, I have probably conducted several thousand interviews with both corporate executives and successful professionals from many different organizations. One of the things I have noticed is that it takes a while for people to access their real opinions and then open up about them. It is often at the very end of a discussion—sometimes as you are leaving the person's office—that you get the most valuable information and insights. This is why, as I mention in Chapter 3, you have to take a subtle, nuanced approach to uncovering a client's true agenda.

A doctor, Danielle Ofri, wrote about this phenomenon in a column in the *New York Times*. Dr. Ofri describes the case of a young woman who complains of strange aches and pains. She seems to be perfectly healthy, and Ofri can find nothing wrong with her. As she leaves his office, however, she lingers at the door, and then obliquely hints at the real problem—a boyfriend who is physically abusive. I can remember my own version of this story—less dramatic, fortunately—when I was interviewing a client executive at the beginning of a consulting project. During the hour-long interview, he painted a rosy, upbeat portrait of his company. As I was leaving his office—literally, at the door with my hand on the doorknob—he blurted out, "Our organization is a disaster waiting to happen." Dr. Ofri says,

> The "hand on the doorknob" phenomenon is well known in medicine. A physician can proceed assiduously through a complete history and physical with a patient, but it is only when the patient is halfway out the door that the important information spills out. . . . Maybe only when patients are fully dressed and standing upright, somewhat removed from the medical setting, if only by a few feet, do they regain enough humanity and strength to reveal such things. Whatever the reason, there is something about that moment—halfway out the door, hand on the doorknob—that is critical. [That is the] time for the real visit to begin. (New York Times, *December 7, 2004*)

FIGURE 11.1 Client Listening Opportunities

This is why you need a comprehensive, multifaceted client listening program, which is summarized in Figure 11.1. Surveys have their place, but there is no substitute for face-to-face conversations that enable you to tap into a client's deepest concerns and feelings. Most clients do not announce to you that they are unhappy with your work—they simply vote with their feet, and begin shifting their business to your competitors. You need to create as many "listening posts" as possible to understand your client's deepest concerns and issues, and anticipate any rough spots in the relationship.

12

Strategy Ten: Creating a Unique Client Experience

Co-Creating Value with Clients

In many markets, we are seeing a fundamental shift in the way value is created for customers. The shift is from value that resides in the product or service to value that is created for the customer during the experience of interacting with the service provider. Increasingly, it is at the *points of interaction* where value is created, not in the factory or R&D laboratory. This transformation is now beginning to affect the world of professional and financial services, and it's important to understand not only the implications it has for service providers, but also how you can think about harnessing it for your own firm. One of the names for this phenomenon is "Experience Co-Creation," an expression drawn from the work of authors C. K. Prahalad and Venkat Ramaswamy on the shift in value creation from the supplier's infrastructure to the point of experience.

I'll introduce this concept by giving you several examples in markets that you will be very familiar with: personal computers and air travel. In 2001, Apple Computer's CEO Steve Jobs, became convinced that large retailers could not properly sell Apple products. He launched a project to create a chain of dedicated Apple stores that would create an entirely new and different experience for customers. Apple built a top-secret prototype store inside a warehouse, and went through multiple design changes before arriving at the final store layout. Focus groups with consumers, for example, revealed that for many people, their *best ever service experience* was working with the concierge in their favorite hotel. This led to the creation of the "Genius Bar" in Apple stores, where customers can get advice on using Apple products.

Every aspect of Apple's stores represents a significant departure from traditional retail space. The luminous, white interiors are built largely out of only three, extremely high-quality materials. Educational seminars are regularly offered to help customers take advantage of their Apple hardware and software products. Clerks are highly knowledgeable about the merchandise, and they carry small, wireless credit card processing devices so that you don't have to go and wait in line at a checkout counter.

The net effect is that Apple has created a radically new "experience environment" for its customers. In large cities, Apple stores are mobbed—sometimes 24 hours a day. Walking into an Apple store, in short, is unlike any other retail experience. The results have been extraordinary: Apple's 219 stores represent the most productive retail space in the world. They bring in an average of *$4,500 per square foot*, compared to Best Buy's estimated $929 and Tiffany & Co.'s $2,746. This year, they are slated to account for nearly $7 billion in sales for Apple.

By the way, Apple's stores are not the only place where Apple has changed the playing field by offering a dramatically different customer experience: the iTunes music store and iTunes music management software that comes free with every Apple computer, for example, represent a very different experience environment compared to other similar products. The same can be said for Apple's iMovie software, which integrates seamlessly with every other software program in its multimedia suite (iPhoto, iTunes, Garageband, etc.).

Another interesting example can be seen in what several of the airlines, including British Airways, Virgin Atlanta, and Lufthansa, have done to create not just an in-air experience but an on-the-ground experience. At the Frankfurt airport, Lufthansa has built a new terminal just for first-class passengers. Here's what Scott McCartney of the *Wall Street Journal* had to say about his visit to this new facility:

> *It doesn't look like an airport terminal at all. Think hip hotel lobby. With leather seats in the lobby, halogen lighting, cocktail glasses filled with nuts and jazz playing in the background, there's nary a Lufthansa sign visible. On arrival, a valet takes your luggage and parks your car. An attendant greets you, walks you through a security check and stays responsible for you throughout your stay, right down to telling you when it's time to leave. (July 10, 2007)*

Alternatively, Lufthansa will send a spanking-new Porsche Cayenne to pick you up at your house at the last minute, and drive you to the airport and then directly onto the runway where you are escorted to your aircraft. A Lufthansa executive says, "The competition will be decided on the ground. Everyone can have the same seats, food, and entertainment. But where you can really do something is to improve the product and the process on the ground." Last year, on New Year's Eve, a couple came to the first-class lounge, had drinks and dinner, and then cancelled their flights for a full refund!

My friend and former colleague Francis Gouillart, who co-founded the Experience Co-Creation Partnership with Venkat Ramaswamy, likes to contrast the old and new paradigms for creating value. In the past, he tells us, value was associated with a company's offerings—the competitive space was oriented around the company's products or services themselves. Increasingly, value is now instead associated with experiences around the purchasing, servicing, and use of a product or service. So the role of a company is shifting from unilaterally defining and creating value to engaging the customer to define and co-create value. The customer—or client—is becoming an active partner in seeking, creating, and extracting value.

Technology is a major enabler of this evolution toward creating value through experiences. Businesses now routinely harvest consumer feedback directly from the Internet through online research, blogs, and other web-based forums. Many companies now enlist their customers to help design their products. John Fluevog Shoes, for example, has nine boutiques in major cities around the world. It invites customers to submit designs for new shoe models, and it then posts these submissions on the company's web site, where visitors vote for their favorites. Fluevog then manufactures and sells the most promising designs. Over 300 finalists have been chosen, and 10 new shoes designed and sold. Fluevog is just one of many examples of this type of customer participation in value creation.

These changes in the business-to-consumer markets are profound. The real question for us, however, is "Are these trends relevant for professionals who serve and advise top corporate executives? If you are a lawyer, consultant, accountant, or banker, for example, can you really learn anything from Apple—or from many other companies, such as Progressive Insurance—who are creating unique, value-laden customer experiences?" The answer to both questions, I believe, is *yes*. Services firms have a real opportunity to differentiate themselves by creating new and value-added experience environments with their clients.

Creating a Unique Client Experience

I was recently facilitating a planning workshop with a client of mine, a large, general management consulting firm that has been enormously successful. One of the senior partners said this to me: "We have a distinctive approach and way of working with our clients that is superior to what our competitors offer. We really are *better*. But it's frustrating, because we should have an even greater market share than we do." My response was fairly blunt. I told the group that their approach probably wasn't as differentiated as they believed, or at least their clients didn't perceive it as particularly different. I encouraged them to look more closely at their business development, delivery, and relationship management practices to see where and how they could truly be different and add more value.

Many professional firms talk about providing their clients with a "unique client experience." I must say, however, that I have seen very few compelling examples of a truly *unique* client experience. Have I observed some very effective practices? Certainly. But most service companies have an exaggerated belief in the uniqueness of their client relationship experience. The first step in changing this situation is to be less complacent.

The fact is most professional services—and many banking services—are delivered today in a similar way to how they were delivered 30 or 40 years ago. Technology has greatly reduced the labor component of certain activities—conducting an audit, for example, or doing a foreign exchange transaction—but for the most part, we market, sell, and deliver using vintage approaches that have been common currency for decades. Yet, as I discussed in Chapter 1, if you look under the surface of many markets, there are revolutions stirring.

That said, some service firms are starting to connect with their clients in new ways and create unique experience environments that enhance value. Let's look at a wide range of examples of how they are doing this.

Client Forums

Many firms hold offsite events for their clients, but most of the time these are based on schmoozing and golf, with a few lectures thrown in to legitimize the event. Environmental Resources Management (ERM), the largest environmental consulting firm in the world, began holding a very special and different client forum about five years ago—one that creates a unique experience environment for its clients. The ERM Forum, now held on a regional basis, usually involves 35 to 40 senior executives who are responsible for environmental affairs and policy at their companies. The event lasts three days and resembles an advanced management program at a leading business school. The ERM executives in attendance keep a very low profile because the forum is not about selling, it's about learning. Expert facilitators take the client executives through a variety of issues discussions, case studies, and role plays. They share experiences in dealing with their toughest environmental issues (from policy setting to remediating contaminated sites), and form relationships with peers that continue well after the forum is over. Most companies struggle to get clients to attend their conferences; In ERM's case, demand has become so great it has to *turn clients down* for its forums.

Insight from Leading Customers

In Chapter 10, I talked about how Lou Gerstner's original strategic agenda at IBM had been very much customer-driven. Co-strategizing and co-innovating with customers has become a well-established practice at IBM. Based on feedback from customers, including IBM director A. J. Lafley, who is the CEO of Procter & Gamble and a major IBM customer, IBM started its "On Demand" consulting business. Launched in 2002, On Demand was designed to assemble a small team of multidisciplinary professionals focused on high-end business and technology transformation consulting services. On Demand later became a marketing slogan for IBM. A number of other IBM businesses, including outsourcing, were developed based on conversations with its customers. Many companies talk about listening to the voice of the customer—IBM has institutionalized this practice, and more importantly, acts on what it hears.

> It's getting cheaper and cheaper for users to innovate on their own. This is not traditional market research—asking customers what they want. This is identifying what your most advanced users are already doing and understanding what their innovations mean for the future of your business.
>
> **—Professor Eric von Hippel, MIT Sloan School of Management**

Joint Business Development

In many organizations, the sales process involves interviewing a prospective client, clarifying the issues, writing a proposal, and then making a sales pitch. BT North America, which provides managed telecommunications network services to large corporations, found itself at a disadvantage because it is a U.K. company whose name recognition among U.S. clients lags behind indigenous suppliers like Sprint and ATT. In response, BT instituted a business development strategy based on a three-day workshop, which it offers, at no charge, to promising prospective clients. BT invests heavily in preparing for the workshop, and during the three days, it facilitates a series of in-depth discussions about the client's technology strategy, key trends, the business environment, obstacles to success, best practices employed by other leading companies, and possible solutions. Convincing a prospective client to commit to this process is not easy (sometimes BT can only can get one or two days for the session), but when it does, the prospect almost always becomes a client. The net effect of this approach is to create a new experience environment for clients that feels tangibly different than what BT's competitors offer.

Simulations

I have seen some firms use simulations, both during the business development process and during ongoing delivery, to create a unique client experience. Here are three examples:

1. A non-U.S. company contacted Fulbright & Jaworski, the international law firm, to potentially represent it in a litigation matter. The client was quite unfamiliar with the U.S. legal system, and its executives had never been inside a courtroom. The Fulbright team created a simulated courtroom to show the client's senior management the process they would have to go through if they decided to litigate. The courtroom included a judge and jury, and the Fulbright lawyers walked the client through the entire experience from start to finish, including testifying under oath and experiencing cross-examinations.

2. Booz Allen Hamilton possesses a highly sophisticated war-gaming program, which can simulate complex, global military interactions. While originally developed for the U.S. government, this capability has also been used for other clients to simulate the impact of alternative strategies in commercial markets. In addition to offering a powerful technological capability, the process results in a very intimate set of consultant-client interactions, especially during the highly suspense-filled workshop when the simulation is actually run.

3. Amdocs, a leading supplier of software and customer relationship management services to the telecommunications industry, has successfully used simulations to reduce risk for clients who are

making a major purchase decision about a billing system that could, at the extreme, make or break their business. Amdocs won a major contract with a U.S. telecommunications client using this approach, beating out several other potential suppliers by creating a simulation that showed the client how the system would work in its business, the stability that it offered, and what it would actually feel like when implemented.

Customizing an Entire Firm

Few markets have suffered the cataclysmic change that has affected the advertising business over the past five years. Procurement has become a way of life for advertising and marketing services firms, and advertising budgets are rapidly shifting from traditional media, such as television, to the Internet. Advertising agencies have been reflecting long and hard—and sometimes struggling in the process—to figure out how to continue to add value to their clients. Last year, WPP, the U.K.-based global marketing services giant, won the entire Dell advertising account. WPP accomplished this through an innovative agreement to create, from scratch, a full-service marketing services agency dedicated to Dell Computer, which is based in Round Rock, Texas. Called Enfatico, the new Dell-dedicated agency has already hired 600 professionals and has 14 offices. Eventually it will have a total staff of 1,000. The value of the deal is estimated in the advertising trade press to be worth $4.5 billion over three years. Previously, Dell's business was spread across 800 agencies around the world, a situation characterized by nasty turf rivalries, a lack of coordination, and inconsistency—not to mention the huge investment of time on Dell's part to manage all of these service providers.

Defining the Relationship at the Start: Setting Expectations

In the early days of a relationship, you have a unique opportunity to discuss the client's expectations and begin tailoring the relationship experience to them. Ernst & Young, for example, uses a carefully developed expectations setting methodology, which is implemented through a co-development or strategic enablement discussion. During this meeting, an Ernst & Young partner works with the client to define what success will look like; what the client's expectations are for the relationship; and how the first year of an audit or tax engagement will typically progress and what the client can expect from Ernst & Young. Two supporting concepts that are used are the YILO and the Single Frame. YILO means "a year in the life of," referring to a year in the life of the relationship between Ernst & Young and the client. Usually, this discussion is facilitated by a Single Frame, an oversized page that captures the client's current state, the future state, and how Ernst & Young and the client will work together to achieve it. It's a very visual, simple, and uncluttered tool for designing and communicating a tailored client experience.

> When we facilitate a strategic enablement session with a client, we get their expectations onto the table. We utilize a very visual approach to examining, together, what the relationship is going to look like. During this co-development conversation, we try to get very specific answers to a series of questions: Where are we going to focus? How does the client want the relationship driven and managed? How do they want information presented? How often do they want to see us? Normally this discussion lasts four hours. Clients tell us that it's a unique process.
>
> **—Tom Hever, Vice Chair, Ernst & Young**

Giving Pricing Control to Clients

Pricing is an area where most firms would never want to relinquish control, yet I have seen several powerful examples of firms that have given clients a collaborative role in determining fee levels. Broadly speaking, alternative pricing arrangements tend to fall into two groups. In the first, fees are linked to achieving certain quantifiable goals (e.g., success fees) or to other metrics such as total fee volume (e.g., the client gets a 5 percent discount or carry-forward if fees exceed $1 million). Interestingly, these still represent a very small percentage of pricing agreements in professional services—they haven't taken off in a big way. This is due in part, I believe, to the desire of large corporations to have fixed, predictable budgets even though success fees could work to their advantage.

The second group comprises pricing agreements that vary based purely on *client satisfaction*. Parthenon Group, for example, is a highly successful strategy consulting and private equity firm based in Boston, Massachusetts, which has over 200 professionals. All new Parthenon clients are offered a 15 percent "satisfaction" holdback of fees. The client is only billed 85 percent of the agreed fees, and at the end of the first assignment, the client pays the final 15 percent only if it is completely satisfied with the work completed. It is, in essence, a form of guarantee that reduces risk for a new client. Another consulting firm in San Francisco, Trium, allows clients to receive a discount—or pay a bonus—based on satisfaction with the work completed. For example, a highly satisfied client could decide to pay up to 125 percent of the agreed fees—or less, if it was not satisfied. In both of these cases, there are no complicated metrics or goals that have to be agreed on in advance—just self-reported client satisfaction.

Creating a New Business Model for Service Delivery

It is rare, but it does happen, that a service firm is able to structure a significantly different business model for delivery of its services. Swiss national Egon Zehnder, for example, set out to "change the rules of the game" in the executive search industry nearly 40 years ago. He redefined the service delivery model for executive search in several ways:

- He would work only for a fixed fee, not a percentage of the candidate's first-year compensation, to better align his and the client's interests.
- Partners at his firm would do the vast majority of the research and interviewing themselves—rather than delegating it to junior research staff—so that they would be intimately familiar with the market and make contacts that would serve them for life.
- All partners would receive the same compensation based on tenure, not sales or production, to create a teamwork culture.
- Each candidate for employment at the firm would be exhaustively vetted by up to 25 partners, to ensure a good cultural fit.

As a result, Zehnder created a firm that had a qualitatively different "feel" compared to its competitors.

Bill Bain, the founder of Bain & Company, set out to reinvent the strategy consulting business in the early 1970s. Bain decided to focus not just on strategy formulation (which BCG and McKinsey prided themselves on), but also on implementation. His premise was that Bain's job was not done until they had worked with the client from strategy to execution. In the early days, Bain would only work for one competitor in each major industry, further cementing the idea of consultant-client alignment around tangible results. Bain's biggest marketing tool (which is used to this day) was a graph showing how, on average, the price of the stocks of Bain clients had gone up far more than the market as a whole.

Just as Southwest Airlines redefined the airline business by creating a low-cost, no-frills carrier, these two firms created new delivery models for executive search and management consulting and therefore a different and more valuable client experience. Since these firms' founding, the competition has adapted and, in some cases, caught up, but their early mover advantages fueled exceptional revenue growth for many years.

New organization models for service delivery are continuing to develop in a number of fields. Eight years ago, for example, Eden McCallum was founded by Dena McCallum in the United Kingdom. Eden McCallum's model is based on 400 independent consultants, almost all of whom have worked for large, well-established consulting firms like McKinsey and Booz Allen Hamilton. The firm's structure reflects its value proposition to clients: High-quality general management consulting that is tailored to the client's staffing needs, for half the price. Clients will often play an active role in helping to select the actual team of consultants. Eden McCallum does not develop nor offer "intellectual capital" or proprietary methodologies the way Accenture or McKinsey might. Rather, it fields consultants schooled in many different approaches, who work closely with the client to define how the project will be executed. Eden McCallum maintains a very slender overhead structure compared to a traditional consulting firm, employing a small group of professionals who specialize in relationship management, business development, and other needed capabilities. A traditional consulting firm might say that Eden McCallum is akin to a vendor that provides extra arms and legs—a kind of temporary staffing agency. But in truth it is far more than that, and it has its share of long-term client relationships that resemble the trusted partnerships that are the focus of this book.

Using Virtual Experience Environments

Some firms are starting to borrow interaction models from online virtual reality worlds such as Second Life. Several, including Bain & Company, are experimenting with virtual recruiting environments that effectively take place online. Both the firm interviewer and the candidate adopt graphic "avatars," which become their visual identities during the interview. While this may seem bizarre, if you think about it, it fits our criteria of altering the experience environment to increase value, lower costs, and/or lower risk. A virtual recruiting environment creates a radically new and differentiated recruiting experience for hard-to-get new recruits, while clearly reducing costs for both sides.

I can't conclude this section without briefly exploring Second Life, which is a three-dimensional virtual world created by Linden Labs. Second Life has over 15 million users who inhabit its 65,000 online acres. Users adopt new identities in the form of graphic avatars, and engage in all kinds of human activities, from having coffee with a friend to building a store and selling merchandise. What's interesting is that Second Life now has over 100 corporate users, such as Ben & Jerry's and Toyota. Some of these companies have created virtual storefronts for marketing their products to the young and hip denizens of Second Life, and in doing so they can conduct inexpensive test marketing of new ideas and concepts. One major hotel chain, for example, has sought input from Second Life participants in building the "ideal" business hotel. In these examples, the experience environment is dramatically altered, costs are lowered, and value created for both parties. I cannot predict whether professional advisors will be conducting virtual advice sessions in Second Life someday in the future, but it's probably well within the realm of possibility. Sir Thomas More would have surely scoffed at the notion of talking to his client, King Henry VIII, through an electronic device called the telephone, but now we do that on a daily basis.

How Do You Design a Different Client Experience?

Many of the innovations in client experience that I have observed have been small steps that have evolved through creative trial-and-error, but there is a way to approach designing an improved client experience in a more systematic manner. My friends at the Experience Co-Creation Partnership have developed a methodology that looks at four dimensions of the client experience: Value, Experience, Interactions, and Network. These steps are worked through both for the service provider and for the client. The process can be messy, but I have had good success with it and it is the most logical and structured approach I have seen. Next I briefly summarize the methodology and the questions it forces you to ask about your service delivery and client relationships.

An Approach to Redesigning the Client Experience

You start this process by examining a current client relationship, including all of the individuals who are involved from your firm and from the client's organization, the interactions that occur between them, and the various processes you use to manage the relationship. Then, ask yourself a series of questions:

Part 1—Value

- Can you envision changes in the relationship experience that would result in more rapid learning and reduced cost and risk for you, the service provider?
- How would these changes create new value and reduced cost and risk for the client?

For example, ERM's client forum experience helps ERM learn more about its clients' issues, and it creates new value for the clients by giving them an opportunity to share best practices for handling their toughest issues. Similarly, IBM's Global Innovation Outlook summits add value for IBM, clients, and other collaborating institutions by creating an exchange of ideas and a learning opportunity focused on regional issues.

Part 2—Experience

- Within your firm, who are the key owners of the relationship experience today? Can you involve new players?
- Who are the key clients who are involved in the process? Can you change who the client is?
- What are the experience environments today, for the professionals who serve the client and for the client executives? What new experience environments can you create for them?
- Can you provide an equally good experience at lower cost?

For example, Bain & Company's virtual recruiting experiment shifts traditional, in-office, face-to-face interaction to an online, virtual one. Webcasting, improved videoconferencing (e.g., Cisco's Telepresence), and e-learning technologies have enabled firms to interact virtually with clients while lowering costs. When Citigroup built a Level 6 relationship with Royal Dutch Shell (described in Chapter 1), it sought out the input of not just client executives but the law firms, accountants, and consultants who were working with the client on the same issue, thus creating a new, higher-level perspective for the client.

Part 3—Interactions

- Can you open up some of the internal steps in your process to new participants within your firm or network? Can you open up new steps to clients?
- Can you create new, two-way interactions—both internally and with the client?
- Can you devise new physical environments and places for the participants in the relationship process?

For example, BT's three-day workshop experience during the business development process essentially opens up a process step to the client that was formerly solely the province of the firm and not shared with outsiders. ZS Associate's "Idea Day" for relationship managers formally brings other partners—and sometimes clients—into a day-long strategy and ideas session about how to add value and grow the client relationship. Towers Perrin's joint account planning process brings the client into a formerly opaque activity that used to involve the account team sitting behind closed doors to brainstorm how to improve the client relationship.

Part 4—Network

- What other environments do you need to design or create to provide a smoothly integrated experience for your own professionals?
- How can you link the various environments you have designed to produce a smoothly integrated experience for your clients?

For example, WPP's Enfatico agency, which has been expressly created for Dell, is designed to integrate and align formerly disparate experience environments that were maintained by hundreds of marketing services companies around the world. Ernst & Young's regional CFO forums, which meet quarterly, create an extended, value-added network for its clients. Recently, Google and Procter & Gamble announced that they are exchanging small groups of employees to give their respective professionals skills in each other's business model—an innovative way to create a new experience environment for employees.

By asking and answering these questions for your particular services and client relationships, you can jump-start the process of identifying ways to enhance your clients' experience and, ultimately, add more value and reduce costs for both parties.

Another useful, related framework for identifying experience co-creation opportunities is the DART model. DART stands for Dialogue, Access, Risk, and Transparency. It forces you to think about opportunities to enhance the client experience in each of these areas, as follows:

Lack of Dialogue: *What interactions with your client are particularly one-sided, preventing the client from engaging in a dialogue with you that might uncover new value?* For example, most sales pitches are one-sided presentations where the service provider tries to convince the client it is the best. A better alternative, which increases dialogue, is to structure a working session with lots of give and take around the key issues the client wants to solve—a session in which you actually role-model what it would be like to work together. (I personally would like to ban the phrase "sales pitch" because it exemplifies everything that is misguided about the traditional thinking about sales.)

Lack of Access: *What interactions are particularly opaque because the right information is not made accessible to either the service provider or the client?* For example, if you are a banker or a lawyer, why not ask to read your client's strategic plan? Why not find out the metrics by which your client is going to be assessed at the end of the year? Why not share an early draft of a report with your client, rather than trying to polish and perfect it for the "big presentation?" These are simple ways of increasing information flows and access.

Lack of Understanding of Risk: *In what interactions is there a risk, on both sides, that the other side does not understand?* In what interactions would a more open sharing of information result in a better distribution of risk? For example, even greater financial disclosure to a company's auditors would enhance their understanding of hitherto opaque risk. Similarly, a technology services firm could make risk more transparent and distributed by sharing information more openly about possible software development delays.

Lack of Transparency: *What interactions are particularly opaque, mysterious, or one-sided? Would sharing more information reveal new opportunities?* For example: A client could be more transparent about its decision criteria and process to select an outside vendor, and therefore improve the quality of proposals that are developed. A service provider could involve the client more closely in the staffing of a project, particularly at the project management level, to ensure a better fit of experience and personalities.

Standardizing the Client Relationship Experience

All too often, a client's experience with a particular company will vary depending on which team it works with. There may be some common threads in terms of methodology and analytical approach, but each relationship partner or account leader will tend to manage her relationships in a slightly different way. While each client is a unique "market of one," standardized processes are necessary if you want to create a firm-wide, uniform client experience. Ernst & Young's strategic enablement process, Parthenon Group's two-partner rule, and Towers Perrin's independent client review process represent standardized dimensions of the client experience. You need to identify what you think are the critical elements of your own client experience, codify these, and make them part of each professional's toolkit across the organization.

Conclusion

Ultimately, you would like your clients to say that working with your firm is a significantly *different experience* compared to working with your competition. Creating a more valuable and differentiated client experience requires a mindset shift, from thinking about value as contained solely within the service you offer to orchestrating value through the client interactions you undertake to deliver that service. As with many of the other ideas I've discussed for adding more value to your relationships, enhancing the client experience requires thoughtfulness and creativity rather than more time or money. It's about working smarter with your clients, not necessarily harder.

PART IV

Frequently Asked Questions and Conclusion

13

Answers to the Most Commonly Asked Questions about Building Client Relationships

In this chapter, I set out and answer 17 commonly asked questions about client relationships. These address issues that I am asked about again and again. They represent the common, day-to-day dilemmas that many professionals face as they work with clients, and their answers should help provide some additional tactical advice to supplement the main chapters of *All for One*.

1. **I have my hands full just keeping up with my current clients and meeting short-term delivery pressures. How do I find the time to invest in long-term relationship building?**

Like a healthy living program, cultivating your relationships is not a one-off event but rather a lifestyle. Here are seven suggestions to help you make more regular investments in building your relationships:

1. Start by developing the right mindset and attitude. Make a commitment to elevating the quality of your relationships to the same level as your professional mastery.

2. Focus significant effort on a small handful of key relationships—15 to 20—as opposed to every name in your contact database.

3. Set aside time each week to invest in relationship building. This could be two hours every Friday morning, or something small that you do every day (e.g., call someone, send an article, write a note, make a lunch appointment).

4. Create small rituals, such as sending handwritten thank-you cards or writing a short summary of every client meeting and distributing it to the participants the next day.

5. Get others to help you. Use your personal assistant to extend your reach and help keep track of key individuals—in short, turn him or her into a "relationship marketing manager" instead of just an administrative assistant. Get your team involved, so that everyone working on a client engagement with you has relationship-building responsibilities.

6. Go about relationship building in a way that is consistent with your character, personality, and style—then it will become enjoyable rather than a chore. If you're introverted, fine—focus on one-on-one interactions, not loud dinner events. If you don't like sports, relate to your clients along other dimensions, such as family and hobbies.

7. Try to communicate with your broader network of contacts in a way that is efficient and conserves time. Create a newsletter or quarterly bulletin about issues and trends in your area of expertise. Once or twice a year, send an article or white paper to everyone on your contact list. If you send out holiday cards, make sure they contain a personalized message. E-mail is gaining currency for just about everything, including holiday greetings, but real investment and effort is required to keep your lists current. There is also no substitute for the occasional, personalized communication sent through the mail.

2. **How do I stay in touch with past clients, in a mean-ingful way, when there is no ongoing business?**

This is a very common dilemma. We may have dozens—even hundreds—of past client relationships or other contacts that are no longer active for one reason or another. There are a couple of things you can do to make this process more successful, and then there are four main ways you can stay in touch.

First, tell clients in advance you're going to check in with them three or six months after you've finished a particular program or piece of work. This way they'll be expecting a call from you and you won't feel awkward about contacting them.

Second, be selective. Distinguish between people who should be on your broader list of contacts, and those who are really key individuals you should stay close to and have a face-to-face meeting with once or twice a year. You might have 15 or 20 relationships at a single client organization you have worked with, but only a few of those are going to be with economic decision makers or high-potential up-and-comers. This doesn't mean you won't stay in touch with the others—it just means you should be willing to invest more serious time with the "critical few."

Finally, think about four ways of staying in touch:

1. *Ideas or content:* Is there a particular issue that this individual is interested in? Follow up around that topic. Send him articles, books, or other publications with a short, handwritten note. Call and suggest having a cup of coffee, perhaps mentioning a recently completed project that he might be interested in hearing about. Add value around an area of concern to that person.
2. *Connection:* Personal introductions are a great way to add value. Who in your network—or your firm's network—would this person benefit from meeting, and vice versa? I've brokered many meetings and conversations between people in my network, and they have usually found it valuable and been grateful for the opportunity.

3. *Personal help:* This can take many forms, ranging from help with private schools for a newcomer to town, to finding a medical specialist for someone in need, to offering advice to a teenage daughter about applying to your alma mater. Always be thinking, "Is there anything I can do to be of assistance to this individual?"

4. *Fun:* This used to be the main way professionals kept up with their networks—by taking clients and prospects out to dinner and sporting events. Many clients don't have time for this any more, but some might still relish tickets to see a concert or a playoff game.

Today's senior executives are extraordinarily time-pressed. Short, casual interactions that don't make heavy time demands on them—such as having a cup of coffee before work or during a mid-morning break—are often a very effective way to touch base and have a brief but substantive conversation.

3. **I'm in my 30s, but many of the clients I need to build relationships with are 10 or 20 years older than I am, and our lives and interests seem very different. How can I more effectively connect with older executives?**

The basic relationship-building process isn't all that different when there is an age gap, but you may need to emphasize certain things:

1. Early on, don't try to come across as offering a wide breadth of experience—focus on your specific expertise and on establishing an identifiable area of credibility. Try to develop strong insights and knowledge around something very specific (e.g., a part of the client's organization, a competitor, or a specific issue the client's own staff hasn't sufficiently dug into). This can give you instant credibility and a "platform" that allows you to be useful to a more experienced executive.

2. Communicate your willingness to invest time to get to know your client. The younger you are, the more important it is to be willing to dig in and learn. When you have 30 years of experience, you can take more shortcuts. But not when you're only 30 years old.

3. Connect around universal and personal themes. When I was 34 and one of the youngest partners in my management consulting firm (The MAC Group, which later became Gemini Consulting, now Cap Gemini Ernst & Young), I started work with a CEO who was in his late 50s. During our first meeting, I somehow mentioned a story that revolved around calling my father for advice on a very important, personal topic. Suddenly, I noticed the CEO wasn't paying much attention—he seemed to be daydreaming—and I asked him what he was thinking. "Oh," he said wistfully, "I was just reflecting on your story about consulting with your father on such an important subject. And I was thinking how nice it would be if, when I'm older, my sons would still come to me for advice and counsel." After that, we clicked right away, despite our significant age difference.

4. Ask especially good questions. This is always important, but perhaps even more so with a highly experienced, older client. Use thoughtful questions to tap into your clients' experiences. Ask why they've discarded certain options and pursued others, what they've tried before, what has worked or not worked, and so on.

5. Understand baby boomer values. Baby boomers, for example, are highly competitive—after all, they grew up competing with 79 million others for the best schools and jobs. For boomers, who are mostly in their late 40s and 50s (born 1946–1963), work is self-fulfillment. They are the 1960s generation at work, and they still want to shake things up and fix them. They are motivated by money, titles, recognition, and the opportunity for self-fulfillment.

6. Show that you are connected within your own organization and can deliver the right people and resources. Demonstrate that you represent an entire firm, not just your own expertise.

7. Be confident, but show humility. The Indian spiritual leader Mahatama Gandhi, said, "To discover the truth one must

become as humble as the dust." Show confidence in your experience and expertise, but also be humble. Ask good questions, occasionally use self-deprecating humor, and earn the right to advise your client by contributing insights and perspective. Everyone likes a talented, energetic up-and-comer, but they will resent a cocky youngster who is overly confident.

4. How do I increase my active lead stream and create more opportunities with new, prospective clients?

Traffic Building is the term I use to describe the activities that help you to build your professional brand and create an inquiry stream from new clients. There are at least five categories of Traffic Building activities you should consider, which are set out next. But above all, lower your threshold for a client meeting. Get in front of current and potential clients more often, and you will invariably see more potential opportunities.

1. **Intellectual capital development:** This includes conducting primary research, doing surveys, and developing and codifying new service offerings. Many of the best professional firms invest heavily in intellectual capital development, but it is equally if not more important for individual practitioners who don't have the name recognition of a McKinsey or Ernst & Young.
2. **Publishing:** Compared to even just a few years ago, your options for publishing have grown immensely. They include:
   - Commercially published articles in magazines and newspapers
   - Books or book chapters
   - White papers
   - Web-based content (articles, commentary, or anything else housed on your or someone else's web site)
   - E-newsletters, e-zines, and e-bulletins
   - Blogs
   - Podcasts
   - Web-based video

Do you need to survey 25,000 managers in order to publish something? Of course not. I've written very popular, commercially published articles based on interviews with a handful of executives.

3. **Speaking:** Again, there are many opportunities to get in front of prospective clients by speaking. These include industry and professional conferences; events that your firm may organize for a single, large client or a group of clients; and other thematic conferences. Becoming a paid speaker is more difficult, and for this you usually need to have authored a book or perhaps have been a CEO, Olympic medalist, or celebrity.

4. **Networking:** There are so many ways to network that you really need to focus on a platform that makes sense for your particular goals and personality. Here is just a partial list of networking opportunities you might consider:

   - Industry and professional association leadership
   - Nonprofit leadership
   - University/graduate school involvement
   - Personal events (e.g., networking dinners)
   - Social/cultural events
   - Content-based events (private seminars)
   - Media and journalists
   - Collaborating firms
   - "Brokers" (banks, private equity, venture capitalists, etc.)
   - Alumni
   - Academics
   - Retired executives
   - Advisors/advisory boards

5. **Other channels:** These could include:

   - Media interviews (print, TV, radio, etc.)
   - Targeted mailings
   - Third-party endorsements
   - Capability alliances
   - Academic alliances
   - Teaching

Each year, you should pick a few activities out of this list and commit to specific goals. Obviously, the best way to create leads with existing clients is to do great work and invest in a broad set of relationships in the client organization. A steady inquiry stream results from a strong personal brand and a steady investment in traffic-building activities that put you in touch with prospective buyers on a regular basis.

5. How do I handle the question, "How are you different?"

Most people squirm uncomfortably when clients pose this challenge, and they give less-than-persuasive answers. Why? Because when you approach answering this question using traditional descriptive logic, you are *never* very convincing. No matter what adjectives you use, no matter what effusive praise you heap on yourself and your firm—"We listen well"; "We are the best at what we do"; and so on—someone else can always say the *exact same thing*. So any effective response to this question must be characterized by *honesty*, by *showing* rather than telling, and by actually *role-modeling* how you are different during the meeting. Here are a number of possible responses that are more effective than simply saying "We listen well":

1. "First, let me say that all of the major companies that we compete with have strong technical competence. Where you would really see the differences come out is in actually working with us day to day. I'm curious, what are *you* looking for in choosing a firm?"

2. "I think that the differences between firms only become tangible during an actual working relationship. Our clients do, in fact, tell us that we are very different to work with than our competitors, and in a sense they are in the best position to answer that question. If it's appropriate, before we finish I'd like to provide you the names of two current clients of mine who would be happy to serve as references and tell you what it's like working with me and my firm."

3. "Trying to describe how we are different is a bit like showing you a photograph of a good meal—it's just not same as spending an

evening at the restaurant and eating it in person! The best way to help you understand this might be by describing a couple of engagements we recently completed for clients in your industry (or, for clients that have faced very similar challenges). These examples will give you a better sense of the way we work with clients."

4. "I believe there are significant differences between us and our competitors, but it does depend somewhat on the particular issue we are asked to work on and the competitor you are comparing us to. Who else are you thinking of ? (Or, Who else have you had experience with)?"

5. "The best way for me to demonstrate how we are different is by showing you how we would think about and approach a particular issue you face. Could I ask you to describe your most important priorities right now, or the highest-priority issues you're trying to make headway against?"

6. "One of the ways we are distinctive is in how we invest to understand our clients' business. So the first step for me is to better understand what your concerns or needs are right now, and see if there is a good match with one of our capabilities. We would then want to invest time in both understanding that issue from your perspective, and in showing how we think we could approach it and be helpful."

If you want to say things like "We have better industry experience than our competitors" you must be prepared to back these statements up with specific examples. You must demonstrate that your claim is real and provides a benefit to the client. Otherwise it won't be a credible response.

6. **What's the secret to getting a first meeting with someone you don't know?**

If the person is a senior executive, it is especially important to get a referral or reference from someone they know. I have asked many senior executives the question, "On what basis would you be willing to meet with a new professional advisor or service provider whom you don't know?" The answer is usually, "They would have to be recommended to me by a friend or colleague. Otherwise I'm very unlikely to have the meeting."

If humanly possible, obtain a "warm" introduction to the individual you are trying to meet. Here are some ideas that have worked for others. Try to get:

- An active referral from a current or past client.
- A referral from another respected party (e.g., a law or accounting firm that also works with the client).
- An introduction from a colleague in your firm who already has a strong relationship with the executive you want to meet.
- The kind of introduction that occurs implicitly when a client sees you working in a related setting (e.g., you are a lawyer or banker involved on the other side of that client's transaction), and the client is impressed with your ability and professionalism.
- A passive reference (e.g., through a letter of recommendation).
- A personal introduction in another setting (e.g., a nonprofit cause, a social event).

If you cannot get an introduction from any source or person in your network, then a cold approach might work. But you'll need a hook. For example:

- You work for one of the top names in your business and the brand strength of your firm alone will open the door.
- You have already achieved renown from a successful book or other types of publicity (articles, speeches, editorials, press interviews, and so on).
- You engage the chairman or CEO of your company to set up the meeting (sometimes rank can help open the door).
- You try to meet the individual at a professional gathering or conference where you know in advance she will be present.
- You join social circles, community activities, or clubs that he frequents.

- You approach the person and ask to interview her for a research project, and hope that you can follow up at a later date and establish a relationship.

- You employ an unusual or curiosity-evoking approach: For example, you get yourself seated next to the executive on an airplane flight, or you send a letter that sets out a well-thought out contrarian view that you think will intrigue the client.

- You offer to share some *really* interesting research.

Remember: A truly cold call should be your last resort. If you're at the start of your career and don't have a network, you should be getting introductions through more senior people at your organization; and if you are a seasoned professional, you should have other means to meet people.

7. **What can I do about a current or prospective client who just won't engage with me?**

This is not an uncommon situation, and it's certainly not the end of the world when it happens. When you have a prospect or client who is aloof and won't engage with you, there are usually three possible reasons behind his or her behavior:

1. The client has not developed enough trust in you—and/or your firm—to feel comfortable opening up and getting personal.

2. The client, because of his particular character and personality, does not build close relationships with outsiders or possibly with *anyone* at work.

3. The client views it as politically unwise or incorrect to associate with you.

Here are some suggestions for dealing with these situations:

- First of all, temper your expectations and remember that the outside advisor is often more eager to develop a personal relationship than the client is. A large project or transaction may be extremely important to you, and it may consume the majority of your time for a period of weeks, months, or even years. Naturally, you want to have a great relationship with your client. For a senior client executive, however, your engagement may represent only a fraction of her responsibilities, and developing a relationship with you may not be a priority at all. Sometimes, relationships are asymmetrical in this respect.

- Remember that different people develop trust and confidence at different speeds. I have known some clients with whom I immediately clicked, and within a few months we had already progressed to a trusted advisor relationship. Others have required a year or two of working together to reach this stage. So be patient.

- If you think someone is capable of developing a strong relationship with you, but for some reason the trust is still not there, then you have to question whether you have really done your job. Have you identified a vital interest, need, or goal and shown the client that you can help with it? Remember, everyone—even the most hard-boiled, aloof client—has something they are trying to accomplish. If someone doesn't trust you, it's usually because you haven't demonstrated the ability to help and/or your intentions are suspect.

- If politics are involved, you may want to consider accepting your fate and staying away until the situation is more propitious.

8. I'm stuck in relationships with middle management. How do I move up in the organization and build relationships with c-level executives?

Usually, when you are stuck at the middle-management level, it's because that's where you entered the organization. Unfortunately, it's much harder to move up than to be referred downward to a middle manager by a senior executive. Some companies grant significant budgetary authority to middle managers; however, and this may have been your natural route into the organization.

To move up, you need to think about actions you can take during three different stages in the life cycle of a project, program, or transaction:

1. *During the sale:* Have you:
   - Asked to meet the senior executive in whose bailiwick the work falls?
   - Insisted on meeting the economic buyer—the executive who must sign off on the decision to hire you?
   - Invested to understand the client's agenda and connected your proposal to the priorities on it?
   - Created a proposal that addresses the client's specific need, but which also aligns with the strategic context of the problem you're addressing?
   - Ensured that the issue you are being asked to engage around is truly important to the client? Commodity work is rarely going to merit the attention of senior management.

2. *At the start of the engagement:* Have you:
   - Included interviews with senior management as part of your start-up process?
   - Discussed, with your immediate client, the need to gain the perspectives of key senior executives?

3. *During the engagement:* Have you:
   - Tried to get on the agenda of other internal meetings or forums where the audience would find your work relevant?
   - As in (2), convinced your immediate client of the need to gain the perspective and buy-in of key senior executives?
   - Used your time on site with the client to network, walk the halls, and meet other executives?
   - Tried to explicitly connect your work to the organization's broader agenda, therefore making it a natural step for your immediate client to want to involve more senior executives in your work?

Sometimes the barrier to connecting with senior management is your immediate client. He may feel threatened that if you go over his head he'll lose control of the project and also lose his power as your main client in the organization. You need to try to convince him that it is in his best interest to connect what you're doing to senior management, and that it will enhance both the chances for success and his own reputation.

Finally, there may be other, more indirect and nonthreatening ways to meet key decision makers. Your firm, for example, could put on an event to which you would invite your client, and your CEO would invite the client's CEO.

9. **When is it the right time to write and submit a proposal? Clients sometimes want a proposal immediately, even when there hasn't been very much discussion of the issues.**

Most professionals jump at the opportunity to submit a proposal to a potential client. It's a chance to book some new business, and besides, who can resist the adrenaline rush that goes along with the prospect of an impending sale? Proposals, however, can be huge time wasters if the proper groundwork has not been established.

Here are eight prerequisites for submitting a proposal to a new or existing client:

1. You are certain this is the right client and issue for you and your firm. Is this an appropriate client, given your strategy? Is this issue in your "sweet spot" in terms of capabilities? Is the executive with whom you will work in an effective, respected individual in his or her organization?
2. You have a thorough understanding of the issues you are being asked to address. This could happen in one conversation, but more likely will only unfold over two or three discussions.
3. You and the client have agreed on the specific objectives of the work—on the outcomes that are sought.

4. You understand the client's buying process. Usually, you will have to ask about this. It is completely appropriate to ask questions such as:

   - "Can you walk me through your decision-making process and time frame?"
   - "Who needs to approve the budget for this work?"
   - "Who will make the final decision about selecting a firm to work with?"

5. You have spoken to or met with the economic buyer. This is the individual who can make the decision to hire you and your firm. This could be a middle manager or it could be the CEO—it will vary from situation to situation. Often, the first person who calls you is not the economic buyer but rather a feasibility buyer—someone who is screening service providers, someone who can say "No" but not "Yes." The worst mistakes made during the sales process often involve ignorance about the identity and role of the economic buyer.

6. You understand what is most important to the client—in other words, what particular value she is seeking. For example: Is speed critical? How important is cost? Does she want a highly tailored solution? You must understand which aspect of your proposed approach is *most* valuable to the client.

7. You have discussed the essential elements of your proposal with the client. Before you submit a written proposal, you must achieve a basic agreement about what's going to be in it. You might say, "Before I send you this proposal, I'd like to meet with you to walk through our basic approach. That way I can get your reactions and input before finalizing it."

8. You have an agreement to discuss the proposal with the client after you submit it. You don't want to spend a lot of time writing a proposal, and then send it into a black hole. Schedule a phone call or face-to-face meeting to encourage the client to read the proposal and share his or her reactions with you.

Just because business is scarce doesn't mean you should jump at every opportunity to write a proposal. On the contrary, you should focus on those opportunities that make the most sense for you and then double-down on them.

10. **Clients often say they want "new ideas and perspectives" from their professional advisors, but that's easier said than done. Where do you get these new ideas?**

Ideas are everywhere, and you don't have to be a Thomas Edison or Leonardo da Vinci to come up with a steady stream of them for your clients. The first thing you need to do is set aside some common misconceptions about clients and new ideas:

- *"If I'm going to go to a client with a new idea, it needs to be really compelling and original."* Rubbish! One client of mine told me, "If I waited until I had a brilliant idea to go see my client, the meeting would never happen." You can bring your client little ideas, observations, and suggestions—you don't have to have invented a new mousetrap.
- *"Some people are just uniquely creative and can dream things up while sitting in their garden."* Sure, some people are naturally more creative than others, but good ideas are not generated in a vacuum—they derive from deep client knowledge, careful observation of the world around you, a broad intellect, and reflection.
- *"Clients won't pay for ideas. Even worse, they just steal them."* It doesn't matter. The more your ideas are adopted by clients, the stronger and broader your influence becomes, and the more likely it is that they will call you back.

So where do ideas come from? A journalist once asked Willie Nelson, the country-western singer who has written over 1,000 songs, how he came up with so many musical ideas. "Songs are everywhere," he replied. I believe ideas are everywhere—we just have to be receptive to finding them.

Here is a list of some idea-generation techniques that may be helpful to you:

1. *Observation:* By exercising "mindfulness"—a keen awareness of the world around you and the particular moment you are in—you can come up with many interesting ideas. In 1948, George de Mestral, a Swiss engineer and amateur mountaineer was hiking in the Alps. After his walk, he noticed his socks and dog were covered in burrs. Curious about how they stuck to his clothing, he examined them under a microscope and observed the tiny hooks that allowed the burrs to hang onto the fabric. In 1955, he patented Velcro, now a billion-dollar industry.

2. *Analogy and metaphor:* Analogies are a powerful way to create new ideas and transfer concepts from one domain to another. Bank branch designers have taken ideas from mainstream retailing, just as manufacturing companies have studied L.L. Bean's customer service.

3. *Suspension of judgment:* Good idea generation requires a suspension of judgment in order to allow "unrealistic" alternatives or ideas to be allowed into the discussion. Many great discoveries were either accidental or the result of "mistakes." Guglielmo Marconi, for example, pursued his (ultimately) successful experiments in the belief that radio waves followed the curvature of the earth (they don't).

4. *Reflection:* "I lived in solitude in the country," said Albert Einstein, talking about the sources of his great ideas, "and noticed how the monotony of quiet life stimulates the creative mind." Some researchers in the field of creativity, in fact, believe that insight occurs during the reflection and relaxation that follows a period of intense activity and work.

5. *Getting your hands dirty:* The more you understand your client's business and life, the easier it will be to come up with good ideas. Invest time to "walk the halls" and gain a first-hand understanding of your client's business.

6. *Using your client's "lens" to view the world:* To me, this is one of the most powerful things you can to do to come up with more ideas. Every article or book you read, every trend or new innovation you read about—think about what it might mean to your client.

11. Clients always seem to want a deal or a discount. How do I manage these pricing pressures?

There are at least five reasons why a client may pressure you to reduce your fees, and you need to understand which of these is at the root of the discount request in order to effectively respond. I've named a client type for each of these reasons:

1. *Red Ink:* This client is under extraordinary budgetary pressure due to a decline in profits and really is having trouble funding your work. Try in earnest to structure your work to help the client meet internal budget pressures. Help the client become more efficient and productive.

2. *Competition Czar:* Your client has solicited proposals from a number of your competitors and says you are more expensive for what appears to be the same service. In this case, you need to invest in a value-added proposal that illustrates how you are different from the competition. Give multiple options in your proposal.

3. *Bargain Hunter:* This client always likes to dig around for the best deal, irrespective of who you are, the service you offer, or the degree of competition. Satisfy this client's bargain-hunting instincts with a small freebie or extra piece of value-added work.

4. *King Commodity:* The client perceives your service to be a commodity or near-commodity, and buys mostly on price. You have three options: Avoid them, add value to show that your service really isn't a commodity, or lower your delivery cost and compete on price.

5. *Chicken Little:* This client likes to fret about how expensive everything is, including you. Sympathize and hold your ground. Describe the quality ingredients that go into your delivery, and frequently communicate the value you are adding.

In every case, be sure to:

- Always link your proposal to the client's critical issues, needs, and objectives.

- Clearly articulate the value of the work you are proposing.
- Make an effort to identify what the client truly values about your proposal. You may have five elements to your proposed program, but it may be that two or three of them represent 90 percent of the perceived value.
- Respond to fee pressure by offering lower-cost options that restructure the work. Propose doing less than what is in the original proposal, suggest that the client take on some of the tasks itself, or start with a small diagnostic phase.
- Talk about the integrity of your fees. One senior executive said to me, "If I challenge an invoice, I actually *don't* want the firm to immediately knock 20 percent off it. If they do, it makes me think I should question every invoice, and then the whole billing process loses integrity."
- Propose discounts, rebates, or other pricing mechanisms that are tied to creating a larger, stronger relationship with the client as opposed to just cutting current prices.
- Reduce the client's risk of doing business with you rather than cut fees. For example, break a large engagement down into small pieces with checkpoints along the way.
- Don't chase down every lead or request for a proposal—if you cannot invest the time to develop a highly tailored, value-added proposal, don't bother.

Finally, don't take it personally if you're asked for a discount. If someone questions your fees, respond with some thoughtful questions about his or her concerns and try to understand why the subject is being raised to begin with.

12. **How do I deal with a client where there is a key decision maker who dislikes our firm?**

One of my clients was once bidding for a multimillion dollar project, only to find that the lead executive was someone who had applied for a senior position at her firm and been clumsily rejected. The executive was not, to say the least, very fond of my client's company.

Here are a few steps you can take when you find yourself with a detractor who may be blocking or undermining the relationship:

1. *Find out the actual history.* If you know what really happened, you'll be better able to identify the best approach. Was there a personality conflict? Make sure that person isn't involved with the current effort. Was it a failure to deliver? Depending on how long ago this was, you may be able to rebuild trust and reposition your firm with new faces.

2. *If at all possible, try to meet with the executive.* It's easy to demonize people you *don't* know, and also to like people you *do* know.

3. *Identify individuals who might influence them.* If you are trying to make nice with someone who harbors resentment against your firm, his cynical side might perceive you as self-serving or insincere. If a trusted colleague, however, tells him that they ought to give you a second chance, he is far more apt to be persuaded.

4. *Make sure you have a fresh team in place.* I have seen situations where the client feels the relationship manager is complacent and takes the relationship for granted, and as long as he is in place, the client won't give the firm more business. Regardless of the exact nature of the friction, it often helps to demonstrate that you are fielding a new team with new skills and a new attitude.

5. *Try to build trust through small, discrete steps.* This is especially important any time there is distrust or animosity. You cannot earn someone's trust and loyalty through words or proclamations about how well you will serve her—you must do it one step at a time, through your actions. Show the person in question that you are committed to serving her organization. Make attempts to meet face to face. Invest to understand an issue of importance to her. Be gently persistent, while making her feel she is firmly in the driver's seat.

Try all of these approaches, but if the person in question is intransigent in maintaining objections to your firm, then you may just have to bide your time and focus on other opportunities.

13. **How can I change and broaden the client's per-ceptions of our capabilities? We've been narrowly pigeonholed by this client around the current, small project we're doing.**

Clients often develop a very specific perception about a service provider that is based on a combination of the particular team they have worked with and the specific project or transaction that was completed. Changing this perception, once it is formed, takes time and effort, and it is a subtle process.

To get out of a pigeonhole you have to do two things: Demon-strate *your personal breadth* and showcase *your firm's capabilities*.

The first step in broadening your positioning is to demonstrate that you are what I call a *Deep Generalist*, a concept described in Chapter 9. This term, which I coined in my first book, *Clients for Life*, refers to someone who combines *depth* in a subject with knowledge *breadth*. In other words, you may be specialized in executive compen-sation or mergers and acquisitions, but you also bring a breadth of knowledge to the table that includes an understanding of:

- Your client as a person.
- Your client's strategy and organization.
- The industry your client's company competes in.
- The general business environment surrounding your client.
- Your own firm's complete array of service offerings or products.

You need to understand and connect with your client's broader business agenda *as well as* the specific needs and goals of the project at hand. You need to be able to have broad-based business conver-sations with your client where you demonstrate that while you have great expertise in a specific area, you offer more than that—you pro-vide insight, judgment, and perspective. Put another way, if your conversations with your client are always focused on the specifics of the engagement at hand, you will definitely be pigeonholed in that area.

The next step is demonstrating your *firm's* breadth and full set of capabilities. There are a number of things you can do to accomplish this—for example:

- Offer to invest time analyzing an issue of interest to the client, and then hold a working session around that topic.
- Introduce specific colleagues who have other areas of expertise. You obviously have to do this in a way that naturally responds to an interest or need the client has, as opposed to simply pushing different services on them.
- Offer a capabilities showcase. One of my clients, a large professional firm, wanted to broaden its relationship with a company for which it had done very limited work. It offered to fly a group of their top experts down to the client's headquarters, at no charge, and hold a one-day session that was a combination of a showcase for the firm's experience in that particular area of practice and an opportunity to better understand the client's challenges.
- Introduce the client to another client with whom you have a much broader relationship. If your client hears another executive say that your firm has done great work in a certain area, it is far more persuasive than if *you* are trying to convince them.

14. How do you recover after you've let a client down or when your client is unhappy about some aspect of your work?

All professionals face periodic crises or rough patches in their client relationships—it's inevitable that not every client is going to be deliriously happy with you and your work all of the time. So how do you respond when things go wrong? Here are eight principles that can guide you when you are confronted with a client crisis:

1. *Respond rapidly.* If a client is unhappy, deal with it *immediately*. Your willingness to drop what you're doing to urgently discuss your client's concerns will by itself improve the situation.
2. *Listen without being defensive.* When people are upset, they want you to listen and empathize without passing judgment on what

they have said. Emotions, in effect, are like facts to the aggrieved party. The worst thing you can do is listen and then start your sentence with "Yes, but . . ." Listen deeply, and thank your client for sharing her thoughts with you.

3. *Say you're sorry.* Even if you think the blame is equally spread, apologizing can help to defuse the situation and begin a new dialog.

4. *Collaborate on the solution.* Don't jump too quickly to a solution (for example, saying, halfway through the conversation, "We'll put a new project manager in immediately"). Involve your client in developing the answer.

5. *Offer amends.* If in fact you have failed in some way, it can help to offer amends. A client of mine told me how one of his clients recently became extremely angry over an unexpected invoice that he received. The invoice was valid, but my client had done a very poor job of communicating just how complicated this small piece of work was going to be. After listening carefully, my client immediately offered a modest fee credit toward their next engagement. The angry executive quickly relaxed, and the incident was over immediately. In fact, the relationship was strengthened.

6. *Avoid excuses.* This goes along with not being defensive. Don't try to explain to the client all the reasons why you are not at fault.

7. *Anticipate crisis.* If you speak frequently to your client and have lots of open communication, you will be able to head off most crises. If there is an atmosphere of openness between you, there's a greater likelihood that your client's concerns will surface when they are baby concerns rather than when they grow into monsters.

8. *Get things out into the open.* When negative emotions are kept in the dark, they fester and grow. When you get them out into the light of day, they shrink and often disappear. The best illustration of this idea is found in the wonderful poem "The Poison Tree" by William Blake (1757–1827). The first stanza is as follows:

> I was angry with my friend:
> I told my wrath, my wrath did end.
> I was angry with my foe;
> I told it not, my wrath did grow.

Like boiling teakettles, upset clients need to vent steam or else they may explode.

15. My firm wants me to break into a new client, but this company already has a very strong relationship with one of our major competitors. What strategies can I use?

Here are nine principles that can help guide you in trying to win business from a new client who already has strong existing relationships with the competition:

1. *Look for trigger events.* There are a number of circumstances that will make it easier to break in. There could include things such as:
   - A conflict
   - Executive changes
   - Reorganizations
   - Economic events or shocks
   - Turnover or retirements at the competition
   - A service or quality failure on the part of your competition
2. *Try to identify something small or nonthreatening that you can work on.* If, in order to hire you, a client has to dump an existing advisor with whom it has a good relationship, your chances of success are very small.
3. *Focus on an area where you are clearly differentiated or have a tangible strength vis-à-vis your competitor.* Ask yourself, "Where do we have a special strength we can leverage?"
4. *Invest to earn the client's trust and respect.* The incumbent has the advantages of knowing the client better than you and having built up a repository of trust that you lack. You're probably going to have to go *above and beyond* in terms of making an up-front investment in understanding the client's issues and organization.
5. *Identify executives in the client organization who are not so loyal to the other provider.* You'll certainly be able to capture the attention and

interest of these executives more easily, potentially dividing and conquering.

6. *Emphasize innovation and new ideas.* Clients are always looking for fresh perspectives, and they will usually not let an existing relationship get in the way of at least listening to someone else's good ideas. Develop a contrarian position about one of their important issues, and you'll most likely get a hearing.

7. *Be patient and persistent.* It may take many visits and many conversations over a long period of time—months or even a year or two—to find the right opening.

8. *Stay in touch so you are there when your opportunity comes up.* This applies to any new business development situation, but even more so when there is a major, established competitor.

9. *Pick your shots.* When there is a strong incumbent, breaking in can be an uphill struggle, and it's no fun to bang your head against a door. Be selective about investing your time, and focus on those few opportunities where the potential payoff is highest.

16. **How can I build a relationship during the selling process if the process is run by procurement and I have no access to the real decision makers?**

In recent years, the use of procurement processes to select and buy services has increased substantially. Here are seven tips to help you work more effectively with procurement executives and make the best of a request for proposal (RFP) process:

1. *Understand the needs and goals of procurement.* All of the basic principles that should guide relationship building with other types of clients also apply here. Good procurement managers are not just focused on obtaining the lowest price, unless they are buying sheet metal—and even then, quality, service, and other factors enter into the equation. Generally, procurement wants good value—quality at the best price, with a reliable supplier that can offer ongoing support and responsiveness.

2. *Help them achieve their goals and improve their own processes.* Can you make suggestions to improve your client's procurement process? Are there additional questions it should be asking the various competitors? Could the program it is seeking bids on be restructured in a more efficient manner?

3. *Within the RFP constraints, be creative.* While you generally do have to fill out all the forms and check all the right boxes, there's no rule in an RFP that says you cannot be creative and demonstrate original thinking in your approach.

4. *Bring the actual team to the presentation.* Often, companies send a "pitch" team to an RFP presentation, but few if any members of this group will actually do the work if they win the bid. You can differentiate yourselves by showcasing the specific individuals who will constitute the delivery team. The message is, "What you see is what you get."

5. *Engage the buyers during the pitch.* During most procurement processes, you will have the opportunity to make a presentation to a selection panel that includes the senior executives who will make the final decision and with whom you will work during the actual engagement. During this time, you have the opportunity to look and feel differently from your competitors. Turn the "pitch" into a collaborative working session. Inquire as to which aspects of your presentation they would like to focus on. Ask the panel thoughtful questions and pause frequently to get their reactions to what you are saying. Describe specific examples to illustrate your points.

6. *If it is a current client, try to help shape the RFP.* If you have a preexisting relationship with the client, you may be able to influence the focus and scope of the procurement before it is finalized.

7. *Don't go around them.* Procurement managers play an important role, and the best ones are just as focused on quality, performance, and finding a suitable fit as any other client would be. Don't treat them like annoyances but rather as important individuals, and never give them the feeling that you are going around them to top management to unduly influence the procurement process.

17. **I've been working for five years with the same client. How can I keep the relationship fresh?**

If you're not careful, the virtues of a long-term relationship can quickly become vices. Over time, you may take your client for granted and become complacent. How do you prevent this and keep things fresh and vital? Here are some strategies you should try:

1. *Treat all old clients like new clients.* You have to bring the same enthusiasm, new ideas, effort, and excitement to the 100th meeting with your clients that you demonstrated in the first meeting when you were wooing them.

2. *Ask yourself, "What would my competitors do to try and win this client's business?"* This is not a rhetorical question because your competitors are regularly trying to win a greater share of your client's business. Think through what their strategies might be, and consider taking these actions yourself.

3. *Change horses.* A few large firms I know will systematically rotate some team members off of a client relationship once they have been there for a certain period of time, usually a year or two. This is good for your staff and also good for the client because it can bring fresh thinking into the engagement.

4. *Add value in new ways.* Is there a well-known academic or industry expert whose ideas would be relevant to your client? Can you use collaboration technologies to better connect with your client? Are there ancillary firms (individuals, boutiques) that you could use to offer something special to your client? Can you connect your client to other clients that you have? Can you bring someone in who can help your client better understand the impact of certain trends (e.g., the impact of social networking or changing workplace demographics)? Could your firm and the client co-develop some intellectual capital (or co-author an article)? Can you invite your client to host or speak at a conference? Are there long-term fee arrangements that would more closely align your interests as long-term partners?

5. *Alter the relationship experience environment.* Over time, you tend to get into habits and routines in the way you manage your relationships. Perhaps you always meet your client in the same office or conference room, and use the same format for presentations and memos. The findings of a recent study of couples who have been married for a number of years may be relevant to this issue. In this study, when couples did the same things they always do—for example, go to the movies on Saturday night, have dinner at a favorite restaurant on Wednesday—their feelings about the relationship remained unchanged. When couples did *new* things together, however—for example, when they visited a museum they had never been to or explored a new restaurant, their reported feelings of intimacy and closeness grew noticeably. I am convinced the same applies to professional relationships with clients. Organize an offsite instead of meeting all day in the client's conference room. Take your client out to dinner with several of your other interesting business contacts. Instead of PowerPoint slides, use oversized sheets of paper that you tape to the walls of the conference room.

Conclusion

I encourage you to ask other experienced colleagues how *they* have handled these issues or situations. Not all of their solutions will suit your character and temperament, but you'll learn something from them, and their examples will be set squarely in the context of your particular firm and profession. Also, ask a client whom you are close to for counsel on some of the vexing relationship issues that you encounter. People enjoy being asked for advice, and there's nothing like getting the client's perspective.

14

Conclusion

Implementing the 10 Strategies

There are many factors in our professional lives that are outside of our control. You cannot do much about the economy, how your competitors choose to act, or your clients' internal politics. But you *can* control most aspects of the relationship-building process. You can decide which clients and individual relationships to invest your time in, when and how to leverage your firm's capabilities, and what types of strategies to employ. Trusted client partnerships are made, not born, and it's up to you to make them.

I'd like to emphasize three ideas to conclude this book. The first is that confidence is critical to building Level 6 relationships. No one has a monopoly on trusted client partnerships. I have seen them developed by very small firms and also very large ones; by market leaders and by unknown upstarts. The first sale is to yourself, and if you believe that you belong in the c-suite and that your firm should be your client's most important advisor, then you've already won half the battle. If *you* don't believe these things, why should your clients?

The second idea is that *focus* is essential. It's almost impossible to develop Level 6 relationships without a significant concentration of resources. Your organization must be willing to invest in its highest-potential client relationships, possibly in exchange for returns that may take a year or more to materialize. Thoughtful, focused investments in the right client relationships almost always pay off.

The third fundamental concept goes back to the basic premise of this book: This is no longer an individual game but rather a team activity. You need to tirelessly reinforce a collaborative, client-centered culture so that everyone's actions are motivated by a *one for all, all for one* ethos. Multiple strategies are needed to create Level 6 relationships, but without a supportive culture, they will fall short.

How do you get started on this journey? Actually, you're probably already well on your way. The first step is to identify and build on your existing strengths. Do you have some client relationships that can serve as examples? Which of your current relationships have the highest potential to become trusted partnerships? Do you have some *good* relationships that could become *great*? Of the 10 strategies described in this book, which ones are you already good at, and which ones do you need to work on? On my web site (www.andrewsobel.com), I have placed several downloadable assessments that will help you to answer these questions.

The second step is to identify the right people to lead the changes you want to instigate—to be part of what Harvard professor Philip Kotler calls the *coalition for change*. Which professionals in your organization have the requisite passion for client relationships and the confidence to aim high? Who is capable of coaching and mentoring? Are there members of your leadership team who could serve as more visible role models? Ultimately, you want to bring your average performers who have potential up to the level of your best relationship builders—but you need to first shine a light on what "best" is.

Finally, start keeping track of your results. If you can demonstrate increased revenue and profit growth from the application of the strategies that we've looked at—and a number of my clients have been able to show this—then you'll gather the momentum you need for even more pervasive changes. But don't stop at short-term financial measures—also look at factors such as client retention and the revenue from referrals. When you factor in all of the collateral benefits of building trusted client partnerships, you'll find that the economic and organizational impacts are even more significant than expected.

Index